Africa's Moment

Africa's Moment

Jean-Michel Severino
and Olivier Ray

Translated by David Fernbach

polity

First published in French as *Le Temps de l'Afrique* © Odile Jacob, 2010

This English edition © Polity Press, 2011

Polity Press
65 Bridge Street
Cambridge CB2 1UR, UK

Polity Press
350 Main Street
Malden, MA 02148, USA

English Translation supported by the German Marshall Fund of the United States.

G|M|F The German Marshall Fund
of the United States

STRENGTHENING TRANSATLANTIC COOPERATION

www.gmfus.org

Ouvrage publié avec le concours du Ministère français chargé de la Culture – Centre national du livre

Published with the assistance of the French Ministry of Culture – National Centre for the Book

ISBN-13: 978-0-7456-5157-6
ISBN-13: 978-0-7456-5158-3 (pb)

A catalogue record for this book is available from the British Library.

Typeset in 11 on 13 pt Sabon
by Toppan Best-set Premedia Limited
Printed and bound in Great Britain by TJ International Ltd, Padstow, Cornwall

The publisher has used its best endeavours to ensure that the URLs for external websites referred to in this book are correct and active at the time of going to press. However, the publisher has no responsibility for the websites and can make no guarantee that a site will remain live or that the content is or will remain appropriate.

Every effort has been made to trace all copyright holders, but if any have been inadvertently overlooked the publisher will be pleased to include any necessary credits in any subsequent reprint or edition.

For further information on Polity, visit our website: www.politybooks.com

Contents

Foreword: Africa's Prospects

Paul Collier

This book provides a French perspective on Africa.[1] The anglophone world is insufficiently aware of this perspective and has much to learn from it. France has had a more intimate and lengthy involvement with Africa than any other country. Further, although francophone and Anglophone Africa have had many common challenges, both French academic analysis and the responses of the French government to these challenges have been distinctive. At the academic level, an emphasis on demography is part of the DNA of French social science: the subject was born in France. At the policy level, both the Franc Zone and the presence of thousands of French troops on the continent demonstrate a radically greater appetite for engagement than do the anglophone powers. Ray and Severino have for a long time been at the apex, respectively, of French academic research on Africa and of French policy engagement. This translation is thus ideally placed to bring important French insights to an anglophone audience.

With the rise of China, India and Brazil as major players in Africa, and with an African American President of the United States, Europe's engagement with Africa can no longer afford to be fragmented. The foundation for a common approach is common understanding.

Africa faces massive changes, both internally driven and externally imposed. Internally, as this book argues, the continuing demographic explosion on the continent is changing the composition of the population dramatically in favour of urban youth. Externally, the rise of Asia has triggered a new 'scramble for Africa', with the discovery and export of newly valuable natural resources. Both an expansion of urban youth and a bonanza of natural resource exports are potentially highly positive economic phenomena. Urban youth are the workforce best suited for innovation and productive employment. Revenues from natural resources could finance the transformative investment that Africa clearly needs. Yet both are evidently also politically testing. Left underemployed, urban youth is the stuff of disorder, violence and crime. Without the strong rule of law, valuable natural resources generate not prosperity but plunder. For no other region can credible future scenarios be sketched across such a wide range of possible outcomes. In the face of such uncertainties, prediction is pointless. Rather, the challenge is better to understand the forces at work so that Africans themselves, and international actors, can strive as effectively as possible to increase the chances of the better outcomes. This book provides a fresh and illuminating contribution to this end.

The forces with which this book is most concerned are demographic and geographic. In that spirit I offer a simple geographic taxonomy of the region. Physical geography is helpful in disaggregating the huge region of Africa into groups likely to face distinctive development prospects. Human geography is helpful in analysing why African prospects are likely to be distinctive from those of other regions.

A view through the lens of economic geography

Many of Africa's economies are resource-abundant. Many others are likely to become so. Resource-rich economies have distinctive prospects. Among those that are not resource-rich, a further distinction is important: between those that are coastal and those that are landlocked. The coastal economies have options of integrating into global markets through manufacturing that are not available to the landlocked.

Countries which are landlocked and resource-scarce

A striking difference between Africa and other developing regions is the high proportion of its population in landlocked, resource-scarce countries. The most promising strategy for such countries is to orient their economies towards trade with their more fortunately endowed neighbours. However, a corollary is that their opportunity for growth depends upon whether their more fortunately endowed neighbours seize their chances. A landlocked country surrounded by poverty and stagnation has little hope of sustained success.

Even if the neighbours grow, in order for the landlocked to benefit, the sub-regional economies need to become radically more integrated. The integration agenda is partly a matter of practical trade policy such as the removal of road blocks and harassment by customs officials. It is also a matter of infrastructure: roads need to be built and maintained.

Although the countries that are landlocked and resource-scarce are the core of Africa's poverty problem, since they depend for success upon their more fortunate neighbours I am going to focus on the other two opportunity categories. Whether these better opportunities are harnessed will be decisive even for the landlocked.

Countries which are resource-rich

Some African economies are already generating large rents from the extraction of natural resources. The potential for further extraction is enormous. The average square kilometre of Africa has only around one-fifth of the *known* sub-soil assets of the average square kilometre of the OECD.[2] It is unlikely that two such large slices of the world should have such discrepant averages, and the most likely explanation is that, to date, there has been less exploration in Africa.

While prospects for resource discoveries are therefore excellent, there is plenty of evidence that resource rents are problematic unless preceded by robust institutions of governance. Governance is likely to be far more important in resource-rich countries than elsewhere because government is critical if natural assets are to be harnessed for the sustained benefit of citizens. The resource rents must be taxed in order for them to accrue to the nation, and the revenues from these taxes must then be spent well by the government.

Effective public spending requires accountable government. Unfortunately, democracy is often corrupted by resource rents. Checks and balances are eroded, and electoral competition turns into a patronage contest rather than a genuine scrutiny of government performance. The classic African example of a failure of democracy to discipline the use of resource wealth was Nigeria under President Shagari. It displayed the classic patronage politics of resource rents in the context of intense electoral competition without effective checks and balances. The regime of President Shagari, though democratic, wasted the Nigerian oil bonanza of the early 1980s.

Countries which are resource-scarce and coastal

I now turn to the resource-scarce, coastal economies. These are the category that globally has had the fastest growth, but also the category in which African performance has been least encouraging, relative to the global norm. The only such African country to succeed has been Mauritius, which followed the Asian pattern in transforming itself through exports of manufactures from an impoverished sugar economy into an industrialized, upper-middle-income country.

Prior to 1980 manufacturing and services were concentrated in the OECD economies, locked in partly by trade restrictions but mainly by economies of scale generated by urban clusters of firms. Around 1980, a combination of trade liberalization and the widening gap in labour costs began to make it profitable for industry to relocate to low-income countries. This process is explosive: as firms relocate, these scale economies build up in the new location and make it progressively more competitive. The chosen locations were in Asia, not in Africa. The factors that determined this choice need only have been temporary and need not have been massive. However, once Asia got ahead of Africa, the forces of clustering made it progressively harder for Africa to break in. Currently, Africa has no significant advantage over Asia in terms of labour costs, while having large disadvantages in terms of cluster-scale economies.

A view through the lens of human geography

Africa's political geography is striking: it is divided into far more countries than other regions, so that the average population of its countries is radically smaller. But Africa's social geography is also striking: despite the division into tiny countries, the typical country is ethnically far more diverse than those in other regions. Hence, small population and ethnic diversity are the two distinctive socio-political features of African geography. Continued population and urbanization will gradually change these features: mega-cities will be melting-pots of ethnic identities. But currently, each gives rise to problems.

Low-income societies that have small populations are, in reality, far smaller than implied by their populations. Africa's political fragmentation has inhibited the growth of cities, and especially of large cities. This reduces productivity: each time a city doubles in size, productivity rises by 4–8 per cent. Collier and Venables[3] contrast African fragmentation with Indian unity and find it has been highly costly. Not only are the ladders of economic development more difficult to mount if population is small, but the snakes of economic collapse are more prominent. The risk that a region will experience civil war increases considerably the more countries into which it is divided: the typical African nation is too small for its government to provide effective internal security.

Africa's ethnic diversity is not a decisive impediment to development, but it does create difficulties. Although democracy is evidently not necessary for growth, in an ethnically diverse society an autocracy usually rests on the military power of a single ethnic group. The more diverse the society is, the smaller the ethnic base of such autocracies is likely to be. Such concentrations of power rationally exploit their position by redistributing income in their own favour, even if this is at the expense of national economic growth. This suggests that ethnically diverse societies are better suited to democracy than to autocracy. However, in an absolute sense, democracy may be considerably more difficult in ethnically diverse societies. Where voter allegiance is by ethnicity, there is little incentive for governments to deliver nation-wide public goods as opposed to favouring a winning coalition of ethnic groups. Ethnic diversity also makes collective action for public service provision more difficult. An implication is that, in ethnically diverse societies, the boundaries between public and private provision should be drawn more in favour of private provision. A further implication is that public spending may be more effective if it is decentralized: at the local level, Africa is much less ethnically diverse.

Bringing physical and human geography together

In conjunction, Africa's distinctive physical and human geography gives rise to some specific dilemmas.

Countries which are both resource-rich and ethnically diverse

As noted above, in the coming decade resource extraction will be fundamental to Africa's economic opportunities. Large revenues from natural resources imply a large state. In turn, this implies that the efficiency of public spending is critical. Yet, such revenues also tend to make democracy markedly less effective: globally, the typical resource-rich country might grow faster under autocracy. However, Africa's high ethnic diversity makes autocracy extremely dangerous. Further, ethnic diversity weakens the ability of the society to hold public services accountable, yet resource-rich Africa does not have the option of a small public sector: resource revenues accrue to the government and will be spent by it.

So what political system would best serve a society which is resource-rich and ethnically diverse? Autocracy is so dysfunctional in the context of ethnic diversity that it cannot be rectified, but although democracy may well be dysfunctional in particular instances, it can also work effectively. The appropriate polity is likely to be a democracy with unusually strong checks and balances, combined with decentralized public spending. How the government can *use* power needs to be heavily constrained, rather than simply how it *attains* power. The key challenge currently facing Africa's resource-rich societies is to build such polities.

Countries which are resource-scarce and have small populations

Coastal, resource-scarce Africa has missed the globalization boat. Why, in the 1980s when industry started to relocate from the North, did international firms decide against African locations? The factors probably differed among countries. In francophone Africa the growing overvaluation of the CFA franc effectively excluded the sub-region from exporting. Lusophone Africa was beset by civil war. South Africa was in the late stages of the apartheid regime. Among the other coastal, resource-scarce countries, Ghana, Tanzania and Madagascar were in crises as a result of experiments with socialism, and Kenya was beset by the ethnic politics of redistribution. Mauritius was the only country not precluded from manufacturing exports by such misfortunes. However, Africa was prone to these disparate syndromes due to the problems generated by its distinctive human geography. Those of its countries that were neither resource-rich nor landlocked were too small and diverse to provide the public goods of security and good economic policy. In the decades since the 1980s, Africa has substantially succeeded in surmounting these problems. The misfortunes that impeded coastal Africa from entering global markets are now over. In the coming decade, coastal Africa is well placed to break into global markets for light manufactures as wages rise rapidly in China and international firms seek to relocate. Due to the dynamics of cluster economies of scale, the most difficult stage is breaking in: after that, as clusters grow, the incentives for relocation increase. In pump-priming the pioneer firms, both African governments and the international community can take supporting actions.

Conclusion

Africa is facing massive changes driven by demographics and global price shifts. These changes will play out in societies that are distinctive due to the fundamentals of their geography. In the coming decade, particular African countries face one or other of two critical challenges. One is how to manage resource rents in the context of ethnic diversity. The type of polity that appears most appropriate is one Africa currently tends not to have: strong checks and balances on how governments can use power and decentralized public spending. The other is how to compete with Asia, despite having let Asia get decisively ahead.

Acknowledgements

In the course of this African journey, we have been relating a plot that is still unfolding. Since any omniscient narrative is illusory in this kind of tale, we have opted for a participant account, inviting the reader to accompany us in meeting its hero – Africa's billion at a particular moment on its journey, that of its awakening.

This portrait of African transformation should be taken as it is offered: a testimony from actors caught up in transformations so rapid that they scarcely have time to register in our awareness. We take responsibility in advance for mistaken perceptions, necessarily contingent, in relation to this moving object so close to us. We freely accept that there is the occasional caricature of a protagonist that is essentially complex, out of a concern to make its story intelligible. We are also aware that we could not deal with all elements of the reality in which it is involved: for example, we have only touched on the most political subjects, and passed over in silence several aspects of cultural and artistic ferment that are also shaping the Africa of tomorrow. We acknowledge that certain of our conclusions are bold: if this book owes much to recent work in the social sciences, we have taken the liberty of going a step further in our prospective analysis – at a corresponding cost in scientific certainty. We have in fact felt authorized to share what we have seen, read and heard. Finally, we chose to describe what is rather than assert what should be, since it seems to us that a change in perspective is a necessary precondition for action.

Insofar as any of this proves correct, we owe much to several of our colleagues at the former French ministry of cooperation, the ministry for foreign affairs and the Agence Française de Développement (AFD) – many of whom work in sub-Saharan Africa, in close proximity with the actors in these changes. We thank them heartily for their passionate discussions on developments in a continent that is dear to them. Even so, it is still important to make clear that this book is the result of its authors' personal reflections, and in no way the position of an institution.

We would also like to thank the travelling companions who taught us to love and understand Africa: Patrick and Sylviane Guillaumont, Béatrice Hibou and Jean-François Bayart, Lamine Loum, Erik Orsenna, and so many others without whom we would know nothing of this continent. We thank all those who supported this project at various steps along the way, whose repeated readings – in matters of substance as well as form – enabled us to improve the text: Jacques Attali; Sophie Cerbelle; Matthieu Discour; Antoine Grimaud; Olivier Lafourcade; Françoise Lapraz-Severino; Bertrand Loiseau; Thomas Mélonio; Daniel Outré; Christine, Laure and Jean-Baptiste Ray; David Robert; Caroline Rozières; Jean-Bernard Véron; and, once again, Jean-François Bayart, Lamine Loum and Erik Orsenna. Our parents and families deserve a quite particular acknowledgement: they infused us at birth, and on its soil, with a stubborn loyalty to and love for Africa. Finally, we thank the countless Africans, friends both famous and unknown, whom we met in the course of years. Many of them are too committed to their political struggles for their names to be cited here without endangering them. They are the real authors of this book.

Introduction

The present book is the result of a certain amazement, and of an encounter.

The amazement we feel stems from realizing that we do not understand Africa and are blind to the extraordinary forces currently in play there. Is the arrival of China on the continent, for example, good or bad news for its inhabitants? Is sub-Saharan Africa over- or under-populated? Will it be able to feed a rapidly expanding population? What will the effects of climate change be in this vast region? Should we expect the spread of civil war and genocide on a large scale, like that which crippled Rwanda in 1994? Or does the decline in armed conflict detectable since the turn of the century show signs of continuing? Is Africa ready for democracy? Should we fear waves of African immigrants? Or is the economic growth of the last few years likely to persist, making Africa the next emerging power? Is there a place for Africa in a multipolar world?

There are countless books devoted to Africa, but they all speak of a different place: yesterday's Africa. These keys to our understanding are now outdated, so much so that we are unable to make sense of the events that are shaking the continent and transforming it before our eyes. Two Africans out of three are under twenty-five years old. In contrast to our sluggish European societies, Africa's demographic dynamism imposes a frenetic pace on the continent's transformation. Côte d'Ivoire had only 11 inhabitants per square kilometre in 1960; it has nearly 70 today, and will have 110 by 2050. If Britain had undergone the same population growth as

Côte d'Ivoire between 1960 and 2010, it would today count 285 million inhabitants – including 75 million foreigners!

Africa is thus changing scale and direction at a dizzying pace. In the light of the speed and amplitude of the metamorphosis under way, it is worth scouting out the route a good way ahead. Yet we generally see this African meteor launching itself at full speed only in a rear-view mirror, so it is scarcely surprising that we fail to understand its trajectory. The gap is striking between the Africa that we see, as if fixed in the last century, and its contemporary realities.

Public debate presents the space south of the Sahara as a blighted and marginalized land, untouched by globalization. Africa is perceived as an object of compassion, calling for a charitable response at best. At worst, it is viewed as a problem that needs to be contained. Charity work has largely been sub-contracted to humanitarian and philanthropic organizations; containment is carried out by UN bodies and by African states themselves. This view, whether charitable or 'lucid', is not unconnected to the harsh realities of a continent that is emerging from several decades of crisis. However, it ignores the upheavals affecting African societies, changes of which few grasp the extent or the opportunities today. Do we realize that, since the turn of the century, African economies have experienced a rate of growth far higher than that of Europe or the USA? In the early twenty-first century, while the emerging actors in international relations are interested in African developments and their own relationships with this continent, Europe seems to have abdicated. The societies on the northern shore of the Mediterranean, and above all their economic actors, have turned their backs. There is no longer any reflective, coherent and prospective public thinking about Africa.

It is high time, then, to get to know Africa again.

This book is an attempt to understand a complex and shifting material, which escapes our traditional ways of reading. It starts from the refusal to be trapped by the evidence of the past. It relies on observing changes that are under way before our eyes. And it sticks to the few signposts that we have for the future. We know that the population of the continent will double in just a few decades. We also know that it will then be principally urban. And the way in which Africans will then live, move, define themselves and interact with their environment will determine the course not only of their societies, but also of our own.

The question here is not to predict whether tomorrow's Africa will be in 'good' or 'bad' shape, nor to determine who might then be praised or blamed. The following pages are not stuck in the sterile debate between 'Afro-optimists' and 'Afro-pessimists' that has monopolized discussion of the subject for so long. The moment has come to understand the consequences of these transformations of seismic intensity – for Africa itself, for its neighbours and for the world. What we can perceive, examining both present and future, is the strategic re-emergence of Africa, with both the risks and the opportunities this involves.

Africa is complex. It has perhaps never been more complex than it is today, at the time of its metamorphosis. Any prospective analysis of a shifting society is condemned to deliver crude diagnoses and erroneous predictions. We accept these inaccuracies and mistakes, convinced that complexity should not paralyse reflection. What matters is to be in step with the moment of history at which we find ourselves, if we are not to risk a chaos at our door that no humanitarian transfusion would be able to contain. An Africa of 1.8 billion inhabitants will rapidly impose itself in the globalization game. If we do not commit ourselves to coherent and appropriate policies, we risk seeing it rudely invite itself into our domestic politics. The great African upheaval forces radical choices in public policy.

We met Ibrahim in a Johannesburg taxi. The route to the city centre from the airport was long and crowded. The driver, a Malian some thirty years old, was a pleasant character. When we asked him his reasons for emigrating to South Africa, he explained the course of events. He left his native village in northeastern Mali after several seasons of poor rainfall, when grain had become scarce on the market. Speculators were quadrupling prices in the 'bridge' season. Despite his father being one of the richest men in the village, Ibrahim's rations, along with those of his six brothers and sisters, were steadily being reduced. He rejected the idea of going off, like his cousins, to fight with the rebels. He was not that angry with the government. 'What do you want them to do? They don't have a franc in the kitty, they can't even pay the village schoolteacher.' Ibrahim's story made sense: Mali was undergoing the dark years of 'structural adjustment' and experiencing the full force of the cotton crisis.

So Ibrahim decided to leave. This led to a period of wandering through the big cities of West Africa. He was in Abidjan when the Côte d'Ivoire crisis erupted. It wasn't good to be a foreigner there. But while the majority of his travelling companions decided to set off on the risky journey to Paris and London, he preferred to head south. He had heard of Mandela's new South Africa, in full economic take-off following the end of apartheid. It wasn't so easy at first: after settling in a township he experienced a new period of hardship and odd jobs. Seeing that we were looking at the little rosary hanging from his driving mirror, Ibrahim explained that he had converted to Christianity. A small evangelical community in the township had helped him a great deal on his arrival. Thanks to money borrowed from its congregation, and from an American charitable organization, he had been able to launch himself in business. He now owned five taxis, linked by an up-to-the-minute radio system. He was planning to buy a people carrier for trips from the airport to hotels – 'like the Chinese', who had also entered this sector. A few months more and he would be able to stop driving and concentrate on managing his business – he already had a small office, fully equipped. And after that? Ibrahim has big plans. He would like to marry and have children, but first of all to move to a different quarter: his priority is to leave the township and buy an apartment in a safer and more comfortable suburb. Return home? No: 'My country is Africa. I am at home here. And then, business is good in South Africa.' Asked about the anti-immigrant violence that caused blood to flow in the townships in winter 2008, he preferred to change the subject.

It seemed clear to us that Ibrahim's history is that of a continent in motion – anything but static or on the margins of the world. The present book aims to relate this great transformation, rich in opportunities and challenges of a new kind. It is a metamorphosis that will mark the planet as a whole – and to which none of its inhabitants will be able to remain indifferent.

Part One

The Peopling of a Continent

What then is Africa? An invention. A space without top or bottom. The Sahara desert. Immense forests, rivers and plains. And, above all, peoples of an astounding diversity. Does this add up to an object of analysis? Not really. And yet we must make a choice and commit ourselves. Conventional approaches may be misguided, but they are convenient. And so, for want of anything better, we shall speak here of the African continent as the space situated south of the Sahara: that of the Sahel; the Horn of Africa; West, Central and Southern Africa; the islands of Madagascar, Mauritius and the Comoros.

This choice finds support, however, in the converging transformations that affect this curious geography and characterize the moment it is currently experiencing. Their common basis is the demographic earthquake shaking African societies. Let us therefore take a small detour through the world of people and figures.

Part One

The Becoming of a Consumer

1

Who Wants To Be A Billionaire?

It might be a television game show. It is in fact the most incredible demographic adventure that human history has ever known.

The prehistory of an earthquake

The face of Africa as we know it today has been shaped by a succession of crises and exoduses. Its current metamorphosis will lead it to experience many others.

African histories, ancient and modern, are inseparable from a whole tradition of movement. These population flows continue to affect the continent's economic, political and social space. The mosaic of communities cohabiting today is evidence of this. The peanut-growing Senegal basin, the cocoa plantations of Côte d'Ivoire and the mining regions of South Africa have developed into centres of dense and prosperous population thanks to successive waves of regional migration. These waves, depending on economic success, war and the vagaries of climate, on voluntary or forced ebbs and flows, lie at the root of a continuous recomposition of African territories. From Mauritius to Liberia, South Africa to Uganda, African societies and economies, with their difficulties and their riches, can only be understood by taking into account the demographic and migratory forces that have always animated them.

External factors have played a large part in this dynamic. The fact of violence is well known, but its scale often forgotten: the

continent was cut to the quick by the slave trade. If historians still
debate over figures, they agree on the order of magnitude. Between
the eighth and the twentieth centuries nearly 17 million Africans
were sold by the caravaneers of the Near and Middle East, or fell
prey to the Indian Ocean trade.[1] Between the fifteenth and the
nineteenth centuries, 11 million left Africa aboard slave ships. This
removal of some 28 million young men and women was considerable, in relation to the population of under 100 million that sub-
Saharan Africa still counted at the start of the nineteenth century.

After slavery was abolished – though not quite extinguished – it
was the turn of colonialism to leave its imprint on Africa's population and space. Work in rough or inhuman conditions, bloody
repression of indigenous revolt, and the exposure of previously
isolated populations to European pandemics led to several million
deaths across black Africa.[2]

It is scarcely surprising, then, that, between 1500 and 1900,
while the world population rose by a factor of 3.5, and that of
both China and Europe by a factor of 5, the population of Africa
remained stagnant or even fell.[3] Sub-Saharan Africa's share of the
world population declined, in the space of four centuries, from 17
per cent to 7 per cent. These two successive bloodlettings, which
affected the continent very unevenly, explain the astonishing contrast in population density between regions. They also explain the
low average density in sub-Saharan Africa, which in the mid twentieth century was some 15 times less than that of Europe or India.
Africa was thus for a long time an underpopulated continent, in
relation both to other continents and to the extraordinary wealth
of its natural resources.

It is in this unique demographic context that the burgeoning
population growth experienced by the African continent since the
end of the First World War should be envisaged. Like Europe in
the eighteenth and nineteenth centuries, or North America in the
nineteenth and twentieth, Africa in the second half of the twentieth century saw an impressive increase in the population density
of its various territories. The typical scenario of the first phase of
demographic transition was both later and more intensive on the
African continent than on the rest of the planet: advances in public
health and medical care made possible a sharp fall in mortality,
while longstanding behaviour patterns kept the birth rate persistently high. This is how sub-Saharan Africa saw its population

multiply by 7 in the space of only a century, passing from under 100 million in 1900 to nearly 700 million by 2000. A baby born in Nigeria in 1950 came into the world in a country of 37 million inhabitants; its grandchild today would be born in a land of some 160 million. Africa south of the Sahara, which then counted only 8 inhabitants per square kilometre, today has 36.[4]

This sudden increase in population density has been the motor of radical transformations in both space and societies. The tumultuous history of African independence movements, the economic convulsions of the 1980s, the bloody crises on the continent that followed the fall of the Soviet Union, and the unexpected spell of economic growth that the continent's economies have experienced since the turn of the century can none of them be understood without taking this veritable demographic earthquake into account.

Africa in mid-passage

The aftershocks of the quake will be no less intense. Africa, in fact, is still a long way from completing its remarkable transformation. While the tempo of growth has declined in relation to the peak of the 1980s, the population of sub-Saharan Africa is continuing to rise at a rate of close to 2.5 per cent each year, twice the average for developing countries. UN studies estimate, as their median scenario, that this population will double again in the space of forty years, passing from close to 860 million inhabitants today to some 1.8 billion in 2050.

It is worthwhile dwelling on this figure for a moment: 1.8 billion is 1.5 times the population of India today, and 3 times as much as tomorrow's Europe. The phenomenon of the African population explosion, already well under way in terms of its growth rate, will continue over the coming decades, both absolutely and as a proportion of humanity as a whole. Sub-Saharan Africa in 2050 will be larger than India, and have at least 25 per cent more inhabitants than China. The equivalent of the Indian subcontinent[5] is forming on Europe's doorstep. Blinded by current transformations in Asia, Europe's citizens and leaders dare not contemplate the African changes to come. And yet Africa is only halfway along its great transformation.

This is a time neither for rejoicing nor for fear, but simply for recognizing the facts. Whatever we might think of it, and whatever the scope and effectiveness of the policies applied to influence its trajectory, Africa's demographic advance over the next fifty years is unstoppable. The worst thing would be to ignore it. But it is also easy to forget that the mushrooming growth of African societies is in fact only a process of catching up after the demographic traumas suffered by the continent – a form of return to normality, in other words, since it is only at the end of this process of accelerated peopling that Africa will regain, in 2050, the fifth of the world population that it represented before 1500,[6] before the devastations of the slave trade and colonization. Africa is in a sense taking back its place in history. With 72 inhabitants per square kilometre it will reach a density close to that of other continents – and a healthy one for its economic development. Africa will then be avenged.

The study of demographic trends suggests, in fact, that the figure of 1.8 billion is in no way a 'high' scenario, but at the lower end of the range of possibilities. Forecasting models are based on behavioural changes – the number of children a couple desire, the rate of contraception use – observed in the demographic transitions of Asia and Latin America, transitions that were backed up by voluntarist policies designed to change behavioural patterns: at the most extreme, for example, the one-child policy in China or India's sterilization campaigns. Yet national programmes to control birth rates are still rare or even non-existent south of the Sahara.

In fact, sub-Saharan Africa has only very partially embarked on the second phase of its transition.[7] The fall in the birth rate is taking place only very slowly in the countries where it is under way. Others are still far from reaching this point: in countries such as Niger, men's desire for children remains far above the actual number of children per woman – a figure of 7.2 in 2007! If Africa is to remain on the path leading to 1.8 billion inhabitants in 2050, African fertility will have to fall steadily from its present level of 5.5 children per woman to 2 in 2050, which implies the use of modern methods of contraception by more than 60 per cent of women. At the present time this rate is under 20 per cent. Thus, if a doubling of the sub-Saharan population between now and 2050 is practically certain, the growth may well be considerably higher, in which case sub-Saharan Africa could pass the 2 billion mark by the middle of the century.

Should we then see the AIDS epidemic, after the fashion of Malthus and his disciples, as a natural regulative process that will curb the African population explosion? Contrary to what is sometimes said – or, more often, thought – this epidemic is unlikely to modify these structural developments. Africa does indeed count two-thirds of the world's total cases of AIDS, and more than 70 per cent of the deaths attributable to the HIV virus. The disease is ravaging the most vulnerable populations, and adding to the many handicaps weighing down the development of certain countries, especially in the southern cone. But the increase in the desire for children that follows a rise in infant mortality,[8] the falling prevalence of AIDS now in many countries, advances in access to health care and the inertia of the demographic process mean that the excess mortality due to the epidemic will not change the nature of the African demographic challenge.

The population of Africa south of the Sahara will therefore have multiplied by a factor of 10 – at a minimum – in the course of a

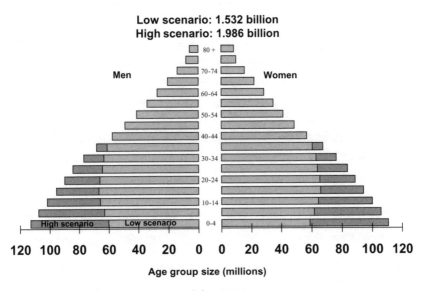

Sub-Saharan Africa: age pyramid for 2050
Source: J. P. Guengant, October 2009.

Africa's Moment

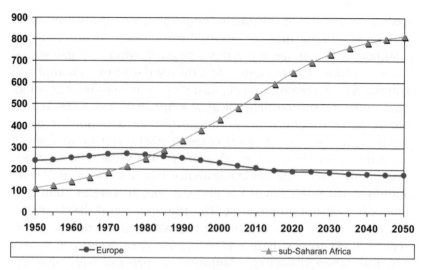

Youth under 25 in Europe and sub-Saharan Africa (millions), 1950–2050
Source: United Nations, *World Population Prospects: The 2008 Revision Population Database* (median scenario), 2009.

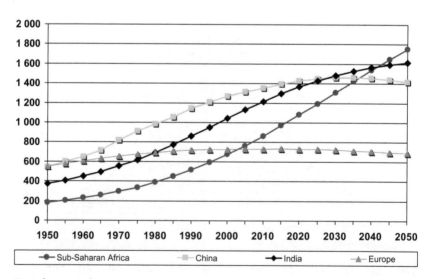

Population change in major countries and regions of the world, 1950–2050 (millions)
Source: United Nations, *World Population Prospects: The 2008 Revision Population Database* (median scenario), 2009.

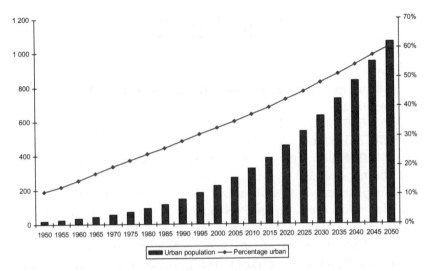

Urbanization in sub-Saharan Africa
Note: The urban population is shown by the histogram (left axis, in millions), and as a percentage of the total population on the right axis.
Source: United Nations, *World Population Prospects: The 2008 Revision Population Database* (median scenario), 2009.

century, from 180 million in 1950 to at least 1.8 billion in 2050. China, by comparison, will have seen a rise of 'only' 2.5 times in the same period, and the Indian subcontinent a rise of 4 times. If Europe's population were to increase by the same proportion, it would have grown from 550 million inhabitants in 1950 to 2 billion today, and reach 4.5 billion by 2050![9] This is the change of scale that will confront Africa in the coming years, and the rest of the world with it – a phenomenon with no equivalent in human history.

Urban explosions

Just as everywhere else on the planet, this vigorous demographic growth is accompanied by a process of massive urbanization. During the second half of the twentieth century, the population of sub-Saharan Africa's cities multiplied by 11. In 1950 the region still did not possess any city with over a million inhabitants. Today there are thirty-eight such cities, half of which boast several million. And the process is not likely to cease any time soon. Africa is still one of the least urbanized continents on the planet, with 35 per cent of town-dwellers, as against almost 80 per cent in Latin America. Here again, the catching-up effect is in full swing: by 2030, half of all Africans will live in towns. In the meantime, its countries will have to deal with a doubling of their urban population, which will grow from around 300 million to around 600 million. In the middle of the last century, Kinshasa had no more than 160,000 inhabitants.[10] Today it is home to nearly 10 million, and preparing to receive several million more in the coming decades.

This phenomenon of urbanization is again the most rapid that the planet has ever known. Previously due primarily to the exodus from the countryside, its main cause today is the natural growth of urban populations that are still very fertile: African cities now have their own momentum. Lagos, which has seen its population multiply forty times over in sixty years, will soon be one of the largest mega-cities in the world, with a number of other African candidates close behind. Unlike European urbanization, this growth of cities will not be accompanied by a depopulation of the African countryside, where population is also rising sharply. Urbanization and increasing population density are thus driving a tremendous reorganization of space and societies. They are redrawing the face of the continent, and the minds of its inhabitants.

Any human community that experiences changes of this magnitude is fatally committed to a difficult balancing act. It is prey to a series of powerful and contradictory forces. It was, after all, against this background of demographic transition that the tragic episode of the Great Leap Forward took place in China (with its 30 million dead), and the Cultural Revolution in which Mao leant on a mushrooming youth to regain his declining power. The Indian subcontinent was also torn apart in the wake of its independence, when its population explosion was in full swing, leading to the flight of tens of millions of exiles, and several hundred thousand massacred. Africa is changing tempo, and the social, cultural and economic upheavals that accompanied European urbanization are shaking this continent in turn – in the age of the Internet and real-time information.

A population that is doubling in thirty years and urbanizing at full speed inevitably places great strains on the supply of public services – strains that penetrate societies and political systems to the core. Even though its demographic growth was far below that of Africa today, Europe in the 'baby boom' years experienced genuine difficulty in carrying out the 'demographic investments'[11] required: don't forget that shanty-towns existed at the gates of Paris until their replacement in the 1970s by the imperfect compromise of the *cités* – which have since become sorry symbols of social segregation. Cities such as Bogotá, Rio and Mexico City have also experienced exponential growth; it will probably take decades for them to regenerate their shanty-towns and *favelas* and to cast off the world records for urban violence associated with this. Egypt's population took off in the 1970s. This period also corresponded to the Muslim Brotherhood's penetration of Egyptian society, by way of intense charitable action among the victims of uncontrolled urbanization. They succeeded in filling the growing gulf between the aspirations of Cairo's 12, then 18, million inhabitants, and what the regime was able to offer in terms of housing, health care and education. Islamism continues, across the Muslim world, to be a powerful instrument of social criticism. Just as Marxism succeeded in mobilizing European youth, this socializing ideal has gripped a section of Arab youth today. What ideologies will shake African youth tomorrow?

How are the vast populations of Abidjan, Nairobi or Lagos to be housed, fed, cared for and educated? How can their ever-growing needs for transport infrastructure, water and sanitation be met? Overwhelmed by the scale of these needs, the municipal authorities of many cities on the continent are very often forced to give way to a makeshift economy. Will the international community be able to do any better, in the periodic fits of generosity that characterize it? Up to this day, all the major international goals of universal education and health care have broken on the rocks of Africa's demographic reality. The Millennium Development Goals, proclaimed with great ceremony in 2000 – with 2015 as the target date – will suffer the same fate in the absence of an economic growth proportionate to the explosion of needs – which African youth sometimes express with rage.

Images of the disenfranchised youth of Liberia or the Congo, jobless yet docile, condemned by pitiless warlords to be cannon fodder for a military campaign, became African clichés of the 1990s. Two out of three Africans today are under twenty-five, compared to less than one-third of Europeans. Many readings

can be made of the tragedy that affected Côte d'Ivoire at the turn
of the century; the responsibilities of the different political actors
can be variously assessed. In any event, this took place against the
background of four factors in combination: economic chaos following a collapse in the cocoa price; large cohorts of unemployed
youth; an urban population that had grown twenty-five times in
the space of fifty years; and large-scale immigration from neighbouring countries. Three of these four factors are likely to persist
in the coming years. And they will affect not only Côte d'Ivoire,
but also Ghana, Chad, the Democratic Republic of Congo and
Kenya. It is no accident that the same years also saw pogroms
of young Ivorian patriots against immigrants from Burkina Faso,
violence by young Kikuyus, Kalenjins and Luos in the shanty-
towns of Nairobi, and anti-immigrant violence in Johannesburg.
The number of new arrivals on the African labour market will
double between now and 2030. Will the informal sector,[12] already
the largest employer in Africa, be in a position to integrate them?

2

Malthus on CNN

Sorry states

These daunting challenges would shake even the most stable and organized of communities. But the territory that is exposed to this earthquake and its impacts is a balkanized continent, divided into forty-nine states that are prey to crises of governance at every level.

The Berlin carve-up of 1885, which saw Africa divided according to the needs of the five industrializing European powers, sacrificed territorial coherence on the altar of colonial peace. Sub-Saharan Africa is still set fast today in a mosaic of political entities that are either too large (Democratic Republic of Congo), too small (Burundi), too arid (Niger) or too landlocked (Central African Republic) to constitute coherent economic units. These national borders inherited from the colonial age constitute a brake on the organization of the sub-Saharan space that is coming into being.

The historical mobility of African populations is more necessary than ever to correct the continent's demographic imbalance: over-populated zones alongside spaces of very low density, stagnant economies and centres of growing employment, saturated ecosystems and broad stretches of arable land, territories at war and havens of peace – these all need to exchange their peoples. And yet this movement, the product of ancestral practice, is ever more restricted by arbitrary border controls. Trade along shorelines and rivers, or across the all too rare regional networks, suffers a whole host of customs duties, supplemented by a multitude of informal levies that are no less arbitrary. A truck journeying from Cotonou to Bamako crosses five countries, four frontiers, eight customs posts and a countless number of highway checks. Jealous of their recently acquired sovereignty, the African nations find the path of regional integration heavy going.

These national divisions are compounded by ethnic cleavages. If these are largely political constructs, they still serve as powerful vectors of mobilization in this period of destabilizing changes, as well as an easy market for entrepreneurs of violence. Too many contemporary analysts have succumbed to the 'identitarian illusion'[1] in their articles or lectures, conveniently listing ethnicity among the causes of the African tragedy. By so doing, they reify the *product* of three decades of economic crisis, bad governance and collective traumas.[2] The sense of deprivation and the perception of growing inequality, political oppression and the fear it arouses, the confiscation of lands and national rents all contribute to the crystallization of ethnic identities that has marked recent decades in a number of African countries. This was notoriously the case in Rwanda and Kenya, where pressure on land, competition for government jobs, economic crisis – or sometimes, fast-paced economic growth – provided a breeding-ground for the intensification of such markers of identity. Historical and contingent as it may be, the formation of new ethnic identities[3] and the resulting erosion of national consciousness arising from it contribute to the continent's growing balkanization. This fragmentation of the political field makes the task of constructing an effective public policy in the service of the national community that much more difficult, and fuels the crisis of the state. We shall return to this later.

The African state is the product of such permanent compromise. Though the burden of the changes under way rests on its shoulders, it struggles to provide even the most essential public goods. Crippled by a whole series of structural weaknesses and predatory practices, it is prey to a double crisis of effectiveness and legitimacy.

The destitution of municipal, provincial and national authorities is desperate. It prevents them from carrying out 'demographic investments' in the modernization of agriculture, town planning or public infrastructures, which would enable them to tackle the double challenge of demographic growth and economic catching-up. Hampered by ineffective tax collection and the great weight of the informal sector, state expenditure in African states rarely rises above 10 to 15 per cent of GDP, compared to an average of 36 per cent for the OECD countries.[4] Despite the processes of decentralization timidly at work across Africa, these modest resources flow only very partially to the local authorities responsible for investment in their territories. Some of these are unable even to keep public infrastructure from deteriorating for want of maintenance. International aid, moreover, which declined in the 1990s, has in the last two decades neglected the basic infrastructural sectors (water, sanitation, transport, town planning) so critical to the demographic process.[5] The funds available for this kind of investment thus fall far short of the challenges that Africa is facing today, and will continue to face in coming decades. This lack of financial resources is matched by a shortfall in human and technical abilities that is equally detrimental to effective administration; many African countries are unable to pay the salaries of skilled employees regularly – a broken-backed public administration, in other words.

Is sub-Saharan Africa then under some kind of curse, the only continent condemned to weather the storm of its transformation without appropriate institutions? Those who maintain this have very short memories. Africa does not have any monopoly on identitarian challenge or weak governance. The processes of demographic growth in Europe, Asia and America – punctuated by social upheaval, periodic economic crises, and the indelible stain of genocide – experienced constraints that are surprisingly close to those that make up the African challenge today.

Darwin's other nightmare

There is, however, a certain difference, which cannot be ignored. Beyond these structural weaknesses, part and parcel of the demographic process and the painful construction of a post-colonial social contract, Africa will have to reckon with an unprecedented context in the twenty-first century. Three factors make the African demographic equation particularly perilous.

First of all, the African cauldron will be refused the safety-valve of distant migration. Europe, in its phase of demographic growth, benefited from a crucial outlet for its own population pressure:

the door of emigration to the New World remained wide open to Europeans until the early twentieth century, making it that much easier to deal with the growing numbers in Germany, Italy and Britain. How many young Europeans went to seek their fortune in this New World that held out its arms to them? How many communities fled the persecutions of which they were victims? It is estimated that during the great famine that struck Ireland in the mid nineteenth century, up to 1.5 million Irish people emigrated to North America in the space of a decade, out of a total population of 8 million. Africa has arrived too late: its population explosion is happening at a time when international migration is far more constrained. The figures for the Irish emigration of 1848, applied to the present-day sub-Saharan population, would represent an emigration of 170 million Africans in the course of ten years! Freetown today is no more than a few hours from New York, but the gates of Ellis Island are well and truly closed. The time of massive intercontinental migrations is essentially past, the window of opportunity closed.

This prodigious increase in the continent's population density is also taking place at the very moment when humankind is discovering the limited nature of the earth's resources. In the face of climate change, the exhaustion of hydrocarbon stocks, the dizzying decline in biodiversity, the rise in sea levels and the saturation of certain ecosystems, will there be room for all at nature's mighty feast? 'The power of population is indefinitely greater than the power in the earth to produce subsistence for man',[6] wrote the English parson and economist Thomas Malthus in his essay of 1798 on the principle of population, adding that 'the superior power of population cannot be checked without producing misery or vice'.[7] Is Africa, with its unavoidable demographic explosion, heading for decades of misery and vice? As we discover the limits of nature, the English parson's arguments still challenge us.

Few economists, however, have been so greatly mistaken in their predictions. The two basic hypotheses of Malthus's population theory have been refuted by human history. Malthus predicted that 'population, when unchecked, increases in a geometrical ratio. Subsistence increases only in an arithmetical ratio.' It was ironic that he should have written these words on the eve of the great demographic transition that eventually took England to a negative rate of increase, i.e. a fall in population if immigrants are excluded.

The experience of all other continents has since confirmed that the sharp rise in a population's natural increase is followed by a second phase, marked by a fall in birth rates. Demographers estimate today that the end point of the demographic transition is an average number of children per woman slightly below that needed to replace the population. Germany and Japan, which are set to lose up to 10 and 20 per cent of their population respectively, illustrate the limits of the Malthusian theory of a geometrical progression in human population.

The means of subsistence available across the world, moreover, have multiplied in the course of the nineteenth and twentieth centuries in proportions worthy of the Feeding of the Five Thousand. Malthus, who postulated declining agricultural yields (each additional acre brought under cultivation being less fertile than the previous), did not foresee the tremendous gains in productivity made thanks to the agricultural revolution. A single litre of petrol used in agriculture provides an energy equivalent to the day's work of 100 pairs of hands.[8] It should come as no surprise, then, that world agricultural production has met the combined needs of demographic growth and the considerable enrichment of human diet. The 'green revolution' of the 1960s, the result of the introduction of new seed varieties, mechanization and artificial fertilizer, put paid to all the predictions of 'inevitable famine' that were made for the Indian continent. When India gained independence in 1947, it was on the verge of famine, but in the space of a few decades the country had become a major exporter of wheat – despite a tripling of its population. Though there is still considerable room for improvement, this kind of gain in productivity is not unknown in Africa: the peasants of the Senegal river valley saw their production multiply fivefold in ten years thanks to advances in irrigation and mechanization. We should therefore be on guard against the Malthusian ideas that are returning to favour.

It would be wrong, however, to deny the validity of Malthus's concept of the 'carrying capacity' of a given natural space. Productivity gains cannot be limitless, given that any space subjected to a steady increase in population will at a certain point come up against its ecological limits. Jared Diamond demonstrates this very well in his book *Collapse*:[9] from the great Mayan civilization to the unfortunate inhabitants of Easter Island, whole societies have self-destructed by drawing excessively on their natural environment.

Like these, and despite major gains in economic and agricultural productivity, certain African countries will not be in a position to feed the populations they are expecting. Will famine, war and emigration have to restore the balance? Let us take the example of Niger, where 80 per cent of the population live from agriculture and livestock. With 15 million inhabitants and a national territory in which only 15 per cent of the land is arable, this country in the Sahel is already experiencing a situation of chronic famine. 'The greatest challenge facing us in the last few years has above all been the lack of land to cultivate. There are ever more mouths to feed and there is not enough land for everybody', explained the deputy mayor of the district of Guidan Roumji in Niger, when asked about the 2005 famine.[10] UN studies predict some 46 million inhabitants for Niger by 2050, where women have on average more than seven children. Even an unlikely 'green revolution' along Indian lines would not be able to support this demographic explosion. Will this country have to rely on its dream of uranium deposits in order to survive?

As we have seen, the continent's increasing population density and urbanization over coming decades threatens to worsen political tensions both within and between African states. Climatic upheavals are likely to have the same effect. The transition from natural to human abundance is one of the structural factors of Africa's delicate situation: while people are ever more numerous, natural resources are becoming scarcer or deteriorating. The consequences of climate change, which is likely to worsen in the future, are in fact already making themselves fully felt in Africa – in zones where the great bulk of the population depend on land for their survival. In Darfur, recurrent droughts in the last twenty years have poisoned relations between herders, driven ever further south, and settled farmers forced to extend their cultivated land to cope with the declining fertility of the soil. The embryonic war that we have been powerlessly watching unfold since 2003 arose in the wake of a long build-up of hostilities between ethnic or linguistic communities, inflamed by entrepreneurs of violence. A new factor in these regions is the deadly clashes that break out today over access to water. Eastern Chad, where ecosystems have been overwhelmed by the massive influx of refugees from the Sudan, threatens to be engulfed in the same cycle of violence. The reports of the Inter-Governmental Panel on Climate Change (IPCC)[11] are clear: given the changes already under way, the African continent will be increasingly affected by irregular rainfall and extreme climate events, as well as the rise in sea level. Coastal zones and the deltas of the great African rivers, the locations of some of the largest cities on the continent, are first in line. The 'green revolution' that enabled India to cope with its population explosion by boosting the productivity of land did not take place in such a context of climatic upheaval.

The concept of 'climate refugees' confusingly suggests images worthy of Old Testament scenes. In all probability we shall not see millions of Africans fleeing the rapid advance of the desert or a sudden rise in sea level. The region of Darfur and Eastern Chad, however, offers a disturbing model of populations escaping in tens of thousands from the atrocities of a conflict partly provoked by the gradual desertification of land. If it is impossible to determine precisely the scope or time-frame of this phenomenon, the most recent studies on the impact of climate changes all emphasize the particular exposure of the African continent and the vulnerability of its populations: between now and 2080, some 1.2 or 1.3 billion Africans will be exposed to water stress, 600 million to hunger, and anything from 2 to 7 or more million per year to coastal flooding.[12] A Pentagon forecast a few years ago, from an institution that rarely risks fantastic predictions, listed flows of climate refugees as among the major threats to the United States' national security in the twenty-first century.[13] For Mohammed, a young escapee from Darfur whose home-made boat was intercepted by Italian coast-guards on the way from Libya, the reasoning is clear: 'We were already dead when we were in Darfur or Libya. If we had died on the boat, it would have been just the same.'

No violence is necessary, no war inevitable. But the demographic and ecological situation of the coming decades brings with it structural vulnerabilities that can only lead to natural disasters, conflicts, and their share of misery and refugees. Doing nothing in the face of these Darwinian adjustments would be criminal, denying the looming Malthusian pitfalls equally so. We shall return to this below.

As the final component of this unprecedented context, Africa will be forced to perform the somersaults of its demographic growth under the lenses of CNN, the supercilious gaze of the international community, and an ever tighter web of international norms.[14] By bringing people closer together, globalization has strengthened the feeling of solidarity that binds them. International public opinion has become far more sensitive to the sufferings of the world's most vulnerable populations – exposed every day before their eyes. Proofs of this are the waves of international mobilization in support of the peoples of Darfur and Tibet, whose cries no one would have heard in the deep freeze of the Cold War. After forty years in which proxy wars supplied the excuse for every kind of abuse and arbitrary action, the world's great powers have changed their tune. To count among the world's acceptable nations, and benefit from state privileges, the continent's governments must conform right away to the 'rights of man', 'good governance' and 'democracy' triptych. We can only welcome this growing international solidarity, as a precious guard against the arbitrary action of the state. This new set of demands made on public authorities follows many decades of culpable tolerance towards criminal regimes. All evidence suggests that it responds to a universal aspiration, which lies at the root of the social contract between governors and governed.

But however legitimate these demands – each year more numerous and stringent – may be, they considerably raise the bar to be crossed by African nations in rapid change. Will these demands enable them to climb more speedily, or rather increase the risk of stumbling? We should at least recognize that these requirements, which bear principally on the rights of the individual, have been of little concern for most countries in demographic transition, most nations in the course of construction. China and India each underwent this process in extremely brutal forms. In the eighteenth, nineteenth and twentieth centuries, when Europe experienced the forces of demographic transition and urbanization, and was churned up by the wave of nationalism, by revolutionary movements and two world wars, it was hardly more concerned for the fundamental rights of its citizens. Vendéens, Basques and Bretons remember the violence with which the French Republic was formed. Even today, in China, Malaysia or Tunisia, economic growth, political stability and national unity – the premises of a 'peaceful' demographic transformation – take precedence over human rights and democracy.

Africa, undergoing its own metamorphosis in a time of calls for increasingly high standards of behaviour, has little choice in this matter.[15] The UN Charter has been supplemented by international treaties on political, economic, social and cultural rights, on the rights of indigenous peoples, and on social and environmental norms; but the lack of capacity of many African states is already apparent when these standards are negotiated in Geneva or New York.

The African nations, which arrived on the scene too late, are undergoing their demographic expansion in the post-Westphalian[16] period, the world of conditional sovereignty. Dependent on international solidarity and subjected therefore to the conditions that accompany this, under threat of military operations under 'chapter VII' of the UN Charter,[17] policed by the 'right of intervention' and the 'responsibility to protect', Africa has little room for manoeuvre. Burdened with the challenges of its youth, the population expansion of its countryside, the urban explosion, regional migrations and problems of governance, in full global environmental crisis and deprived of any migratory outlet, the African state has to jump a hurdle that is constantly being raised.

Part Two

Africa on the Move

As we said, Africa's demographic history will not be comparable to Ireland's in the nineteenth century. And yet, as far as a prospective analysis can see, Africans will not stop moving within and beyond their borders. Africa in this century is and will remain a land on the move.

3

A Black Peril?

After the famous 'yellow peril', has the time come to fear a 'black peril'? Will the African 'population bomb' become a 'migration bomb'? We are all familiar with images of dead African bodies on Spanish beaches, illegal immigrants climbing the barbed-wire fences of Ceuta and Melilla, young Nigerians exploited on the pavements of European cities. These do indeed correspond to harsh realities. But faced with the power of these images, and impassioned speeches on the tidal wave that Europe is expecting, we should not lose sight of statistical reality.

Dams against the Mediterranean

It is a little-known fact that the countries of sub-Saharan Africa have always been open to immigrants. Africa south of the desert has already between 16 and 35 million migrants,[1] whereas only 4 million (i.e. a quarter or an eighth as many) of its citizens are settled in the OECD countries. In all probability the continent will continue to contain the great bulk of immigrants that its trans-formation produces; only a small part of this wave heads for the countries of the North. In terms of absolute numbers, however, this part is not negligible and has to be managed. Is this possible? In absolute terms, the world has experienced periods of migration in the nineteenth and twentieth centuries that were far greater than today's. On the eve of the First World War immigrants amounted to more than 5 per cent of the world population, i.e. nearly twice

the present proportion.[2] The net annual balance in France,[3] currently 1.7 per 1,000, is both much lower than during the decades
of the post-war boom, and one of the lowest in the industrialized
world.[4] France therefore is not facing a massive wave of migration but rather an 'ongoing transfusion',[5] continuing its historical
tradition. The figures for sub-Saharan migration actually remain
particularly modest, far indeed from the invasion that some people
feel: even if there has been a rise in immigration from black Africa
since the beginning of the century, only 8.5 per cent of immigrants
settled in the OECD countries originate from the African continent (including North Africa), as against 16.8 per cent from Asia
and 25 per cent from Latin America.[6] Sub-Saharans thus make up
a far smaller share of international migrants than they do of the
world population (12 per cent).

What will the situation be tomorrow? The permeability of
borders is a fact. Europe, only 14 kilometres away from Africa
at the Straits of Gibraltar, will feel the shocks of the earthquake
under way south of the Mediterranean. However reassuring it
might be for some people, 'fortress Europe' is simply a myth:
no strengthening of the security system at the borders, no legal
restrictions will shelter the nations of the North from the flows
of migration, whether economic – regular or irregular[7] – or the
movement of refugees.[8] Studies conducted in the wake of several
decades of South–North migration show in fact that these flows,
whose causes are numerous, varied and complex, are only weakly
affected by state policies – whether on the part of their states of
origin, states of transit, or states of reception.

We have then to accept that sub-Saharan immigration is a social
phenomenon that will mark both the south and north shores of
the Mediterranean. It will structure new economic and social relationships between Europe and Africa. Is it possible to predict the
scale of this movement? The estimates of international migration
that sometimes accompany population forecasts are basically no
more than extensions of present trends: since we cannot envisage
future changes, it is impossible to predict the size or nature of
migrations to come. We know, however, that the number of new
entrants on the African labour market will double: the continent
is looking at 27 million more active young people per year by the
early 2030s.[9] This change of scale will inevitably place African
economies and societies under heavy pressure. The countries of

the Maghreb began their demographic transition some decades before those south of the Sahara. Their recent history shows that when the labour market is unable to absorb the ranks of young school-leavers, many of these seek their salvation in exile. And the forecasts leave no room for doubt: Africa's demographic and economic context in the coming decades will inevitably create a class of young urban unemployed – multiplying the number of those wanting to leave.

The primary reason is simply poverty. Désiré, Mahmat and Ange, whom we met one evening at Agadez in Niger, already knew where they were going. Aged seventeen, twenty-one and 'nineteen, I think', they had just one idea in mind. Leaving was a sufficient project in itself, never mind the destination. Europe, the Eldorado of the north, is big, and they did not doubt for a moment that they would find a place in it. 'In Europe people are old. They need arms like this' – Désiré proudly indicated his biceps. Paris beckons them – they know it already from films on Canal+, the news on TV5 or the stories of their immigrant parents. All they have to do is cross the desert and the Straits of Gibraltar. 'Then there's the motorway.' If they don't reach Paris, there's London, Brussels or Madrid – what difference does it make? After the hardships of unemployment in Abidjan (Désiré), the army in Chad (Mahmat) or odd jobs in Ouagadougou (Ange), the adventure alone is worth it. And it is an adventure above all[10] – but also a flight from an everyday life marked by a poverty all the more intolerable for being contrasted with the opulence of European and North American societies that is so glaringly visible. And what of those immigrants abandoned by smugglers in the desert? Those whose frail barques could not withstand the capricious Mediterranean? The faces of our adventurers cloud over for a moment. The danger of the crossing is well known, allowed for. It is useless to insist. Only a few more weeks, and they'll have enough to pay for it. 'As far as Algeria. Then we'll see.' Will Désiré's five younger brothers, in the village and in Abidjan, follow his example?

If Africa's crisis is the source of major population movements, increasing mobility towards the OECD countries will also be – perhaps above all – the product of Africa's own growth and development. Paradoxically, emigration is not chiefly the result of extreme poverty. International migrants generally come neither from the poorest countries nor from the most deprived communities in their country of origin, let alone from the most destitute in these communities.[11] The journey is costly, and can only be considered when the family earns enough to save up for the expense, or at least its first section. The going rate can be several hundred dollars, even thousands. In 2003 the boat trip from Morocco to Spain cost around $600 for Moroccans and $1,000 for sub-Saharans. The voyage on a cargo ship from Mauritania to the Canary Islands was as much as $3,000, paid partly to local smugglers and partly to the crew.[12] Economic development, by freeing people from traditional ties, giving them a limited amount of money and education, and bringing them modern means of communication and exchange, increases both individual aspirations and abilities to emigrate.[13] The increasing number of Mexicans leaving for the north despite strong economic growth is a telling example. It is only later on, once the difference in living standards compared to the OECD countries begins to lessen, that economic growth can reduce the incentive to leave – as we are beginning to see now in Morocco, Tunisia and Turkey. The economic growth of African countries, therefore, will still have the effect of accelerating migration for some decades to come.

Demographic transfusions

An African influx, no doubt. But an 'African peril'? Seduced by clichés, forgetful of figures, those preaching along these lines ignore the exceptional social demand of the northern shore of the Mediterranean, and the strength of its call to the southern side.

The formidable demographic challenge of Africa, in the early twenty-first century, matches the no less delicate population problems of Europe and North America. In this stage of their development, the countries of the North, with their ageing populations, demand an influx of young and increasingly skilled labour – East European, Asian, Maghrebian and black African. The typical 'home help' in the French cities today comes often from Mali, Cameroon or Burkina Faso, sometimes from Algeria or Morocco, rarely from Asia and only exceptionally from France itself. If the Paris region's garbage is sorted each day, this is thanks to the work of an invisible army of Malian, Cameroonian, Beninian or Maghrebian first-generation immigrants. From the fruit harvests of southern France and Spain, through catering, to the building trades, the economic viability of whole branches of industry depends on immigrant labour, with Africans making up a growing share of this. A quick look into the kitchens of any New York restaurant likewise reveals a growing African presence: several generations of Mexicans, Cubans and Puerto Ricans are now joined by Nigerians and Senegalese, busy night and day feeding the formidable American economic machine. The Western systems of production depend on a regular transfusion of new blood from abroad. The effectiveness of the remedy depends on the proper dose of this vital fluid. Long recognized by economists studying the labour market, this fact is no longer taboo, and even finds a place in the official report on recommendations for French economic growth delivered to the President of the Republic in 2008, with its 222nd paragraph headed: 'Take in more foreign workers'.[14]

The African continent will see its working-age population rise fivefold in the course of the next forty years, while that of Europe will fall by a quarter.[15] The societies on both sides are inevitably going to become more closely connected; the issue at stake in the population policies being drafted across the world is to get the best result from this for the countries of origin, transit and reception, as well as for the migrants themselves. However debatable the content of these treaties, the agreements for concerted management of migration flows sought by France since 2007 are witness to a new era.

Three closely linked factors will combine in the next few decades to make immigration increasingly necessary for the countries of the North: the spectre of a gradual decline in their populations, a rapid fall in the ratio of active to inactive individuals (hence problems in financing pensions and social expenses), and finally the growing shortage of labour in whole sections of the economy. As the demographer François Héran explains, 'With the inevitable increase in the number of deaths due to the deferred mortality of the baby-boomers [thanks to medical advances], the natural balance[16] in France will decline and become negative in a generation's time. Only immigration can prevent the French population from decreasing.'[17] Migration already contributes some 85 per cent of annual demographic growth in Europe,[18] a rate that will soon pass 100 per cent. Besides the demographic weight of different countries, what is at stake here is the proportion of active to inactive, and thus the balance of the working population in our ageing societies. Without immigration, the active population would decline throughout the developed world in the course of the coming decades: the relationship between economically active and senior citizens, which was 8 to 1 in France at the start of the twentieth century, is 4 to 1 today and will be no more than 2 to 1 in 2050.[19] With the retirement of baby-boomers in the next five years, these problems are already approaching. Germany anticipates a massive shortage of labour: by 2020, it could require an additional 2.4 million skilled and unskilled workers, and up to 6 million if German economic growth were to return to 3 per cent per year.[20] Europe will lose 30 per cent of its working-age population between 2010 and 2050.[21] Immigration alone cannot prevent the ageing of the developed countries, but, by the inflow of workers and their social contributions, it will help to balance the budget in the countries of the North.

An unlikely new European baby boom would not be able to reverse the second demographic shift that our continent is undergoing. But it is equally hard for it to resign itself to a decrease in population, with the economic recession and loss of competitiveness this would imply. We must therefore maintain that, as in past history, the future of Europe is indissolubly linked with immigration. It is this image that the candidates from black Africa who present themselves at our doors see so clearly before them. We can't hide from them the fact that restrictive immigration policies are a crude attempt to regulate a structural need. This need gives them confidence – albeit sometimes excessive and unrealistic – in their ability to profit from their long and perilous journey to our shores. They will succeed in crossing our threshold, risking their lives if need be.

Brain drains

Our immigration policies in the North are quicker to recognize the need for skilled workers than the need for arms to cradle our young and assist our old. Yet it cannot be said that the 'cerebral yield' of European 'selective immigration' policies is very high. Teachers, engineers, computer programmers – studies report an increase in the course of the last decade in the number of educated immigrants, particularly originating in sub-Saharan Africa.[22] Half of all immigrants from Nigeria and South Africa, and around a third of those originating from Kenya, Ghana and Ethiopia, have college or university education. But many of these skilled Africans are performing unskilled work in the countries receiving them, evidently representing a less than optimal allocation of skills at the international level.

The impact of this exodus of skills on development in the countries of origin is certainly a problem for them. Nowhere is this brain drain more shocking than in the medical sector, at a time when doctors, pharmacists and nurses are desperately needed in Africa. Whereas in France 62 million people are cared for by 209,000 doctors, there are scarcely 96,000 in sub-Saharan Africa for a population of 860 million, i.e. a ratio less than a twentieth as large.[23] There are twice as many Angolan doctors working in Portugal as in Angola, and almost as many Senegalese practitioners in France as in Senegal.[24] And yet France, in common with the greater part of the industrialized world, continues to recruit African doctors – even while investing substantial sums in the continent's public health. Abdoulaye, a former student at the Dakar Faculty of Medicine, is working now as a 'replacement intern' (FFI) in gynaecology in a hospital in the Paris suburbs. Since his qualifications are not recognized as being on the same level as those of his French colleagues, he has in effect been working for more than ten years as a gynaecologist on a student's wage. By taking on additional night duties to earn – with difficulty – a monthly salary of 2,300 euros, he and his FFI colleagues enable the Sécurité Sociale to make substantial savings. But at what cost to Senegal? That country has seventy-five gynaecologists for its whole territory, and the risk of a woman dying in childbirth is 120 times greater than in France.

This problem will get worse in the years to come. Europe has a growing need for medical personnel to care for a population of old people that is greater each year. In the face of a growing demand for these skills on both sides of the Mediterranean, and in the absence of measures to tackle the harmful effects of this brain drain, African public health risks being the great loser from a laissez-faire policy, with all the negative effects that can be anticipated in terms of the spread of epidemics and a fresh rise in African fertility – an increase in infant mortality having the paradoxical consequence of slowing down the fall in the birth rate. Cooperation in the health field between Great Britain and Malawi, for example, now includes increasing the provision of training for the country's doctors and nurses while raising the incentive for them to work at home in Malawi – particularly by improving the management of the medical sector and offering higher salaries. But this joint effort has a price, since it is accompanied by a ban on British recruitment of Malawian medical staff for both private and public services.

New models of cooperation and exchange seek to replace the current 'exodus of skills' by a 'circulation of skills'. Starting from a recognition of mutual needs and the existence of comparative advantages, the concept of 'circulatory migration' proposed by certain specialists in international migration opens up tracks in this direction. African professionals, for example, would be trained in Africa or in the OECD countries, and work for a time in the North before benefiting their home country with their experience and know-how. If the history of European immigration suggests a certain caution in relation to supposedly 'temporary'[25] migration scenarios, this pattern of mobility is by no means unrealistic: it is already typical of Indian professionals, for example. India exports massive numbers of students to the United States and Great Britain, re-importing from the best universities in the world professional staff in mid-career who wish to benefit from the opportunities presented by the economic take-off of their country of origin – and, incidentally, the opportunities for male students to marry Indian women who have remained at home. This is not yet the pattern of the developed world's migration exchanges with sub-Saharan Africa, which suffers from a net loss of skilled workers to the North, often permanent.

The virtuous immigrant?

Several voluntary schemes, sometimes encouraged by the host countries, have been proposed since the turn of the century with a view to encouraging immigrants to invest in their country of origin, or even to return there. The economic success of these projects is so far only modest,[26] due to the extremely complex role played by returning financial flows. But these flows have transformed economic and social reality in many countries.

Contrary to what is often thought, the countries of the North have no monopoly on migration policies. Certain states, for example the Philippines, have in fact specialized in the export of migrants, just as others have concentrated on trade in timber, minerals or textiles. One Filipino in six with higher education is working abroad. Whether skilled or not, Filipino emigrants send home over $15 billion each year in various forms, amounting to 13 per cent of the national GDP.[27] Whether the result of a deliberate national policy or an old history of exile, these transfers today represent enormous sums on the world scale: developing countries received $328 billion in 2008 in the form of transfers from their emigrants,[28] or close to three times official development aid in the same year. The export of migrants can thus be a highly lucrative industry: it brings Senegal the equivalent of 8 per cent of its GDP, or twelve times the volume of direct foreign investment.[29] Are these inflows of capital, which continue to grow considerably from year to year, beneficial to the host country? Answering these questions requires a careful analysis of the data available, and a patient study of socio-economic impacts on the communities receiving these transfers. The verdict is still far from clear.[30]

Many people have argued that expatriates sending back money to their region of origin, by making up for a lack of local resources, contributes to economic development and thus helps the area they came from to catch up with their host countries. This new form of international solidarity[31] has certainly proved particularly valuable in times of humanitarian disaster, playing the role of a safety-valve. During the 2005 famine in Niger, the resources of relatives living in Europe, or in less affected countries of the region, helped whole villages to cope as best they could with the steep rise in the price of foodstuffs. The transfers from emigrants also represented a considerable inflow of money in zones suffering a serious lack of investment. These resources had the advantage of being on average both more stable and more predictable than other sources of currency available to the countries affected, i.e. official development aid and private investment from abroad.

But for these resources to affect the socio-economic development of the countries of origin, they have to be invested in productive activities. Studies conducted in recent years show that this is only rarely the case. The transfers from emigrants are more usually used for purposes of insurance, to deal with illness or death (the payment of various funeral costs) or to support the current expenses of the family who remain in the home country (food, house repairs, children's school fees), even for ostentatious consumption (buying a motorbike, building a second home). The inflow of large sums from abroad, moreover, leads to negative effects that have as yet been little analysed, starting with the creation of considerable inequalities between families in the same village, or between different villages.

In the space of a few months, for example, Sékou became a notable figure in his small village, a few dozen kilometres from Timbuktu. His elder brother, recently settled in the Paris suburbs, sends him money. Each month he proudly mounts his new motor scooter to go and collect his money order from the city. Soon, he tells us over a glass of Coca-Cola, he will have a new brick house built to replace his mud hut – an investment inconceivable for his neighbours. 'He is richer than the village chief or the imam', one of these explains to us later, visibly disturbed by this change in the local hierarchy. 'And with all that he doesn't share anything at all. It will make problems for him, I tell you.' In recent years, the successful exodus of a close relative has replaced access to a government job as the leading model of economic success and social mobility in Mali. Sékou's neighbour also confessed to us that he was preparing the departure of his own son, along with three other young people from the village. The money sent back each month by an emigrant represents several local wages, often more than a civil servant with a university degree can expect. The risk of dependence on these flows of money does not just affect individual families or villages; as we shall see below, the governments of these countries are themselves tempted to specialize in the 'migration business'. Currently, 20 per cent of Mali's GDP comes from these remittances, if we include flows channelled through informal networks – a major resource for the fifth-poorest country on the planet.[32] 'If you sow emigrants, you harvest money', one of our interlocutors in Timbuktu told us.

You often hear people say that encouraging the flow of savings makes it possible to reduce the flow of departures, by promoting economic growth in the regions of origin. This statement of faith rests on three assumptions that are hazardous to say the least, and certainly need to be qualified. First of all, as Sékou's story shows, the link between inflow of funds and economic development is in no way automatic; it depends on a series of conditions – in particular the money being put to productive use – which are particularly difficult to combine. Second, as we saw above, the tie between the economic growth of a particular zone and the rate of emigration of its population is itself more complex than is usually believed. The correlation between the two phenomena is sometimes in fact a *positive* one. A population better-fed, better-educated and better-off tends to be a more mobile population, at least for an initial period.[33] Third, the arrival of financial resources from an emigrant relative, whatever may be the realities of their life in the host country, is accompanied by an image of success whose main effect is to encourage young people in the village to pack their bag and head off on the road of exile. Far more research will be needed, sociological in particular, to decipher the complex relationships that exist in Africa between the remittance of savings, economic development and emigration. One thing is sure – these are not as simple as we might like to believe.

From another point of view, what impact do these transfers have on the emigrants themselves? Experience shows that the 'virtuous emigrant', who sends part of his income each month back to his home country, by this very fact erects barriers to his own success in his country of settlement. One of the handicaps to the integration of immigrants in the countries of the North is indeed their level of savings: 60 per cent of sub-Saharan immigrants settled in France send money back to their home country, transfers that amount on average to around a quarter of their income.[34] These represent a brake on investment, both economic and emotional, in the host society – in addition to the challenges faced by anyone trying to settle in a foreign country. An immigrant is in fact expected to integrate into the population of the country where he is living, adopting behaviour as close to that of the latter as possible. Many migrants, however, with incomes already below the national average, drastically limit their spending in order to send money back to their families, reducing their ability to adopt a mode of life and economic behaviour typical of the host societies.[35] More than just 'savings', this money set aside is in reality a shift of spending power from the host country to the country of origin – and a deduction from the resources that the immigrant can invest in his own integration. It is estimated that 8 billion euros are sent from France each year, or the rough equivalent of French official development aid!

Whatever the effects on their integration and their communities of origin, sub-Saharan immigrants will continue to give financial support to their families who remain in Africa. This solidarity is often one of the reasons for emigrating. A rising number of immigrants will thus automatically increase the volume of these flows, which suggests attempts should be made to reduce the cost of transfers and to make the best use of them in the communities of origin. Should public policy actually aim at increasing this transfer of funds? That is not at all certain. Inciting immigrants to send their savings home, a policy with uncertain consequences for the healthy development of their home countries, amounts to discouraging them from investing in their new life – and thus inflaming the real problem of migration, which is that of integration.

4

Crowded Roads

As trees can hide a forest, so the migrations of sub-Saharans to Europe and North America eclipse a social phenomenon of far greater scale – and far more strategic as well. We mentioned already how migration within the region amounts to a flow four to eight times as great as the movement of its citizens to the rest of the world. The number of immigrants from Burkina Faso in France is estimated at 3,000, whereas there are more than 5 million scattered across West Africa.[1] There are powerful underlying currents at work over the years that are reshaping the African continent – involving an intensive exchange of populations. Whether it is a question of rural exodus, regional migration or trans-Saharan crossing, these invisible movements amount to an important way of regulating this space as it changes. At a time when the continent is being transformed, the way these regulatory movements develop will be a crucial factor. Who are these travellers now journeying on the roads of Africa? Where will they go tomorrow?

Crossroads of migration

Yesterday – as today – Africa's roads were taken by thousands of villagers heading for the continent's cities. This exodus swept up 80 million Africans in half a century;[2] it will affect far more in the decades to come. Though the natural growth of these cities has taken over from rural exodus as the major factor in their expansion, the growing attraction of urban life and the gradual using-up of agricultural land lead us to believe that rural exodus will continue to represent one of the main causes of African mobility. In Rwanda, Burundi and Kenya, civil peace is dependent on the successful operation of this urban outlet: the city and its satellites, in fact, are a natural destination for populations deprived of their means of subsistence in the countryside. Each day this inflow of people is shaping African cities. Drawing on existing connections, the new arrivals most often gather by community, region or village of origin – the first steps towards learning to live together within these urban mosaics. Such cities are a unique mixing place in countries that often comprise several hundred ethnic and linguistic communities. The city, as window on the world and its information networks, is also the melting-pot of African nations.

On their way, these populations travelling on the roads south of the Sahara cross the millions of migrants shifting from country to country within the sub-continent – depending on the vagaries of climate, political tensions, the availability of land or economic opportunity. These comings and goings across spaces that historically were only weakly populated correspond to ancestral tradition, which the many nomadic peoples of Africa, heedless of national borders, continue to embody. This is how the Peul herders of the Sahel or the Bozo fishers of the Niger River have lived for centuries. But the colonial powers, with their strategies of profiting from territories and forced labour, greatly accelerated this mixing of populations, with South and West Africa being its two principal poles. Regional migration to South Africa began as early as the late nineteenth century with the development of gold and diamond mining, and continued to grow as the twentieth century went on. Whether forced or voluntary, this movement of men and women into richer zones of activity was also at the root of the long-established movement of populations from the landlocked and arid Sahel regions towards the coastal zones of West Africa, where trading activity and production for the market developed.

Ghana, for example, was populated in the inter-war period by substantial movements of people into its cocoa plantations, when it was still the British 'Gold Coast'. A few years after independence, Côte d'Ivoire in turn experienced a genuine economic miracle. The prices of coffee and cocoa tripled in the space of two years, prompting the country to increase rapidly the area given over to major agricultural holdings. Building on the colonial practice of importing foreign labour-power, Côte d'Ivoire encouraged an inflow of workers from the neighbouring Sahel countries, which were experiencing serious climate problems. In a gesture of pan-African solidarity, President Houphouët-Boigny extended an open welcome to these new arrivals. Mossis from Burkina Faso and Peuls from Niger left their devastated countryside to help populate the Côte d'Ivoire cocoa belt. The need for labour was so great that, between 1976 and 1980, 1.3 million migrants flooded into this country with its economic miracle, contributing to the take-off of its economy. Nigeria and Gabon similarly saw the number of immigrants on their territories rise by eight and ten times respectively in the wake of the petroleum boom. The number of West Africans who have changed their country of residence between 1960 and 1990 is estimated at 30 million, i.e. an average of a million each year:[3] a 'breathing' phenomenon essential to home and host countries alike, given their different capacities for absorbing people.

Breakdown

If historic mobility patterns persist, and continue to represent considerable flows of men and women, several elements lead us to fear a 'breakdown' of internal migration.

'Internal' migrants, who made up close to 3.5 per cent of the population of sub-Saharan Africa in 1960 and 1980, had fallen to 2 per cent by 2010.[4] In a period of rising population, increasing density and insufficient economic development, places that lack labour, like Côte d'Ivoire in the days of its 'miracle', are increasingly rare. And at the same time, reasons for leaving – lack of access to essential services, lack of jobs for a young and mobile population, recurring political instability – persist right across the region. Added to this dangerous situation is the influence of European statements seen as resolutely hostile to immigration. Why should only Europeans and Americans limit the right of entry to their territories and keep out unwanted immigrants? Massive expulsions of migrants are not new in Africa,[5] but several events in recent years reveal a rise in xenophobia and nationalism across the continent – with potentially dramatic consequences.

The violence that followed the end of Houphouët-Boigny's rule in the 1990s is perhaps the most striking example of this.[6] In actual fact, the 'Ivorian model' of openness and sharing of agricultural profit between autochthonous and allochthonous[7] populations was knocked off course by the fall in coffee and cocoa prices of the late 1980s. In the space of a few years, the 'farmer state'[8] saw its resources steadily dwindle. Foreign debt sky-rocketed along with international interest rates, and the Bretton Woods[9] institutions summoned to the rescue made their rescheduling of debt conditional on drastic economic reforms. Four successive 'structural adjustment' plans[10] required a radical reduction in the bankrupt state's spending – affecting programmes of health care, education and agricultural subsidy. Their effects on the Ivorian social fabric were devastating. Whereas in 1985 less than 1 per cent of the urban population lived below the poverty line, this proportion had risen to 20 per cent by 1995. The young unemployed of Abidjan, returning to their native villages in search of work, found their land occupied and worked by immigrants, provoking a variety of conflicts between 'autochthones' and 'allochthones'.

This double impoverishment, urban and rural, took place at a time when the international community was pressing for a greater degree of democracy in African political systems. But the introduction of a multiparty system did not have the anticipated results in Côte d'Ivoire. In a climate of deep economic and social crisis, the electoral competition between parties gave rise to xenophobic rhetoric. The concept of *ivoirité*, quite alien to the country's tradition, mobilized thousands of 'patriotic' youngsters against the 'foreigners' who had come to steal land, women and jobs from 'native Ivorians'. One of the founding texts of this ideology illustrates very well the rhetoric of racial nationalism underlying it: '*Ivoirité* appears as a system...whose coherence even presupposes closure. Closure and control of our borders...Self-identification naturally presupposes differentiation from the other, and this demarcation postulates discrimination, whether this is intended or not.'[11] The first episodes of political violence at the turn of the century served as an excuse for anti-immigrant pogroms carried out by an army of young out-of-school city boys, readily malleable in the hands of political leaders seeking power. Many mass graves were dug, and hundreds of thousands of individuals originating from Burkina Faso or Mali, the majority of whom had been born in Côte d'Ivoire, were forced to 'return home' – or else continue their exodus. More than a million people were forced to migrate in the wake of the Ivorian political crisis, half of these moving to other countries.[12]

Africa will continue to receive the great majority of its own martyrs, whether they originate from the Great Lakes region, Darfur, the Gulf of Guinea or the Horn of Africa. Expelled from their native lands or host countries, these refugees are also a part of sub-Saharan mobility. Their number has regularly kept pace with post-colonial political storms, rising from 80,000 in 1960 to 6.5 million in the 1990s, before falling again below 3 million at the start of the new century, thanks to the relative calming of the previous decade's main centres of instability. It is quite unlikely that the flow will dry up in the decades to come.

The wave of xenophobia that enflamed the townships of South Africa in May 2008 seems to confirm this gloomy forecast, as well as the risk of a 'breakdown' of regional migration. Despite the expulsion of several hundred thousand foreigners to the neighbouring countries of Zimbabwe, Lesotho and Mozambique in the course of the 1990s, South Africa still counts almost 5 million immigrants on its soil, or 1 inhabitant in 10.[13] As in Côte d'Ivoire, movements to and fro from one side of the border to the other were traditional, and an integral part of the economic systems of both home and host countries. Like their grandparents, between a quarter and a third of Mozambicans and Zimbabweans have spent some of their lives in South Africa.[14] This is why the scale of violence unleashed against these 'African brothers' who had migrated to the country of Nelson Mandela surprised so many observers – including those in the country's own political establishment, with their background of historic struggle against the xenophobic violence of the apartheid regime.

The 'rainbow nation', country of the African renaissance whose constitution proclaims that it 'belongs to all who live in it, united in our diversity', was actually in optimistic mood in spring 2008. Eyes were riveted on the football World Cup to be held in summer 2010, for the first time in an African country, and the South African government was preparing an agreement for the free movement of citizens of fourteen southern African countries. In these years of economic growth, marked by a severe shortage of skilled labour, the country's policies allowed the immigration of workers from neighbouring countries. These skilled workers from the surrounding region arrived in South Africa's big cities at the same time as a large number of refugees hailing from the Democratic Republic of Congo, Zimbabwe, Ethiopia and Somalia. They were accepted rather than welcomed,[15] but this was in keeping with South Africa's resolutely pan-African stance on the international stage.

But anger is rumbling in the continent's leading economy, an anger fuelled by the deep fragility of a post-apartheid society riddled by extreme poverty and growing economic inequality. Racial segregation was rapidly replaced by a spatial segregation between the 'rainbow' quarters of the new South African middle class, including 2 million blacks, and the still one-colour townships. The high growth rate of the continent's premier economic power has been slow to improve the living conditions of the most deprived: 40 per cent of the population are unemployed, and a third of South Africans live on less than 2 dollars a day. Inequality between the black South African middle class and the population of the townships is among the greatest in the world, and translates into a difference of eighteen years in life expectancy. The groups of young people prowling Alexandra township, armed with knives, stones and petrol cans as they hunt for foreigners, are those left behind by the South African dream. At a time when economic boom goes hand in hand with acute social crisis, scapegoats for these disappointed hopes are all the more easy to find as many immigrants into the country are better educated than the average township inhabitant who grew up under apartheid. Images of riots shown on our TV screens show clearly that xenophobia is well and truly back in vogue in the rainbow nation.[16]

With globalization and its ruptures challenging identities, and the transformation of African societies and spaces shaking up communities, we should beware the emergence of an African ideology of exclusion. Europe is still bandaging the wounds of a century of nationalism. At a time when the full force of the African population explosion is making itself felt, and a new kind of environmental crisis is coming to a head, it would be dangerous to insist on rigid borders. And a reduction in regional mobility would be disastrous for Africa, its peoples and their neighbours.

The new nomads

The tens of thousands of travellers taking to the African roads each year also head for their immediate neighbours. Mobility between the sub-Saharan continent and the Maghreb goes back to ancient times. The Sahara desert, which saw caravans linking Noukachott and Timbuktu in the darkest days of the trans-Saharan slave trade, as well as ancestral pilgrimages to Mecca, has always been crossed both northward and southward. But these trans-Saharan routes have been brought back to life today by trade of a new kind, undertaken by a new type of adventurer. These new nomads are piled into a bus making for Tripoli, or stacked by the dozen in the back of a pick-up moving without lights through the darkness of a rocky plateau towards the Algerian border. Crossing the no-man's land of the Sahel, from the borders of Chad, Niger and Mali into the deserts of Algeria and Libya, are nomadic peoples, military forces of all kinds, rebels, traffickers in arms, drugs, cigarettes...and migrants. Agadez, a staging post for the Sahara in Niger, and a veritable hub of international migration, sees some 65,000 Africans pass through each year en route to the Mediterranean coast.[17]

These new nomads are the pioneers of a great shift in patterns of movement.[18] As well as places of departure and transit, the big cities of the Maghreb – from Rabat to Cairo via Oran, Annaba and Tripoli – have today become destinations in their own right. It is estimated that only between 20 and 40 per cent of trans-Saharan migrants reach Europe,[19] whatever their original intended destinations might have been. Their predecessors worked for a while in the big migratory turntables of the Maghreb, before continuing their odyssey. More and more often today, however, migrants settle here. Hard though it is to obtain precise figures, there seem to be more sub-Saharans now living in the Maghreb than in Europe.[20]

Caught between the demands for genuine Islamic fraternity, the implications of an African solidarity sporadically claimed, their needs as developing economies and the challenges of a new immigration, the societies that host these migrants vary in the hospitality they extend. Libya, for example, has become a genuine pole of immigration by virtue of the pan-African policy of its leader.[21] Colonel Muammar Gaddafi, disappointed by the weak support he received from fellow Arab countries when the United Nations placed his country under embargo in 1992, chose to radically reorient his foreign policy towards the African continent, part of this being the acceptance of immigrants from south of the Sahara. Libyan cities became in the 1990s a destination for countless arrivals from Sudan, Chad and Niger. This sudden influx of sub-Saharans, however, was badly received by the local population: violent riots broke out in September 2000, leading to the death of dozens of black Africans. This was followed by the expulsion of many of their number – a factor that helps to explain the sharp rise in sub-Saharan emigrants intercepted off European coasts in the year 2000.

In Algeria, too, sub-Saharan immigrants have been alternately tolerated and rejected – even both at once. These new arrivals on the labour market have helped to revitalize the south of the country, making up for the shortage of labour-power that for a long time delayed the construction of major infrastructure projects in southern Algeria. The population of Tamanrasset grew from 3,000 in 1966 to 65,000 in 1998, by which time half of the town's population were sub-Saharans.[22] But this growing contribution to the country's development did not prevent a policy of severe repression towards networks of sub-Saharan immigration.

The highly precarious situation in which the majority of black African immigrants settled on the southern shores of the Mediterranean find themselves makes them ready targets for arbitrary measures. Libya, for example, has continued this alternation between periods of openness and periods of closure, of invitation and expulsion. Between welcome and repression, stumbling forward through mistakes, the Maghrebian states have learned to a certain extent to manage this new phenomenon of migration that is set to grow further. In Cairo, Oran, Algiers, Rabat or Tripoli, the host societies are also absorbing the new arrivals. But racism is still bubbling underneath. 'A black man does not have a name; he is still called a slave, even by children', one migrant settled in Libya explains.[23] The slave trade across the Sahara continued until the late nineteenth century. Yet this open xenophobia on the part of the population does not prevent everyday interaction between Algerian, Moroccan or Libyan employers and Malian, Senegalese or Ivorian workers, in construction, agriculture and fishing.

In the wake of the countries of southern Europe, which in the second half of the twentieth century changed from lands of emigration to lands of immigrants coming from the southern shores of the Mediterranean, the Maghreb is now in turn faced with immigration in all its complexity. Since it is quite unlikely that trans-Saharan migration will slow down in the decades to come, and since Maghrebian societies will one day themselves need foreign labour to make up for shortages on their own labour markets, the states on the southern shores of the Mediterranean will be led to develop public policies to manage these flows. Tunisia, whose citizens now emigrate to Europe in ever smaller numbers, and whose economy attracts new arrivals each year, is in the process of becoming a country of net immigration. Its ageing population will require a change in its policies in just a few decades; its birth rate fell sharply from the 1960s on, and its population of old people will double in the next thirty years. The need to replace economically active Tunisians could rapidly become a beacon for the new trans-Saharan nomads.

Beijing–Dakar

It is a little-known fact that these hopefuls cross on their route north new arrivals who see Africa as a land of opportunity. These new Africans actually follow a long history of reception on the continent: for centuries sub-Saharan Africa has been a land of immigration.

There were, for example, the 'Malian Jews' who settled there in the first centuries CE,[24] or the Dutch colonists who established themselves at the Cape in the mid seventeenth century. There were also the freed slaves from America who, with the help of the American Colonization Society, left the United States for the shores of Africa where they established the republic of Liberia. Later came waves of Indians, transferred from one British colony to another to exploit the broad territories of East Africa that the Crown had newly acquired. The construction of the British East African Railroad from Mombasa to Kampala in the late nineteenth century required tens of thousands of 'coolies' drawn from Gujarat and Punjab.[25] It was his championing of the Indians of South Africa, moreover, that began Gandhi's non-violent struggle against the various forms of discrimination under the British Empire.[26] Their descendants today number several hundred thousand, in the big cities of East Africa. Despite the expulsion of 50,000 of their number by Idi Amin Dada in 1972 (when they made up 2 per cent of the Ugandan population), they are still the largest foreign community in Africa. Sikh and Hindu temples in Nairobi, or Ismaili mosques in Kampala, are evidence of this old-established presence.

These immigrants also include the communities of Syrian and Lebanese traders who have prospered for over a century in many cities of West Africa, their numbers increased by new arrivals fuelled by the repeated episodes of violence in the Middle East. Present right across the continent, the Lebanese community today numbers between 300,000 and 500,000 – Maronite Christians, Shiite or Sunni Muslims. Immigrants of first, second, third or fourth generation, sometimes married to African women, these businessmen have carved out an essential place in the operation of West African economies. Still today, many young Lebanese continue to join their acquaintances settled in Senegal, Côte d'Ivoire or Cameroon, to set up in the wholesale or retail trade, hostelry, textiles, foodstuffs, etc. Africa, the last frontier for these unparalleled pioneer traders, is in their eyes a promised land in the early twenty-first century, offering their businesses a stability that is sadly lacking in their own country, as well as expanding markets. It is also a place of social mobility: the 'success stories' of Lebanese in Africa are legion. The most fortunate of these immigrants re-invest considerable sums in their country of origin.

The fabled African melting-pot is still bubbling today, recently fuelled by a massive influx of Chinese immigrants. The number of Chinese living on the continent is said to have risen fivefold in five years – almost as fast as the growth in bilateral trade. While the Chinese presence in Africa was still no more than hearsay in the early 1990s,[27] there are today five times more Chinese in Africa than French, making up the second-largest foreign community. Their number was close to three-quarters of a million in 2009 – though neither African governments nor the Chinese are able to measure it accurately. Both know, however, that these hundreds of thousands of new arrivals are only the advance party, and that many more of their compatriots will follow. Arriving in connection with a construction project or under their own steam, sometimes illegally, these expatriates have initially settled mainly in South Africa, Nigeria, Angola and Madagascar. They are ever more visible in all the continent's big cities: from Abidjan to Douala, Luanda to N'Djamena, thousands of Chinese restaurants have flourished in the African cities in recent years.

If Serge Michel and Michel Beuret were surprised to hear a group of African children in Brazzaville greet them with *ni hao*, the two journalists explained in their book devoted to these new immigrants that 'for them, all foreigners are Chinese'.[28] From the rich Beijing businessman to the humblest of workers, by way of a class of restaurant owners and shopkeepers, China's congested population has found a new outlet in Africa. This continent, seemingly so rich and empty, has become their new Far West. 'Africa really is an immense opportunity, just at the right time. It is the last place like this on earth where you can do so much business', says Jacob Wood, the Chinese owner of a large hotel in Nigeria.[29] Supported by both Chinese authorities and African elites, this growing diaspora plays the role of a Chinese bridgehead on the continent. The agreements between Yaoundé and Beijing state that Chinese are the only foreigners to enjoy the right to stay for eighteen months in Cameroon without a work contract.[30] Agencies in Shanghai and Beijing, as well as other Chinese cities, have already been specializing for several years in the export of Chinese workers, working flat-out in the enormous projects that are starting up every day.

Besides workers and managers in civil engineering, extractive industries and clothing, there is a veritable army of shopkeepers besieging Africa's towns, aiming to conquer a market of 860 million that is ever growing. Who knows the irresistible force of population growth better than the Chinese? This market will double and then triple in the coming decades. Sellers of cheap 'made in China' trinkets, T-shirts and shoes, dolls and 'super wax' *pagnes*, they busy themselves in opening up to Africans the gilded gates of mass consumption. In Dakar, where there are over 1,000, their shops have taken firm root on the Boulevard Charles-de-Gaulle – the main artery where the Senegal army parades. Bedecked with fluorescent neon signs or painted in bright pastels, and offering a profusion of goods, the same shops can be found in Yaoundé, Abidjan or Brazzaville.

But not everything is rosy in this new African melting-pot. Anger is regularly expressed towards these tyrants of labour, accused of unfair competition by Senegalese, Ivorian or

Congolese traders. Violent anti-Chinese revolts in the Zambian copper mines served as a warning. Even Chinese prostitutes undercut local prices, threatening the famous Cameroon *wolowos* with unemployment.[31] Despite these occasional and sometimes violent tensions, a mutual learning process is under way, on the basis of well-understood common interests: thousands of young Africans are learning Chinese, which is taught in the major African universities and sometimes in high school.

Faithful to its history, which is one of a melting-pot, the continent of 2,000 languages[32] thus forms a vast mosaic. As proof of its ever deeper involvement in globalization, Africa has enrolled in turn in the International of migration. Faced with the tightening of controls in Eastern Europe, it has become, in the space of a few years, a privileged place of transit to Europe for international migration networks. The town of Agadez shelters Pakistanis en route to the Algerian coast. The airports of Dakar or Douala see Asian migrants pass through on their way to Paris or London. Piled into boats making the crossing from West Africa to the Canary Islands, African travellers now rub shoulders with Chinese, Bangladeshi, Palestinian or Iraqi migrants.[33] Playing its part in the age of globalization, Africa is more than ever a place of passage.

Its population exploding, traversed by peoples in motion, Africa is swarming. But this is not the swarm of a vast column heading for the gates of Europe. Rather, as a place of asylum and exodus, of pioneers and refugees, Africa is swarming like an ant-hill: each odyssey has its destination, its direction and – for those who understand it – its own meaning. This seeming din made up of contradictory movements back and forth is by no means without purpose: whether desired or forced, these regulatory movements fuel the transformation of spaces being occupied – re-formed as the routes of migration evolve. Stirred by the changes it is undergoing, at full throttle, Africa is on the march.

But will it be able to function?

Part Three

Africa against Growth?

The African continent appears to lag behind in the world growth stakes: a desperate case in the eyes of public opinion, a bad example for the economists. Both are guilty of blindness. Europe seems as unable to recognize how African growth has taken off again as it was inept at grasping the causes of its breakdown – not to mention its own role in this. And yet both breakdown and take-off are readily understandable. Analysis of the former helps to explain why we now have the latter, how sustainable it is, and what its weak points are: a small detour, therefore, through the land of the economists.

5

The Undiscoverable Curse

In relation to Africa, compassion is always *de rigueur*. Essayists[1] and charitable enterprises fall over themselves to depict a continent that is permanently poor, outside of globalization, abandoned to famine and war. Prisoners of a corrupt political class, an inhospitable nature and archaic traditions, its peoples are promised a fate made up of poverty, hunger and violence. Study of the economic history of the last fifty years has even led two celebrated American economists[2] to speak of a genuine 'tragedy' of African economic growth.

Is sub-Saharan Africa, like the tragic hero struggling in vain against his destiny, in mortal combat with an accursed fate sealed in advance? Despite overcoming the 'childhood illnesses of independence'[3] that René Dumont diagnosed in 1962, the persistence of great poverty has confirmed the theory of 'African exceptionalism' in the eyes of many commentators.

A fatality of race?

There is indeed a striking contrast with other regions of the global South, even though these were generally richer than the African nations when they gained independence.[4] During the 1970s and 1980s, while Latin America and East Asia had respective growth rates of 2 and 5 per cent, African living standards were stagnant. When China launched the great economic catching-up process that enabled it to lift first hundreds of thousands, then millions, out of poverty each year, the number of people living in extreme poverty south of the Sahara actually *increased*. This African malaise was so long and so traumatic for the continent that sub-Saharan Africa in the early twenty-first century had built up several sad records. Thirty-one of the thirty-five countries classified lowest in terms of human development are in Africa. The standard of living of a sub-Saharan is on average only a third that of an Asian and a quarter that of a Latin American. Life expectancy, which has *declined* in relation to the 1980s, is just forty-seven, i.e. 24 years less than in East Asia and 32 years less than the inhabitants of the OECD countries. African children are 33 times more likely to die before the age of five than those in the advanced countries, and five times more likely than their Latin American counterparts. Need we continue this sad awards ceremony? Sub-Saharan Africa is the part of the world where agricultural yields are lowest and increases in production slowest. Nearly half of the fifty countries most deeply affected by corruption are on this wounded continent,[5] which could also boast more deaths from war at the turn of the century than the rest of the planet combined.[6] All this, despite the fact that development aid in the 1990s made up more than 15 per cent of the African countries' GDP.[7]

Is underdevelopment, then, an African fate – a curse whose source lies in its climate, its culture or its institutions? Countless experts have peered over the bedside of this suffering Africa, seeking the underlying causes – in some cases, just one cause – for the chronic underdevelopment that cripples the continent. From Robert Barro[8] to Paul Collier,[9] by way of Jeffrey Sachs,[10] William Easterly[11] and Patrick and Sylviane Guillaumont,[12] eminent economists have sought the key to this 'African tragedy' in complex calculations. But a decade of statistical analysis[13] and bitter academic debates have not managed to get to the root of the 'African dummy variable' – this unexplained statistical residue indicating that the mere fact of being African penalizes a country in terms of growth. Like tarot cards, tea leaves and constellations, the databases have been far from eloquent on this enigma, supplying in each case contradictory findings,[14] circular arguments and a chaos of truisms. We thus learn that a low rate of economic growth is correlated[15] with a country being landlocked, with low levels of education and – surprise! – periods of war. A still further imaginative step has been taken by a young Zambian economist, who found development aid itself to be the cause of Africa's poor economic performance.[16]

Behind the scientific quest for 'the cause' we can see the shadow of an old hunt for the guilty party: who is responsible for African underperformance? Each hypothesis has its own suspect. Arguments of bad luck (Africa's geographical misfortune condemns it to underdevelopment) have been answered by those of a plot (Africa as victim of the countries of the North, who work to keep it in a state of underdevelopment), and these challenged in their turn by the champions of Africa's own responsibility (Africa as victim of Africans, incapable of entering modernity), in a dialogue of disconcerting sterility. Yet these reductionist discourses, erected into dogmatic explanations, have strongly influenced debate and penetrated popular wisdom, so it is far from useless to review them briefly here.

Geographical accident

Bad historians are worse geographers, yet their literature has long stamped its mark on ideas of African underdevelopment. Africa, according to them, is condemned by its geography. The 'African tragedy' is explained quite simply by the unfortunate position of these countries on the globe.

These arguments are supported by the power of intuition – what Pierre Bourdieu called the 'truth effect': how can we fail to note that the economies of the world's temperate zone are rather rich, whereas those of the tropics are generally poorer?[17] But this infamous 'curse of the tropics'[18] still needs explanation. Aristotle already appealed to it in his *Politics*, maintaining that cold climates developed the intelligence.[19] Niccoló Machiavelli later developed this theme in his own political reflections, but it was Montesquieu who developed this line of thought into a genuine 'theory of climates', leading our encyclopaedist to write:

> We have already said that great heat enervates the strength and courage of men; and that in cold climates there was a certain strength of body and mind that rendered men capable of long, arduous, great and bold actions... We should not be surprised therefore that the cowardice of the peoples of hot climates has almost always

rendered them slaves, while the courage of the peoples of cold climates has kept them in freedom.

It equally follows that 'the peoples of hot countries are timid like old men; those of cold countries are courageous like young men'.[20]
QED: it is climate that explains the 'African torpor'.[21]
Its dubious scientific parentage has not discouraged certain celebrated contemporary writers from giving new credibility to this old intuition – greatly reinforced by statistical calculations. According to Jeffrey Sachs, one of its modern heralds, 'at the root of African impoverishment lies...its extraordinarily disadvantageous geography'.[22] Starting from the fact that only two tropical countries (Singapore and Hong Kong) figure among the thirty 'developed' economies, the American academic seeks to demonstrate how a country's geographical latitude constitutes – statistically, of course, as it is the figures that speak – a handicap for its economic development. The tropics are particularly unfavourable to agriculture, health and the transfer of technologies, since tropical soils, being more fragile, do not permit cereal cultivation, while infectious diseases are more widespread (malaria, but today also AIDS, on which Sachs leaves epidemiologists to determine the precise link with tropical geographies, accepting that this is a highly complex question) and transport costs there are particularly high, especially in the rainy season. Since sub-Saharan Africa is the region of the world with the largest share of population and land lying in the tropics, it is particularly penalized. 'Divine injustice', we can then reply to Africans concerned for their fate: you are poor due to an 'accident of latitude',[23] coming into the world in the wrong part of the globe... *Tristes tropiques!* To sum up, if Africa does not grow, it is because it is located in Africa. Tautology no. 1.

The existence of particular geographical constraints in Africa is undeniable – starting with the landlocked position of certain countries, the presence on the continent of one of the world's greatest deserts, the hostility of the forest cover and the fragility of its soils. But to make geography the underlying cause of African underdevelopment would amount to prolonging the general confusion about these unhistorical half-truths: the greater parts of Asia and Latin America have encountered the same kind of geographical characteristics on their growth path, if not worse. Malaysia, for example, is much like Kenya or Côte d'Ivoire in this respect.

Colonial drama

Dissatisfied with these 'hard luck' theories that fail to recognize the force of human history and conflicting interests in play, other writers have seen in the persistence of African underdevelopment the invisible hand of the industrialized powers in search of markets and raw materials, who have sought to keep the Third World in its ties of dependence. The African tragedy is in their view the logical result of colonialism[24] – the continuation of loss of sovereignty by other means. Africa is condemned not by its geography but by its history.

Much in vogue in the 1960s and 1970s, these arguments continue to fuel certain contemporary reflections by the global justice movement – African in particular – on the continent's underdevelopment. As a sequel to the slave trade, followed by the enforced loss of sovereignty, the 'African exception' would then be the product of a disguised neocolonialism. According to these theories, the stagnation of the African economies in the 1980s and 1990s did not take place despite the rapid growth of other economies on the planet but actually *because* of this: continuing the colonial project, the states of the North carried on exploiting the continent by structures of unequal exchange, underpinned by a world economic order biased in favour of the richest – all justified by an omnipotent neoliberal ideology. Constrained by the Western multinationals firmly established on their territory to buy high-priced manufactured goods and overcharged services, Africans were thus confined by the world trading system to the export of unprocessed raw materials, whose prices were determined in Chicago and London. A 'rich continent of poor people',[25] sub-Saharan Africa did not benefit from the natural resources extracted daily from its subsoil; and in this way the elites of the rich countries exploited the poorest of poor countries, with the criminal complicity of these countries' rich elites. According to the Argentine economist Raul Prebisch, international trade is a zero-sum game, the enrichment of the rich countries being inversely proportional to that of the poor.

In this view, there would be no mystery in the fact that Africa, stuck in these relations of unequal exchange, experienced a fall in its standard of living while Europe and the United States were

enjoying the unprecedented growth of the 'thirty glorious years';
economic take-off for Africa would thus depend on uncoupling
from the world's other economies. Africans may well feel angry,
but no escape from the continent's economic crisis will be possible without a radical change in the ties of dependence that bind
the sub-Saharan nations to their former colonial capitals. This
analysis leads its most radical champions to demand the suppres-
sion pure and simple of the World Bank, the IMF and the World
Trade Organization, all three accused of perpetrating this unequal
order.[26] Why are you poor, Africans? Because your history is
African. Tautology no. 2.

Theories that development aid is an instrument of capitalist
domination are paradoxically joined today by arguments born at
the other extreme of the ideological range, which are just as hostile
to aid: neoliberal theories of 'dead aid'[27] also denounce such solidarity as a cause of dependence – an argument heard in all the
industrialized countries when they established systems of social
insurance and welfare.

Denunciation of a form of 'neocolonial curse' lies at the root of
certain powerful critiques of the many imperfections that persist
in the world market, which the most vulnerable economies are the
first to suffer. These also relate to in-depth analyses of the limits
and negative effects of aid, as of any form of external injection
of funds. But by locating the causes of underdevelopment at the
heart of the international economic system, and proposing an
interest for the rich countries in prolonging the underdevelopment of the poorest regions of the planet, they actually prevent
any escape from poverty for the countries situated at the bottom
of the chain, in the absence of an anti-capitalist world revolution.
This is a highly fatalistic conclusion which equally fails to account
for the economic take-off experienced by several other developing
countries.

Cultural adjustment programme

Refusing to absolve Africans of all responsibility for their own
fate, other writers have sought elsewhere the causes of the stubborn underdevelopment that undermines the very identity of the
peoples living south of the Sahara: in their institutions and their

underlying culture. Africa, wary of progress, is in their view, above all, its own victim, prey to a series of traditions that are deeply incompatible with development.

> For us, the overall cause, indeed the single cause, that lies at the root of all deviations, is African culture: characterized by self-suffi-ciency, passivity, its lack of eagerness to go and meet other cultures before the latter impose themselves on it and crush it, and its inabil-ity, once the harm is done, to develop under this contact without falling into an abject imitation.[28]

Does Africa thus need, as the – African – author of these lines maintains, a 'cultural adjustment programme'?

A whole collection of writings vigorously denounces the neg-ligence of the post-colonial state in Africa: its factionalism, its ever-present corruption, its ready resort to violence. They count the costs of these daily scandals for the continent's economy, and describe the most abominable forms of these. These cries from the heart, born from the anger that the spectacle of human wastage arouses, are in principle only too justified. Too few, alas, avoid the trap of culturalism[29] – the most deceitful of reductionisms. This denunciation quickly changes into an unrestrained discourse, marked by a shameless racism that parades freely under cover of uttering the 'truth that no one dares speak'. Used in the singular, 'African culture' then becomes single and immutable. Africa's diversity being complex, a complexity hard to penetrate, African unity is assumed, despite all signs to the contrary, giving free rein to all these stereotypes of 'African man' – modern synonym for the 'black soul'[30] that colonial anthropology used to seek out in an earlier age. In thrall to their community, the slaves of tra-ditions, Africans are unable to realize themselves as individuals. Fatalistic and servile, they defer to the most corrupt and auto-cratic authority. Enclosed in superstitious obscurantism, they are impervious to reason. Capable of the most inhuman violence, they rediscover the original barbarism of the first man, 'man in the raw state'.[31] Imprisoned by ethnic loyalty, forced into unconditional solidarity, their spirit of enterprise is broken. Lacking the aware-ness of time, and heedless of the future, they live permanently in the present.

Need we go further in search of the mystery of African stag-nation? The American intellectuals Harrison and Huntingdon[32] explain that certain cultures, because they produce inappropriate social institutions, are deeply incompatible with economic growth. Few cultures are further from the Weberian ideal type of the Protestant work ethic than this sub-Saharan culture. In the opposition between 'local tradition' and 'universal modernity', with the process of civilization inevitably leading societies of the first kind towards the second, Africa is thus hemmed in and cornered by its own sins – rejecting development.[33] If we follow Fukuyama in believing that the organization of societies in the capitalist and democratic mode is the ultimate stage on the long road of development, then Africa, dragging painfully behind it its cultural ball and chain, finds it hard to join in with the end of history. It has only itself to blame. Why are you poor, Africans? Because your culture is African. Tautology no. 3.

This set of arguments with a Hegelian flavour, which surge up without warning in the most conventional discourse, pollutes debates on African underdevelopment. Falling into a foolish identitarianism, they fail to appreciate the plurality of cultures and their meanings; the manipulation of norms and traditions; the play of interests. Just as Islam has become for certain people the only interpretative grid for the thoughts and actions of Muslims, so this immutable African-ness explains every stance and action, insidiously trapping Africans in a deceitful social construction. What is this supposed African culture? That of Bamako or that of Cape Town? That of the 1950s, of the late twentieth century, or of today? And who is this African whose soul is so familiar to us? A farmer? A driver? A teacher? Is *Homo africanus* the same *Homo economicus* throughout the continent?[34] Throughout history?

Fifty years ago, great intellectuals explained to us, with weighty arguments, why Asia was condemned to famine and underdevelopment;[35] how Asian culture and institutions, imprinted by Confucianism, formed insurpassable obstacles to the region's development. Thirty years later, their intellectual heirs explained how the Confucian ethic was crucial to the economic take-off of East Asia and its entry into modernity. Will we let ourselves be gulled again by the sirens of culturalism?

Geographism, structuralism, culturalism: these three theses, that both confront one another and mingle in contemporary discourse on Africa, clumsily support the argument of its fated underdevelopment. And in the way that they make fragments of truth into 'explanation', these reductionist visions resemble each other. Their common foundation is a fatalism so characteristic of scientistic discourse: whether the African crisis is due to the continent's geographical misfortune, to the imperial ambitions of industrialized powers, or to a specific sub-Saharan culture, Africa actually has little chance of rapidly curing itself of the disease affecting it. Claiming to raise the veil of the 'African mystery', they actually perpetuate it. The 'African tragedy' is a tenacious myth, and it justifies inaction.

6

The Great Wheel of Growth

The tragedy of African underdevelopment is certainly not as it is commonly depicted. Africa is condemned neither by its geography nor by its history, and not even by its institutions – still less by the economic aid it has received, more parsimoniously than what is often believed. No curse keeps Africa's population in poverty. But in that case, how are we to understand twenty years of economic regression? And how can we judge whether the present improvement will last?

Let us simply take a look at the pitiless mechanism of economic cycles. We shall then see that African underdevelopment over these last thirty years does not derive from some kind of 'mystery' specific to Africa, from a plot by the industrialized countries or an African lack of aptitude for development. Caught in a machine it did not control, victim of both internal and international policy mistakes, Africa could not follow the path of those countries that have emerged from poverty in the course of the last few decades. Rather than a complete and utter failure, what we have here is a succession of crises. Where certain writers see the sign of an 'African tragedy', we see only a banal tragedy of economic cycles. Let us take the time to relate it.

Act one: a good start in Africa

Champions of the 'African tragedy' often forget that the early years of independence were actually a real golden age for the continent.

The 1950s and 1960s were full of hope for the young African nations – hope largely fulfilled for over a decade. Buoyed up by a favourable international conjuncture, economic growth on the continent was sustained. The renewal embodied by charismatic founding fathers, on the model of Nkrumah in Ghana or Nyerere in Tanzania, involved the new African elites taking charge of state apparatus and the economy. Several foreign businesses were nationalized, swelling the ranks of an expanding civil service. Priority was given to the establishment of genuine national industries, considered at this time to be the most direct path out of under-development. Advised by an army of technical assistants from the developed countries, African leaders defined the priority sectors and directed investment towards them, using five-year plans to make best use of the scarce resources that their young nations were able to mobilize. Electrification, the building of roads and ports: infrastructure was the proclaimed priority of these planning states, in perfect accord with the dominant economic theories of the time.

This productive upsurge translated into strong economic growth, helped by several years of good harvests and favourable prices for Africa's main exports. The 'catching-up' phenomenon was fully at work: the investments in the African economic machine that were so sorely needed allowed for a rapid rise in production. Exports rose from year to year, and the economic growth rate reached an average of 4.6 per cent per year between 1960 and 1973 – well above population growth. This economic performance was concretely expressed in a major improvement in the main social indicators: life expectancy rose by several months each year, and school enrolment shot up remarkably.

Ten years after African independence, indeed, the concerned gaze of international experts did not focus on this continent in full economic upswing, but rather on the Far East. Overpopulation, famine and economic backwardness: an alarmed report by the World Bank in 1969 viewed Asia as the endangered continent.[1] Who would believe this today? At that time the African GDP per capita was higher than that of Asia, excluding Japan.[2]

We should note that this proud Africa, launched at full speed on the path of economic catching-up, suffered from the same ills that some people today consider as absolute barriers to its development. The continent's geographical constraints, from the landlocked position of some countries to the fragility of its soils, were already a reality for this growing Africa. One should add that, at that time, Africa possessed neither the treatments that medical advance has brought in the last fifty years, nor the transport infrastructure, fertilizer and agricultural techniques that it has mastered in that time. Neocolonial practices were still in full swing, in the midst of the Cold War. The former metropolises, in fact, were not prepared to sacrifice their economic interests for the sake of independence, a lesson that Sékou Touré, who brought down on himself the wrath of France by opting for 'total independence' in 1958, learned to his cost. As well as the de facto political control granted by a series of military treaties, France also exercised a monetary stewardship over a good part of the continent by means of the CFA franc – managed from Paris. Foreign economic aid was at its height – whatever those who more recently condemn this 'dead aid' might say. African traditions, which several contemporary observers perceive as so damaging to the continent's development, were also far more weighty in rural societies that remained isolated from the outside world, compared with today. The continent's labour-power remained very poorly educated, with only a very small proportion of the population having access to primary education. Despite all this, Africa in the 1960s experienced vigorous growth.

But the African economic landscape was not all rosy; plague had penetrated prosperous Thebes. Serious structural weaknesses underlay this first act of post-independence economic history, exposing the young African nations to the coming conjunctural downturn.[3]

Colonial Africa had in fact bequeathed them its export-driven infrastructure and cash-crop economy. A rational solution in the age of colonization, this economic model turned into a slow poison once independence was won. The French colonies, for example, had a system of duties on the movement of goods from and to the metropolis, designed to finance their administration.[4] The production system in Africa after independence, and thus the structure of state receipts, mechanically followed this economic model built around the export of unprocessed materials: cocoa, coffee, cotton, hydrocarbons and minerals. The former colonies continued to sell their exports to the old colonial powers and, despite an arbitrary policy of import substitution, continued to buy from these the great bulk of the manufactured goods they consumed, for want of alternatives. These exchanges fuelled the state budgets by way of customs dues. The Lomé conventions, the first of which was signed in 1975 and viewed as an exemplary system of cooperation between countries of North and South, illustrate the prolonging of this economic system that privileged cash crops, focused on the former colonial powers. The preferential trade of colonial times, which consisted in the export of raw materials from agriculture and mining free of duty, was in effect replaced by a 'privileged trade regime' that favoured the African and Caribbean countries. Their main exports enjoyed a system of guaranteed prices. This mechanism, unique of its kind, was initially created in order to guarantee the African economies a supply of foreign currency, but actually trapped them ever more in a very marked economic specialization that privileged cash crops over food cultivation.

The growing industrialization of African economies was in fact financed by major taxes on the agricultural sector, which rapidly suffocated its more fragile participants. Food crops, with very low yields and neglected by public investment, soon proved unable to supply the big cities of a continent undergoing a rapid urban expansion. Encouraged by an overvalued currency in the greater part of the continent, African states continued to import food from abroad, rendering themselves unable to reduce their foodstuffs deficit. The young sub-Saharan industry, for its part, struggled against an unpropitious environment for economic take-off: uncompetitive internationally due to high transport costs, with a low productivity of labour and an overvalued exchange rate,[5] it could not count on the internal African market either. Domestic demand for manufactured products, weak because of a population that was still largely rural and lacking in funds, was not in a position to take over from exports in order to drive the sub-Saharan economies. On the import side as well as that of exports, the vulnerability of this economic system to fluctuations in terms of trade and international prices was therefore considerable.

Another great weakness of the African economies in the 1960s was the size of their public sector. At the time of independence, the state seized from the hands of the colonizers focused the expectations of a generation of African intellectuals: they set out to free Africa from the colonial yoke, educate the masses, industrialize the continent. Less idealistically, the new ruling elites had every interest in taking up fashionable ideologies in order to assert their control of the national economy – ensuring themselves, in passing, of a stable source of revenue. Under cover of either Keynesian or socialist economic theories, vast public apparatuses with expanding bureaucracies were established, with a multitude of state companies and various stabilization funds, largely pilfered by the ruling classes. The most skilled politicians, like Houphouët-Boigny, were able to use this bonanza to obtain critical political support.[6] Others used the goldmine of public resources for their personal enrichment and that of their clan. In both cases, this organization of the economy proved particularly draining on public resources: the salaries of civil servants absorbed an average of 40 per cent of the African state budgets,[7] and sometimes far more. This has been equally paralysing for economic initiative: in the 1960s and 1970s, anything that was not expressly permitted was banned. Of course, such permission could still be bought. Corruption then ravaged the social system. Exorbitant customs duties decked with legal – or, more often, irregular – exemptions; permits of all kinds open to purchase; licences that were obligatory only for the deprived; plundering, though negotiable, taxation; all these ills lethal for growth developed at high speed. This model, besides being particularly costly, was viable only on three conditions. First, the revenues from exports had to continue to flow into stabilization funds; second, the big international banks had to continue to grant major loans to the African states or their big national companies; third, the African states had to continue to receive the revenue from 'strategic rent' that their position as allies in the Cold War granted them. These three conditions were all more or less fulfilled through the 1960s and 1970s.

Act two: out of control

The decade of the 1970s saw this African economic machine run out of control, with a forward flight into debt. Act II of our tragedy, in fact, took place against a more comfortable background. The rise in prices of raw materials and the steady expansion of cultivated land led to a rise in export revenues – rapidly raising the question of the best use of the currency thus generated. This was, unsurprisingly, a time of 'white elephants' that were characteristic of the ambition of the new African nations and the hopes raised by rising prices. These were also symptomatic of a climate of confrontation between Cold War blocs that was partly played out on African territory. The development aid generously granted to African leaders aligned with the positions of Washington, Moscow, Paris or Beijing served as a weapon in the ideological battle between competing economic models. The coronation of Emperor Bokassa of Central Africa in 1977 (the cost of which, amounting to a full year of the country's budget, was partly financed by French aid)[8] was a typical symbol of these fat years – even if the escapades of Idi Amin Dada were just as horrific and wasteful. The former Belgian colonialists also had their cross to bear, in the actions of their turbulent protégé, President Mobutu.

The period of inflation that followed the first oil shock of 1973 greatly reduced the cost of borrowing, easing the mobilization of foreign resources for African expenditure. Western banks, needing to recycle the petrodollars that they managed, lent freely to African states whose credit ratings had been increased by the higher prices of their exports. The OECD states also took part in this great economic merry-go-round: the commercial scramble of the 1970s led them to finance the worst lunacies on credit. How many billions in tied aid[9] led to the building of unviable cement plants, hospitals devoid of staff, or roads leading nowhere? Such a count was never made, but it would undoubtedly spotlight the recklessness of Western lenders, rendered blind or imprudent by the smell of money and the indulgent climate of political compromise that marked the Cold War. The Eastern bloc did not lag behind, responsible for some spectacular performances in this genre, with Guinea-Bissau a telling example. You can still see the snowploughs rusting away!

As for multilateral development aid,[10] it also forgot the principles of economic sustainability that it proclaimed, and closed its eyes to the absurdity of several economic sectors that it supported. The African governments, who assumed revenues would be stable and interest rates low, got heavily into debt in order to finance gigantic projects. The earliest of these, benefiting from the catch-up effect, could show high rates of profit. But a large number of the major works thus financed were ill conceived, unsuited to the African context or oversized – involving high running costs and hence a strong pull on public expenditure. In order to face up to the steep rise in prices at the time of the second shock – oil and

cereals – of 1973, several African states also adopted policies of
price support, increasing still more the weight of public expenditure and consequently the risk for the sub-Saharan economy to a
fall in export receipts. Between 1972 and 1980 this led to a rise in
African debt of some 20 per cent per year, to reach nearly a quarter
of African GDP.[11]

But this sword of Damocles hanging over the young African
economies was hidden until the end of the decade by a combination of rising export revenues, abundant development aid that
paid little heed to the use of the funds granted, and generous loans
from banks with money to spare. With its existence camouflaged
and its fall delayed, the 'debt economy' of the 1970s charged this
sword with a colossal weight.

Act three: the fall

Then came the fall. It was only in the early 1980s that the defects
left by the colonizers in the African economic system and the initial
choices of the sub-Saharan ruling elites revealed their destabilizing potential. The 'scissors crisis',[12] provoked by the sudden and
lasting fall in export prices for African raw materials along with
the dizzying rise in interest rates, plunged the continent, within a
few years, into a long period of stagnation, from which it has been
struggling to emerge.

Between 1979 and 1982 the prices of Africa's main exports fell
in real terms to their lowest level since 1950. States that were
highly dependent on this sweet poison saw their revenues fall
away. Government treasuries emptied. Borrowing, the miracle
solution of the 1970s, became impossible: Mexico's default on
its national debt in 1982 led to capital becoming much more
expensive. This escalation in the interest rates paid by the countries
of the South had a snowball effect on the debt built up during the
previous decades. Servicing an overblown and still growing debt
added to the strong inertia of public expenditure. It drained state
finances and devoured budgets. Deprived of the export earnings
and foreign capital from which they lived, African states no longer
had the means to carry out the least productive investment. The
investment rate in their economies fell from 20 to 15 per cent in

the space of a few years, leading to a net decapitalization: a meagre public investment was insufficient to make up for the rapid deterioration of infrastructures. On top of this, public development aid surrendered investment. It was used above all to relieve the major Western banks whose balance sheets were weakened by doubtful debtors, and to refinance African sovereign debt to public creditors – a system that conveniently made it possible to gloss over the respective shares of responsibility in this unsustainable indebtment. International aid also served to a smaller degree to cover the current expenditures of African states crumbling under outstanding payments, in order to stave off a bankruptcy that would have been catastrophic for all concerned.

Called in by Africa's creditors to rescue a cash-strapped continent, and concerned not to assume the unenviable role of liquidator, the Bretton Woods institutions delivered a diagnosis without appeal: given the scale of the crisis, the African economies needed structural adjustment. The objective was to create the foundations of a liberal economy, which would guarantee a better allocation of resources. The great pendulum of economic theory swung from one orthodoxy to another: out with dysfunctional interventionism, in with the market. The Washington institutions, deeply marked by the neoliberal consensus of the Thatcher–Reagan years, were adamant: it was urgent to reach a balanced budget; to drastically reduce public expenditure, including the social sectors; to abandon the costly model of 'redistributive bureaucracy'; to end the practice of price subsidy; to privilege the repayment of foreign debt (debt due to foreign lenders) over that of internal debt (salaries due to civil servants, payment of local businesses); to privatize; and to dismantle customs tariffs. Triggered by the dilapidated state of African public finances, this package of reforms was conceived and applied in the initial conviction that an Africa with rectified public finances could rapidly find a new path of growth. The change had to take place at a forced pace: for the adepts of 'shock therapy',[13] only a brutal transformation of structures could end the bad practices built up over decades: a form of catharsis, from the ashes of which would arise prosperous liberal democracies.

This economic liberalization was necessary to tackle the stalemate of corrupt dirigisme and ethnicized economic interventionism. But it was done in the worst possible conditions. The structural adjustment programmes involved waves of privatization, at a time when buyers were not exactly knocking at the doors to purchase state enterprises. The hasty opening up of economies that had long been protected from international competition, carried out prior to the liberalization of domestic markets, sometimes led to the conversion of public monopolies to private ones, and thus public rents to private; it meant the dismantling of the little manufacturing industry that the twenty previous years of interventionism had generated. The insistence on a strictly balanced budget turned out to be particularly ravaging for African societies launched on a double path of economic and demographic catching-up. The shock was certainly brutal, but it did not produce all the effects that were hoped for.

The economic bankruptcy of African states rapidly engendered a symbolic bankruptcy as well. Deprived of their means of action, African governments were compelled to accept the structural adjustment programmes proposed by the twin Washington institutions. But the funds tied to these plans were conditional on the accelerated dismantling of heavy state apparatuses built up in the post-colonial period, and of the economic model of patronage that they favoured. Though ineffective in economic terms, these had nonetheless played a structuring role over the years in the delicate political balancing of young multi-ethnic states in the making: these mechanisms of formal and informal redistribution between regions and clans underpinned fragile national social pacts. Had the consequences – and costs – of their hasty dismantling been measured? Carried away by the dogma of 'less state', the structural adjustment programmes were – at least initially – blind to the social and political consequences of the ruptures they brought about. Unable to respond to the growing needs of their populations, and placed under foreign direction, the African states lost their credibility.

The erosion of the social contract was followed by a form of 'generalized institutional disintegration':[14] in the face of the collapse of underfinanced public services and in an atmosphere of growing political instability, the institutional economy gave way to a makeshift one. The rise of practices of corruption, which many attributed to the African state culture, consisted largely in the adaptation of rational agents to a system in crisis, in which each person sought to survive and feed their family. The collapse of economic growth, with no compensation from public policy, led the greater part of sub-Saharan Africa into a growing impoverishment and a gaping increase in inequality. Mass unemployment made its appearance, and malnutrition gained ground. Yet national solidarity organized around the state apparatus was crumbling at a time when their traditional equivalents had also collapsed. The loss of legitimacy on the part of penniless states, combined with the growing social vulnerability of their populations, logically fuelled a renewal of community loyalties. Solidarities crystallized around ethnic and religious membership, reinvented and exploited by political entrepreneurs. This situation was central to the violence unleashed in the 1990s. Interestingly, this violence was also privatized: from Liberia via Angola and Congo-Kinshasa to Sierra Leone, bands of young mercenaries sold their services to the highest bidder.

This was the context in which suppliers of funds chose to let their aid dry up.

Paradoxically, Africa was the first victim of German reunification: with the fall of the Berlin wall, the continent lost its status as a field of ideological, economic and military confrontation between capitalist and socialist blocs. Overnight, one of the most powerful motors of development aid ground to a permanent halt. The new geopolitical priority was the rescue of the East European economies. Aid to Africa, now seen in compassionate rather than strategic terms, aimed at little more than helping African states to deal with the most glaring social impacts of structural adjustment. It was also largely privatized or externalized, left to the world of the NGOs, now flourishing, and to the humanitarian arm of the UN system. This change in the register and priorities of international support translated into a steep fall in the sums allocated to Africa: from $34 per capita in 1990, aid to sub-Saharan Africa fell to $21 in 2001. With export receipts also falling since 1979, and recourse to further loans impossible since 1982, the strategic rent that African states had enjoyed also disappeared after 1990, and with it the largest major source of hard currency.

Behind this African collapse figures that of the Bretton Woods system, as it was conceived at the end of the Second World War. It was neither able nor willing to come to the rescue of Africa as it had with post-war Europe. Had the structural adjustment programmes of the 1980s and 1990s been accompanied by higher volumes of aid, it would have been possible to manage the financial crisis while still pursuing investment in physical and human capital. But the international community chose to keep to the management of the financial crisis, and restraining the most violent convulsions provoked by its remedy.

It was particularly under the impulse of the Nordic countries that the international development agencies adopted the only policy that its declining resources left open: that of 'adjustment with a human face'. What was the objective? To improve the living conditions of Africans after twenty years of declining per capita growth. But what was the reality? A concentration of aid on health and education expenditure, to the detriment of infrastructure and agriculture, which had become too burdensome to support on top of refinancing the debt and subsidizing basic social services. Was the problem a lack of resources at the international level? Those who believe so mistake the orders of magnitude; better support for structural adjustment would have turned out far less costly than these clumsy attempts to rescue bankrupt states. The reality is that the 1990s saw a massive disengagement from Africa, particularly on the part of Europe and North America. Freed from the ambiguous sentiment of post-colonial solidarity, the international community decided that Africa was no longer worth more than a bit of compassion.

The refusal to treat the African crises as a subject of public policy was a major historic mistake, involving blindness even to the industrial economies' own interests. This tragedy comes with its share of errors from which the industrialized countries cannot absolve themselves.[15] It has led to a continuing political instability on the continent: once the support of outside powers was withdrawn from authoritarian regimes, these collapsed, discredited by their economic and financial failure. It is not without a strong dose of cynicism that Mobutu and his like were chided after being embraced only the day before. Yet the young democracies that were born in the upheavals of this period did not enjoy the political dividends promised by repeated speeches along the lines of Mitterrand's at La Baule.[16] They had to manage a worsening economic crisis at the same time as the support that their dictator predecessors had enjoyed was being withdrawn. We should not be surprised by the outbreaks of civil war and other domestic upheavals.

Curtain

Rather than an Africa irremediably 'bankrupt', the third act of this African tragedy thus offers us the more complex image of an Africa facing several concomitant crises. An 'organic' crisis arising from the sudden and profound changes experienced by the continent at the time that its nation-states were established. A structural crisis, bound up with the modes of production inherited from the colonial period as well as the economic choices made in the wake of independence. And finally a conjunctural crisis arising from the world economic upheavals that struck the African nations at a moment of extreme vulnerability.

This reveals the true tragedy of African underdevelopment. In no way does it remove human responsibility: the errors of economic policy are blatant, and shared by actors in both North and South. But it shows that no country, no people could have grown and developed in such circumstances. African economic decline in the 1980s and 1990s is in no way mysterious. It was the logical and almost inevitable consequence of a combination of circumstances that were quite particular and historically dated. If this tragedy of sub-Saharan economic growth is worth relating here, it is because it enables us to maintain that the Africa we see today has moved far from the stage on which the drama of its underdevelopment was played out.

Paradoxically, it was only at the turn of the century, when the Bretton Woods institutions published their first acknowledgement of the excesses of structural adjustment, that their benefits began to be felt – and that the foundations of a lasting growth appeared. Can Africa finally emerge from its economic crisis? We offer in evidence the course of the last ten years. Many people are unaware of the fact that the sub-Saharan economies grew at an average rate of more than 6 per cent each year between 2003 and 2008, as against less than 5 per cent for Latin America and less than 2 per cent for the Eurozone. This represents more than four points of annual economic growth per inhabitant. At such a rhythm, the average standard of living will double in a little more than fifteen years. It is true that the world crisis at the end of this decade has temporarily reduced this trend. Besides, growth is still uneven between different countries, and its benefits remain far too unequally distributed within each society. But sub-Saharan Africa has taken its place in recent years among countries with a relatively high growth rate, thus marking a radical break with the two previous decades. More than one African in three lives in an economy that has had a growth rate over 4 per cent for at least ten years.[17] These successes, moreover, are not just the mark of resource-rich countries: their economic performances are matched by certain countries that are poor in raw materials. Tanzania and Mozambique, for example, figure among the most dynamic on the continent, despite being net importers of oil. In 2008 and 2009, while the industrial economies were suffering the effects of the subprime crisis and their low growth rates pulled down the world economy, Africa continued to display almost impertinent rates of growth. Why then this change of pace? We shall now see.

Part Four

When Africa Awakes

History continues. If we understand that Africa's development has been restricted by a 'tragedy of economic cycles' rather than an inherent 'African tragedy' condemning the continent to misery, we have to see the profound changes at work as the seeds of the following period.

Relieved of many burdens that held it back only yesterday, Africa and its burgeoning population have entered a new cycle, which may be that of its emergence: the foundations for strong economic growth have returned. Though structural vulnerability and new risks exist, the continent has genuinely entered a new era.

7

The Great Shake-Out

Tolstoy explains in *War and Peace* why it was impossible for the Grande Armée not to reach Moscow, and how it was equally impossible for it to remain there. In the same way that the French defeat in Russia could not have been avoided, Africa could not spirit away two decades of recession. But just as Kutuzov's armies could not fail to achieve victory over Napoleon, it is impossible for Africa to do anything but hurl itself full-pelt into the adventure of growth.

Structural adjustment did succeed

It is fashionable today to cast the structural adjustment programmes that we have just reviewed into the dustbin of economic history. Depicted as icons of failed economic policy, their negative features – which we only touched on – have been well documented,[1] and their human costs calculated. With respect to the loss of GDP per capita, rate of investment and life expectancy that accompanied them, the balance-sheet appears terrifying.

Yet it has to be noted that these programmes eventually 'succeeded', to the extent that they managed to extract the African states from a deep economic failure. If they took place in pain and were sometimes the occasion for errors in economic policy,

these radical adjustments of economic practice began to bear their
fruits at a time when no one any longer expected them to. The
symbols of this recovery – in Uganda, Ghana or Burkina Faso,
for example – are witness to what twenty years of sacrifice and
upheavals finally made it possible to enjoy.

The first of these fruits – bitter for certain established rulers –
released the stranglehold that was stifling so many governments on
the continent. The scrupulous supervision of the World Bank and
IMF made it possible in fact to clean up African public finances
considerably. As an unavoidable preliminary to the bailing-out of
over-indebted states by the international community, this clean-
up allowed the majority of the continent's economies to get back
on the bumpy road of financial sustainability. The successive
programmes of debt relief undertaken by the governments of the
North, under pressure from a strongly mobilized public opinion,
did the rest, delivering the continent from a situation of permanent
indebtment. After the Heavily Indebted Poor Countries (HIPC)
Initiative and the Multilateral Debt Relief Initiative (MDRI) – the
latter alone covered $43 billion, i.e. 40 per cent of the GDP of
the African countries involved – African indebtment is today no
longer a handicap to the continent's development. The sovereign
debt of the sub-Saharan countries has fallen from over 85 per cent
of GDP in 2000 to 40 per cent of GDP at the end of the decade,[2]
creating new room for manoeuvre for public expenditure in these
countries. Do we really appreciate this? Public debt at around 40
per cent is some 40 points less than France's debt in 2010, where
economic growth has hovered around 2 per cent since the start of
the century. In this new economic environment, public investment,
so essential to economic catching-up, has finally begun to take
its place in African government policies: steadily rising now for
several years, the rate of investment reached an average of 22 per
cent in 2008. This figure is previously unequalled for the region –
and close to that which the emerging Southeast Asian economies
displayed at the start of their take-off.[3]

Still better, the removal of the debt burden has been combined
in recent years with a radical fall in inflation.[4] Why is inflation
a problem? The sub-Saharan economies, like many other economies in crisis, have experienced in the past episodes of runaway
prices that proved extremely harmful for their development and

for the standard of living of their citizens. The inflation–devaluation spiral contributed to the impoverishment of many African societies in the 1980s and 1990s. Too high a rate of inflation actually penalizes first of all those who possess no tangible goods, i.e. the poorest. Zimbabwe, which plunged into a severe political and economic crisis in 2007 and 2008, is a sad example: inflation here reached something like 100,000 per cent in the month of December 2007 (more than the Weimar republic experienced in 1923), hurling Zimbabweans with no access to foreign currency into a parallel makeshift economy. While high inflation was par for the course in Africa towards the end of the last century, the inflationary crisis in Zimbabwe is today an isolated case. Apart from this singular tragedy, the relative stabilization of prices on the continent has thus contributed to a normalization of the sub-Saharan economic situation.

Another important indicator on the economic barometer, the terms of trade,[5] has also improved substantially over the last few years. Its tumble was largely responsible for the collapse of economies over-dependent on the export of raw materials. But from oil and natural gas to aluminium and gold, the prices of the minerals and hydrocarbons in which African subsoils are so rich experienced a significant rise during the first decade of the century. Despite the knock-on effects of the world crisis at the end of the decade, this rise has every likelihood of continuing in the longer term, propelled by the combined effects of strong demand from the emerging economies and growing awareness of the limits of world supplies. Nothing is more risky than trying to predict how commodity prices will develop; they are notoriously volatile. As we have seen, a false anticipation of their progress contributed to the dramatic forward flight of the continent in the 1970s. Prudence is thus the norm. Nevertheless, the fact remains that the upward tendency in fossil fuel and mineral prices is driven by strong structural factors, and there is little prospect of a reversal in the medium term. Whether tomorrow's world runs on oil, coal, uranium or biofuels, Africa will count among the leading world suppliers of energy. If China, India, Indonesia, Brazil and other emerging countries continue their economic catching-up in the decades to come, their construction of buildings, roads, railways and machinery will continue to require the raw materials in which Africa is so

abundant.[6] Stimulated by the growing demand for raw materials
from these major emerging countries, African exports have risen
by 25 per cent in a single year.[7]

A similar development can be seen in the market for agricultural
raw materials. The world food context has in fact turned round
in the space of scarcely a decade, with the result that the prices of
basic foodstuffs, which had steadily fallen in the previous thirty
years, have suddenly shot up again. Spurred by structural factors
on both the supply side (competition for fertile land between food
crops and biofuels, increasingly frequent climatic events, etc.) and
that of demand (world population growth, increasing consumption of meat, etc.), there is every prospect of these prices remaining
at high levels. If this development places a considerable burden on
food bills for African countries accustomed to importing part of
their consumption from international markets, it represents in the
longer run an opportunity that African agriculture has to grasp –
and the 400 or 500 million Africans[8] who earn the greater part of
their livelihood from it. Wasn't the low level of agricultural commodity prices denounced for several decades?

For the first time since the early days of African independence,
the main economic indicators have thus turned from red to green
in the majority of sub-Saharan economies. Is Africa in the process
of becoming the next emerging market – the new frontier of risk
capital?

It would certainly be too soon to say this. Yet the comparison
with the ASEAN countries around 1980 (Indonesia, Malaysia, the
Philippines, Singapore and Thailand), for which the term 'emerging markets' was first employed, is a telling one. It shows that sub-
Saharan Africa has a lower rate of inflation and greater reserves
of foreign currency, and receives more direct foreign investment,
than the ASEAN countries did on the eve of their economic take-
off – countries whose economic governance at the time, moreover,
did not display the 'good' practices that the World Bank and IMF
define today.

Ready for take-off

This new macroeconomic context, the vital soil for the fragile
sub-Saharan recovery, is crucial if the continent is to see

lasting growth. But it is not sufficient by itself to make the African economies take off. The real engine for catching-up lies elsewhere, in a human phenomenon with a far greater structuring effect.

The many pressures that the continent's demographic explosion and the increasing density of its populations have imposed on African societies and their environment are all too familiar. But there are few observers who have understood the opportunity that this represents. A strong and sustained economic growth is not possible in a human desert, and yet Africa has until recently been underpopulated and very weakly urbanized. Côte d'Ivoire, for example, had in 1950 a population of 2.5 million for a territory of 322,000 square kilometres, i.e. less than 8 inhabitants per sq. km, or three times less than the least crowded département of France today; 7 out of 8 Ivorians at that time lived in the countryside. How can a space like this be developed, with an active policy for health and education? The cost of linking up its scattered citizens, and organizing exchange between them, would be astronomical. On what basis, then, can a national economy be organized? Given these constraints, the choice of exploiting the subsoil and exporting its wealth unprocessed was for a long time a rational economic strategy. With 8 inhabitants per sq. km, it was almost impossible to free African economies from small-scale family farming and cash crops. At the time of independence, 8 inhabitants per sq. km was the average population density of sub-Saharan Africa. The economic conditions that this involved provide the background to the tragedy of economic cycles that Africa has since experienced: underpopulated and rural, the continent was for a long time lacking the human support to generate its own growth.

Adam Smith's postulate[9] means the same for Africa in the early twenty-first century as it meant for England in the eighteenth: the concentration of population encourages the development of trade and a rise in productivity. Though far from being a sufficient condition for growth, a greater population density and the urbanization resulting from it are certainly a necessary condition. No country has developed without this broad economic and social transformation, accelerating the division of labour[10] and creating an opening to the world. Angus Maddison's[11] historical studies show how the population density of the Italian peninsula was three times that of Gaul at the time of the death of Caesar Augustus in 14 CE – a time when the former certainly dominated the latter. Rome, the imperial capital, counted around a million inhabitants. Nearly 2,000 years later, the industrial revolution of the European economies was also made possible by a strong population growth and a rapid urbanization: Western Europe saw its level of urbanization triple in the course of the nineteenth century.[12] This development made possible the appearance of a large working class, concentrated round the sites of production – an indispensable step for industrialization. How could we imagine the American 'gilded age', built on sweat and tears, that would pave the way for a century of economic growth, without the industrial districts of New York, Chicago or Detroit? Or the emergence of the British Empire without the 'workshop of the world' formed by London and the Manchester region?

The economic take-off of Southeast Asia in the late twentieth century was also preceded by a phase of rapid population increase, followed by the development of large industrial centres. The densely populated Chinese countryside continues to supply each year, in the form of the *mingong* migration – the 'worker-peasants'[13] who arrive daily in Chinese manufacturing cities – the cheap labour that fuels the double-digit growth rates of the national economy. What made the power of the Roman Empire possible 2,000 years ago, the birth of European and American industry in the eighteenth and nineteenth centuries, the emergence of the Asian tigers in the 1980s and the recent rise in China's international economic power was thus lacking for a long time in the sub-Saharan economy and preventing its economic take-off – a young and abundant labour-force concentrated in the urban centres.

But this is indeed what we can see forming under our eyes in Africa today, in the chaos and suffering that is characteristic of great historical developments. If these naturally involve political risks, the other side of Africa's urban explosion, its galloping birth rate and unemployed youth, is the formation of large urban markets and the impending reversal of dependency ratios. As elsewhere on the planet and at other periods of history, this process of human concentration, by its mere existence, automatically generates substantial gains in productivity, opportunities for trade, and thus a certain tempo of economic growth.

It is not just people who see their productivity shoot up: public policy also becomes more effective in the urban zones, insofar as the cost of infrastructure is that much less per inhabitant served, and the population easier to reach than in sparsely populated zones. Roads, schools and health centres are far more cost-efficient in town than in the countryside. This impact of population density on the efficacy of public expenditure is rarely taken into account. And yet, for several decades, the simple fact of difference in population density meant that a dollar spent on education or public health had a much greater impact in Asia than the same dollar spent similarly in sub-Saharan Africa.[14] Certain regions of Africa today are coming to display a population density and rate of urbanization closer to the Asian average.

When Africa goes shopping

This double explosion, demographic and urban, makes possible the emergence of a vast regional market. To recall the figures: sub-Saharan Africa will have 1 billion *extra* inhabitants between now and 2050. These new Africans will have to feed themselves, house themselves, travel and communicate. Whether formal or informal, local, national or international, an economic activity will emerge to respond to these needs. Utopian? This 'spontaneous generation' of economic activity is very striking in Pikine, a poor working-class suburb of Dakar. This outgrowth of the Senegalese capital counts close to a million inhabitants, settled in makeshift houses as a result of the rural exodus and 'clearings'[15] in the city centre. Trade and industry, though largely informal, are extremely dynamic; the fish market is the largest in the country. Chinese exports, moreover, have been quick to seize on this new niche in world demand. As elsewhere on the planet, 'made in China' is the dominant label in the markets of Dakar and Yaoundé.

But sub-Saharan Africa is not just a market for cheap and poor-quality goods. Very profitable investments have taken place this decade in telecommunications, construction and major infrastructure. These sectors have recruited on a large scale, and a large number of young Africans draw their income from them. Though the initial investment was from foreign businesses, this market is becoming a growing field for new African businesspeople – and the engine of growth that national economies have long lacked.

Strangely, African agriculture will also find its salvation in the galloping urbanization. The populations of the expanding African cities will have to be fed, opening up unprecedented outlets for the continent's farmers. A Danish economist remarked in the 1970s, against the Malthusian ideas that were in vogue again at the time, that 'demographic development is the determining factor for technological change in agriculture';[16] sub-Saharan Africa will be the next illustration of this. When towns house only 5 or 10 per cent of the population, the urban market, often remote from the site of production, cannot provide sufficient remuneration for farmers. The volumes produced and the sale prices are both too low for investment in irrigation (which also needs energy), seed and fertilizer to be profitable. But rapid urbanization means that we can envisage today a real transformation in the African agricultural situation. Investment in agriculture is becoming ever more profitable; the sub-Saharan countryside is in the process of gaining the means of its modernization.

This is the story of Alassane, an elderly farmer whom we met in the market of a small town in Burkina Faso. As a market gardener, he had long been selling in the town a few chickens that he reared, and also – when his harvest permitted – his meagre surplus of tomatoes and potatoes. The rapid growth of the market in the local town, which now has a few thousand inhabitants, and the recent soaring of food prices, have changed his situation entirely. With a big, if rather toothless, smile, and sparkling eyes, he explained to us that the price of chickens had tripled in just two seasons, that the surplus he received would soon make it possible for him to buy sacks of fertilizer and have his chickens vaccinated – nearly half of them still die of disease each year. His younger sons, he told us – raising his arm in the direction of his village – would one day be able to construct a real stock farm, and – *inch'allah* – perhaps also a shop for cooked chicken near the market. Or even buy a vehicle to take his eggs to the capital: it is said that eggs sell for double the price on the market in Ouga. One thing at least is sure: with a growth rate of nearly 6 per cent per year,[17] the population of Ougadougou will have a healthy appetite for Alassane's sons' eggs. We can thus believe that tomorrow, through a major transformation of African agriculture, its countryside will feed its towns, which will become the countryside's main suppliers of services.

The demographic explosion is also having a significant effect on the age structure of African societies – a crucial factor for an economy's dynamism. The continent's population is the youngest on the planet. In the 1980s and 1990s this was expressed in the highest dependency ratio[18] in the world. At the worst of its economic crisis, Africa counted something less than one worker for each dependent child or old person, whereas Southeast Asia, in full economic take-off, had more than two workers for each dependant. With the steady fall in the birth rate, a reduction in the dependency ratio has now set in. This will continue at a steady pace for the next forty years, and around 2050 reach a ratio between active and inactive identical to that which permitted the Asian 'economic miracle' of the 1980s. Africa could then benefit in turn from a 'demographic dividend'.[19] A window of opportunity is opening for Africa, on one condition: that this swarming youth is equipped to face the labour market, and able to contribute to the creation of added value for the continent.

Africa has suffered a great deal in the past from the volatile nature of its growth, and been particularly vulnerable to violent conjunctural swings.[20] This should be no surprise. Its economy did not possess any of the ingredients for home-grown development. But since the turn of the century, a great upheaval has been taking place before our eyes. Where certain analysts see the growth rates of the last few years simply as the effect of a boom in raw materials, we see here the beginnings of a process of economic growth that is much more lasting. Africa's demographic explosion, the increasing population density of its territories, and its galloping urbanization are changing the nature of the economic growth within its reach: a growth that is more structural, more internally produced, and thus far more solid than one based simply on the export of raw materials.

A powerful engine is throbbing beneath the rattling hood of the African economy. Only great misfortune can prevent sub-Saharan Africa from a growth rate of at least 5 per cent per year. In this sense, its development has become inevitable.

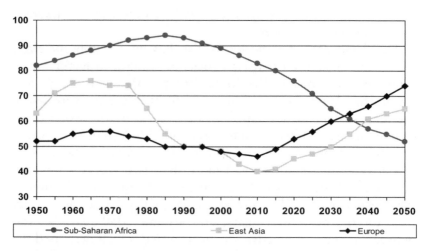

Dependency ratio by region
Note: The dependency ratio is the ratio between the 'dependent' population (from 0 to 14 and over 65) and that of 'working age' (from 15
to 65). It is expressed as the number of 'dependents' per 100 people of
'working age'. East Asia = mainland China, North and South Korea,
Japan and Mongolia. Europe includes Russia.
Source: UN, *World Population Prospects: The 2008 Revision* (median
scenario), 2009.

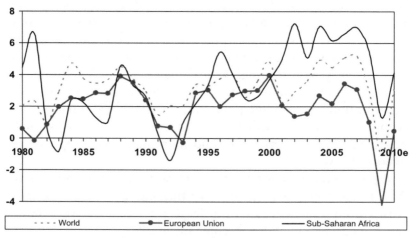

Economic growth by region, 1980–2010
Source: IMF, 2010.

8

Emerging Africans

Are we cradling dangerous illusions? Projections that breathe the naïve hope of inspired soothsayers or peddle a dyed-in-the-wool Afro-optimism?

On the contrary – all observers of the African continent have noticed in recent years the effects of the profound transformations at work south of the Sahara. These start with the emergence of new kinds of business, evidence of the new era that is under way.

'Black diamonds'

Foreigners have no monopoly on business in this African take-off. From finance to industry, via new technologies, art and science, this renaissance is borne by a whole generation of actors. These members of African business milieus or intellectual professions singularly confound the clichés that have such a hold over the collective imagination. As much at ease in New York, London or Paris as in Abidjan or Johannesburg, these cosmopolitan and multilingual entrepreneurs have often studied abroad.

These are the artisans of the continent's renewal – people like Achankeng Leke. This Cameroonian hoisted himself into the list of young world leaders, drawn up each year for the Davos World Economic Forum, by advising big international corporations seeking to establish themselves in the African market. A graduate of Stanford University in California, he won his spurs in consulting work in the computing start-ups of Silicon Valley. Moving on

to the large American consultancy group McKinsey, he was sent
in 2002 to develop its activities in South Africa. Today his teams
advise the largest international businesses on their growth strategies for the African continent. It is with the emergence of entrepreneurs like Achankeng Leke in international business circles, and
white-collar recruitment in the businesses they establish, that we
see the face that Africa presents the world diversifying today.

Like their counterparts in Asia or Latin America, the new African
middle classes are called to play a leading role in their countries'
politics and economics.[1] For these young men and women, the
city is their window on the world, the place of business, of social
success and of accumulation of wealth.

This was already the case some years ago. We travelled for
several kilometres on a badly maintained road from N'Djamena,
crossing sprawling residential districts lacking sanitation, running
water and electricity. When we arrived at the bar, in a part of
the town with a Christian majority, the bass speakers made the
car windows tremble. 'Everything works on generators', we were
told; 'the district isn't connected to the grid'. In front of a large
square compound fronting on the Chari River, a long queue
had formed. With their feet in the sand, the switched-on youth
of N'Djamena were waiting to cross the threshold. Inside there
was a festive atmosphere. Everyone was wearing their Sunday
best – whether a jazzy *boubou*, a miniskirt and tight T-shirt, or
an elegant evening dress. Cameroonians come high in the stakes
for the most sexy outfits. For men, dark glasses are *de rigueur*,
and Diesel jeans an evident plus. Others go for tailored suits. The
décor is reminiscent of an American video clip. The scene could be
Miami or Los Angeles – with the little difference that we're asked
not to take photos. Hidden behind their veils, anonymous Muslim
women have come to the fête incognito. African rhythms follow
one another: *makossa, soukouss, zouk, coupe-décalé*, as the fashionable youth of N'Djamena mingle. Around the dance floor small
groups are sipping beers and cocktails, talking and laughing. Some
of them will later move on to compounds that are not lit up, wash
their evening clothes at the public taps and tomorrow resume their
mundane jobs: the middle class in Chad is still frail, caught up in
the tribulations of a country in crisis. Elsewhere on the continent,
however, it has surfaced more clearly, and is already swinging in
the most fashionable nightclubs.

These people are known in South Africa as the 'black diamonds'.[2] The beneficiaries of black economic empowerment here are today estimated at some 2.6 million, a rise of a quarter since 2005. This represents 12 per cent of the country's black population. Without turning their backs on their townships of origin, where they keep family ties, they have moved into the smart suburbs of the country's big cities. The schools there are better for their children, and security conditions less troublesome. This move is also a symbol of success – how can they turn it down when all social ascent was formerly banned? On Saturday they window-shop in American-style commercial centres, eat in French or Italian restaurants. Their purchasing power has grown considerably: fifteen years after the end of apartheid, the black population of South Africa owns 10 per cent of its businesses (as against none before 1994). Employed or running firms in the service sector, mining or the media, this privileged class has swallowed capitalism whole, courted by banks, cosmetics companies and car manufacturers. Some struggle to save, others to consume – with an ostentatious dimension totally assumed. 'Having a BMW is a mark of success; young people look at you with esteem', explains the country's first black champion racing-driver – recruited as an ambassador for the German company.

In Kampala, Dar es Salaam and Nairobi likewise, these new African yuppies have arrived in the age of mass consumption. Joseph Nassanga is a young Ugandan businessman. He lives in Kampala with his wife Sandra, manager at a bank, and their two children. Like his counterparts throughout the world, he never puts down his Blackberry. He goes to the gym once a week, goes jogging at the weekend and regularly invites friends to dinner. He has a nice house perched on the hillside, surrounded by walls topped with barbed wire. They had to borrow in order to buy it, but the growth of Joseph's business makes him feel secure; if things go well, he will pay back the loan ahead of time. Nor do Sandra and Joseph stint on holidays: they go abroad once a year – often to other African countries, but they have also visited London and New York. A Lonely Planet guide is left on their dining table; they are planning a week in Paris. Like their colleagues and friends who are journalists, consultants, engineers or lawyers, they borrow, take out life assurance policies, invest for their retirement. They hope in due course to be able to send their children to the international school in Kampala. Sandra is impatiently waiting for the big new Oasis shopping centre to open. Fully air-conditioned, it will host all the major clothing and audiovisual brands, a big cinema, a gallery of restaurants and even a play area for children. Nakumatt, the major Kenyan distribution company that is build-ing it, has just opened a hypermarket at Kigali, open twenty-four hours a day. After trebling its turnover in the space of four years, this company has announced the construction of three hyper-markets in Uganda, four in Tanzania and a second in Rwanda. It already has nineteen branches in Kenya.

It was in Kenya, indeed, that customers of the Nakumatt shop-ping centres were particularly affected by the post-election vio-lence of January 2008. Some 4 million Kenyans out of 37 million belong to the middle class, one of the most well-established in Africa. The number of university students in Kenya has more than doubled in the last ten years, reaching a total of 100,000.[3] Focused on their career ambitions, their investments and other future proj-ects, the major winners from the 5 per cent annual growth rate that Kenya has known since the turn of the century did not see the crisis coming. Or at least they no longer believed their country capable of plunging back into such archaic violence. Images of killings with machetes, arrows or clubs existed only in their worst nightmares – repressed memories of Kenya's 'old days', the years of crisis. They didn't appear in their software. These millions of white-collar workers no longer identify themselves by their mem-bership of a particular ethnic group, but rather by the work they do, the brands they buy, or the school to which they send their children. Inter-ethnic marriage has increased, and many are happy to vote for a politician from a different community. The riots hit the Kenyan middle class in their ideals, and badly affected their businesses, but they did not accept this passively; they put pressure on the two main political parties to end the violence and begin talks. It was also they who made sure that the commitments made were kept, and that the country did not fall back into chaos. They have too much to lose to leave politics to the politicians.

This is the issue at stake now with the emergence of the African middle classes. In Europe and the United States it was their counter-parts who forged the societies of the twentieth century by expand-ing the right to vote, imposing the welfare state and creating the foundations of mass consumption. In India, the fragile equilibrium of the world's greatest democracy rests on their shoulders. According to the World Bank, which sticks to a conservative definition, the African middle class will increase four times between 2000 and 2030[4] – from which we can envisage economic, political and social upheavals similar to those that the industrial societies of the North experienced with the emergence of their middle classes. Housing, health care, schools, savings, loans: the South African 'black diamonds' and the Kenyan white-collar workers are laying each year the bricks for a solid economic and political system. While sub-Saharan Africa has long suffered from a lack of savings, its people are opening bank accounts. While its economy has been marked by a shortage of investment, they are embarking on new projects. While some still lament the weakness of Africa's 'human capital', the sons and daughters of the new African middle class are emerging with quality degrees in all disciplines. While low tax revenues continue to weigh down the continent's public finances, their formal activities and salaried jobs form the fabric of a modern tax system.

But just like anywhere else, the new African yuppies expect a return on their investment. For nothing in the world will they sell their hard-won dream. If the emerging middle classes contribute to public finances, they will increasingly demand accounts of the use of their taxes: in 21st-century Africa, as in the American colonies in the eighteenth century, the demand 'no taxation without representation' will be heard. They present themselves freely to their compatriots, with a certain pride, as models to be followed, the incarnation of a resolutely African modernity.

'Hello Paris, Dakar calling'

This new African economic effervescence is fuelled by a system of finance that is growing more varied and sophisticated by the day. As additional proof that Africa is no longer excluded from globalization, in recent years it has focused the full attention of financial markets. Could we have imagined this just ten years ago? The continent is steadily raising its profile as a new frontier for risk capital.

Investment funds including 'hedge funds', the symbols of financial globalization, have targeted Africa. The years 2007 and 2008 saw the creation of a number of funds specializing in the region by investors wanting an early entry to markets with a strong growth potential. Betting on the take-off of beer-brewing in Tanzania, tele-communications in Senegal or the banking sector in Ghana,[5] the funds invested now amount to billions of dollars. Stock exchanges are also flourishing in the African capitals, with over 1,000 compa-nies quoted. The thousands of Kenyans who queued in the street at the time of the first public issue of Safaricom[6] are evidence of this: these new investment opportunities favour the growth of African savings. The crisis of 2008–9 brought a timely reality check to a movement that was getting carried away, and led to a number of bankruptcies. As it gets under way again, the boom will be more cautious, but everything leads us to believe that it will confirm the trend that began in the mid 2000s.

Direct foreign investment on the continent, which is growing fast, also broke records each year until the world economic crisis.[7] And now, for the first time, this was no longer restricted just to extractive industries, but fuelled the development of the tertiary sector as well. The same call centres that employ tens of thou-sands of Indians and Moroccans in their home countries have also flourished in Senegal in recent years.[8] Élodie Martin's real name is Alima Fila. This young Senegalese graduate works in the country's first call centre, in a suburb of Dakar. She sells mobile phone subscriptions in France for a French company, speak-ing faultless French. She earns three times the average wage in Senegal, but costs eight times less than an employee in the call centres of the Paris region. In an industry where labour makes up three-quarters of the costs, it is hard for French companies to compete with their African counterparts. Alima's employer even offers an offshore secretarial service: thanks to the fibre-optic sub-marine cables linking Senegal with Europe, a Parisian architect can call on the services of a secretary working in Dakar. Just as if she was working in the next office, she picks up her phone, takes his message and sorts through his emails. Made possible by the coun-try's digital connection and its young graduates' perfect mastery of French, the establishment of call centres heralds further waves of delocalization to sub-Saharan Africa – a real boon for societies who have over a third of their young people unemployed.

The picture of the continent heading for normalization would not be complete without some comment on the (r)evolution under way in the finances of the African states themselves – states that are not far behind in the hunt for capital. As well as access to loans from 'emerging lenders' such as China, the new ability of many African governments to borrow has enabled them to issue treasury bills in local currency. Subscribed to by both African and foreign savers, this kind of financing of public administration, which would have been inconceivable hardly a decade ago, has tripled in West Africa in just two years. But that is not all: several African states now also have access to world financial markets. In a context of low interest rates in the North, international investors have been looking for higher yields, and take the risk of lending to states that have only just recovered from a crisis of solvency.

The issuing of bonds on international markets by countries that have benefited from debt relief programmes may well seem disturbing. The viability of this private commercial debt subscribed outside the context of the IMF is not yet proved, essentially based as it is on the self-discipline of the borrowers. But should we take fright at this most blatant sign of the long-awaited reintegration of the 'forgotten continent' into the globalization process, while its economies see their 'ratings'[9] climb from year to year? At the time these pages are being written, Nigeria and Mozambique have seen their ratings reach the same levels as those of Turkey and other emerging economies.[10] As we see, governmental development aid has clearly lost its monopoly on financing African growth. While sub-Saharan Africa long depended on volatile (and conditional) public flows, private funds are now making their way to the continent. In 2006, private lending to sub-Saharan Africa overtook government loans for the first time, reaching $50 billion, i.e. four times higher than in 2000.[11]

As the new century gets under way, the African continent is starting to realize its potential: beyond the vagaries of the global economic situation with its bubbles and crashes, the 'success' of the structural adjustment programmes, urbanization and increasing population density, the build-up of domestic markets and the clean-up of economic policy are all starting to produce their effects. Some people have doubts about the prospects for this sunny period in the African sky.[12] And, indeed, the renewal of sub-Saharan growth is not without its weaknesses. The factors of structural vulnerability remain, in the form of the several 'poverty traps' that economic studies have pointed out.[13] We have also shown the political risks bound up with African population increase, the sharp acceleration of migration being not the least of these. We have also emphasized the importance of climate problems and natural resources, bad management of which could make the present growth short-lived. A decline in aid transfers would also constitute a profound shock, capable of threatening the still-fragile growth of private flows. Nothing is certain.

Nonetheless, and despite all these qualifications, the face of Africa has changed in the early years of the twenty-first century. The sharp rise in trade with emerging countries, the integration of African economies into international financial circuits, and their accelerated connection with the world thanks to the trio of Internet technologies, telephone and television, undermine the image of Africa as being on the margin of the world, excluded from globalization. The emergence of African actors in the front rank of international relations, in both public and private sectors, illustrates this normalization – the result of profound changes.

Like the majority of their less-favoured compatriots, these Africans look to the future with optimism. Having escaped from a decade of hell, the future belongs to them. That is the conclusion of a poll[14] carried out in 2007 by an American institute in ten sub-Saharan countries: the Africans questioned saw themselves as better off than five years earlier, and placed great hope in the future. Whereas the majority of Canadians, French and Americans expected their children to have less good lives than themselves, those polled in Senegal, Kenya and Uganda were resolutely optimistic for their future and that of their children. Nine Malians out of ten expected their lives to improve in the next five years. Isn't this the best sign of a new era? Though rapid growth may not be any guarantee, it has again become possible for the first time in thirty years.

Under the eyes of a demoralized Europe, Africa is undertaking its great shake-out. And this accelerated economic change is triggering a new awareness: the African transformation is fundamentally changing the ways of life of its inhabitants, the terms in which they define themselves and project the future. It is shifting political, economic and social trajectories in the component countries.

Part Five

Between God and Mammon

Books and speeches persistently invoke a mysterious 'African identity'. But what exactly does this mean? Africans who come into the world in the early twenty-first century set out to build their lives in a continent that no longer has anything in common with that of the time of independence. They have little in common with their parents and grandparents, born respectively just before the fall of the Berlin wall and in the first years of the young African nations. Nearly half of sub-Saharans do not remember the end of apartheid in 1994, nor the Rwandan genocide.[1]

A people with two thirds of its members under twenty-five makes up a society changing at high speed: values, norms, relationships and social organization are far more fluid than in our own ageing populations. And such changing societies, rapidly hitching themselves to the cart of globalization, experience violent cultural and social ruptures. These regular upheavals provoke an accelerated diversification of the continent's sociological landscape. Out then with the unchanging 'African-ness' of Senghor's poems and the hymns to *négritude*: more than ever, African identities are multiple, diverse and complex. Like Africa itself, they are plural. If something like an African identity ever existed other than in our imagination, it no longer does. What we have today is a whole host of interacting identities. Yet it is useful to seek to understand their components and trajectories; it is on this basis that tomorrow's Africa will be constructed.

Who then are today's Africans? It is an ambitious task to assert anything specific about them: city-dwellers differ from country folk, the company director from the small shopkeeper, the young prefect from the old traditional chief. The 'median African' of economic and social statistics has vanished in the whirlwind of the transformation under way, evaporating into the multiplication of ways of life, thought and affiliation. One thing, however, is certain. While we continue to think of Africans as essentially rural, animistic, poor, cut off from the world and dispersed in a vast ethnic mosaic, unsuited to democracy, the inhabitants of the black continent are in actual fact increasingly urban; they are rapidly leaving traditional religions in favour of Islam and Christianity; a middle class is being formed in the African cities, connected with the world and its networks; ethnic markers are experiencing the competition of a whole catalogue of new markers of identity; local political struggles are linking up with international aspirations in forging a generation of democrats.

This age, when different sources of authority, status, rights and aspirations all seek to assert themselves, is an age of many dangers. It is indeed a 'crisis' in the sense that Gramsci defined this: as an 'interregnum when the old order is dying while the new one is not managing to be born'.[2] But should we really expect the old order to die before the new one appears? 'A woman who is ill goes both to the doctor and the sorcerer', we were told in N'Djamena. In an interval when norms and actors, both traditional and modern, coexist and compete for the regulation of society, Africans draw from each of the two the elements that structure their lives and give them meaning. But in the city as well as the countryside, this interpenetration of the old and the new generates an uncertainty about the norms in force, what Émile Durkheim called anomie.[3] It is in this uncertainty, between loss of bearings and the emergence of new values, that contemporary Africa is advancing. Nowhere is this transition yet complete, but it is everywhere under way.

Africa is thus changing at full speed. But for several decades to come it will still be in this intermediate period. The interweaving of tradition and modernity, of the local and the global, makes possible the slow construction of the new – a modernity[4] not imported but reinvented, and resolutely African.[5]

9

Urban Compositions

From one jungle to another

On a recent visit to Mathare, one of the great shanty-towns of Nairobi, we asked its inhabitants about their origins. They replied that they came...from Mathare. Born into the world in this urban jungle, a heap of wooden planks and metal sheets that is transformed into a great field of mud as soon as a storm arrives, this is where they say they belong. If this is less of a surprise with the throng of children that follow us, it is rather more so with the adults; to hear their stories, more than half of them seem to have been born in this shanty-town of the Kenyan capital. Only twenty years ago, this would have been inconceivable. These men and women no longer recognize themselves in the symbols of their ancestors, and no longer practise their rituals. For them the sacred forest, the spirits of earth and water, no longer have much to say. At most they are vestiges of an already distant past, told to their children so that it is not quite forgotten.

Given the demographic dynamism of the African cities, the majority of the sub-Saharan urban population has been born in town. What does this mean? It means that a genuinely urban identity is in the process of formation, steadily replacing that of the countryside. This emergence of a new order generates profound and sometimes violent breaks in the organization of African societies. Traditional norms and systems of education, adapted to rural modes of life, are poorly suited to the transformations of urban life. They have to be reinvented, readapted, sometimes left behind. Pablo Picasso said that 'every act of creation is first of all an act of destruction'. This African creative destruction, extremely rapid by the standards of our own societies, will take several generations to bring about a genuine 'new order'. During this transition period from a system of customary rules and traditional justice to a system of written law and national justice (commonly called 'modern'), two different networks of authority exist side by side.

The success with which they manage to regulate the young African societies may be greater or lesser. When Côte d'Ivoire was tearing itself apart over the question of *ivoirité*, a traditional chief from the southeast of the country illustrated the power that certain traditional authorities have managed to preserve.[1] At the peak of the crisis, when violent clashes between indigenous and immigrant communities were taking place in adjacent regions, King Nanan Boa Kouassi III gathered representatives from the different communities. They agreed on preserving the fragile inter-ethnic balance in the region, each village or county chief undertaking to keep watch on agitators within his own community. In a context where national powers were abandoning their function of maintaining peace, and xenophobia was being unleashed, it is likely that the king's moral authority and that of the chiefs over their communities made it possible to avoid the region going up in flames. It was in fact spared any communal violence. Could this authority keep its stabilizing power for some time to come? It is not certain that such an undertaking would have had the same success in the city, if we are to believe the remark of a county chief from Ndényé: 'A district chief in Abidjan is not a chief, as he does not have any authority over his population; he does not command...You are a chief in your home region, but not in the district of a city.'[2] It was the big cities of Côte d'Ivoire that saw the greater part of xenophobic violence against civilians.

This is the opposite of the phenomenon that we witnessed in Chad. Here, customary justice was relatively effective in the capital, where it replaced a national system that was collapsing, but came into crisis in the countryside to the east. The 'race chiefs' of N'Djamena are the equivalent of the 'district chiefs' of Abidjan. With their authority anchored in their territories of origin, these leaders of the different ethnic communities that make up the country – and thus its capital – govern life in N'Djamena. The great bulk of the differences between members of two communities, and even more so within each one, are thus settled by their mediation, in return for representation costs. This system of customary justice fills its role so well, in a capital where a considerable share of the population are recent immigrants, that it serves as a daily reminder of the crisis of Chad's governmental institutions: 'Often, when the problem is settled by the gendarmerie, people come and hunt out the guilty parties in prison in order to kill them. They have the impression that justice has not been done, that the wrong has not been repaired.' Our interlocutor, however, a Chadian intellectual, believes that this is a temporary situation: 'It is a problem for our country. Before long, we shall have to have a modern legal system.'

Defective in the city, the 'modern' system of justice functions even worse in the region of Ouaddaï, a Sahelian zone in the far east of the country. Bordering on Darfur in the Sudan, this rural province is prey to sporadic episodes of armed violence. The customary authorities, 'village chiefs', 'county chiefs' and 'sultans', thus find themselves in the front line in managing conflicts and preventing violence. For a European observer, the moral authority that they exercise over their populations, and their effectiveness in settling everyday disturbances, is surprising. Each day they perform their task as mediators in litigation between communities, particularly in periods of transhumance when frequent disputes break out between settled farmers and nomadic herders. Ruling on cattle theft or a fight between two young people that got out of hand, they form a moral interface between the two parties. As the conduit for complaints and demands, they negotiate with a view to reaching a just retribution. This transactional justice is above all a matter of honour: it is not rare for a fine, once paid, to be refunded. Because there has been negotiation, repentance, followed by just compensation, the wrong has been repaired.

But this mediating power of the Ouaddaï traditional authorities has been clearly overtaken by events in recent years. Violence between communities, armed and exploited by the governments of two bordering countries, has crossed a symbolic threshold. The strength of traditional chiefs was also their weakness: the power they wield rests on a moral authority anchored in tradition, in a world in which everyone knows their place. There is no mechanism for compulsion, or what Max Weber called 'legitimate violence'. When traditions decay and people's 'positions' are overturned, while the land loses fertility and Kalashnikovs echo, customary authority is out-of-date. It is impotent and forced to give way.

In both Chad and Côte d'Ivoire, as elsewhere in Africa, there are thus two powers, 'one from above' and 'one from below',[3] that are negotiating to regulate, as best they can, societies in movement. In the best of cases, they find rules of subsidiarity: what the traditional authorities do not manage to deal with becomes the responsibility of the state. Sometimes, however, both forms fail – giving way to the law of the strongest. Most frequently, the two compete. The population appeal to the most effective power – whether as independent agents or as subjects of administration. But what happens when the gap between law and custom grows, when norms contradict one another? 'Changing the world is not just creation and progress', wrote Alain Touraine, 'it is firstly and always decomposition and crisis'.[4] Africa has not reached the end of the difficulties raised by its great gulf between tradition and modernity.

A legendary solidarity

Everything changes with the move from village to city – starting with relations between generations, the lynchpin of many African customary systems. Old people are out of their element in the continent's great metropolises. Whether they come from the countryside or not, whether they are rich or poor, they are more rapidly overtaken by the pace of development. The young, for their part, quickly adapt and find their bearings. They become 'those who know', prematurely reversing authority relations.

Idriss is a young man whom we met in Saint-Louis in Senegal. He is seventeen years old and goes to high school. When he comes home in the evening, he sells mobile phone top-ups in the town centre. The money enables him to buy trainers, and sometimes a cinema ticket. When things are tight at the end of the month, he also has to pay the compound's water bill. But Idriss always keeps enough to pay for his session at the Internet café next to his school. He wouldn't miss for the world the emails from his girlfriend, who left with her family for Belgium. A Skype conversation when the connection allows, the time to exchange a smile and a few broken words, keeps him going until the next day. But his father, a part-time gardener for an expatriate couple, doesn't see things the same way. The money that he earns scarcely feeds his family – those in Saint-Louis, and those still in the village. Care for the grandfather depends on Idriss's father, whose heart remains in the countryside. It is senseless for his son to waste his pay on electronic gadgets. The holidays are approaching; there's the matter of bus tickets to return to the village. This is not a prospect that appeals to Idriss. To sacrifice two weeks of his pay – two whole hours at the Internet café – to get bored in the bush with a family whose language he doesn't speak and with whom he has nothing in common any more? The father is out of his element, the son rebels, the father gives in: Idriss will remain in Saint-Louis, with his phone cards and his time on the Internet. His father is displeased, and cannot understand what bad spirit has got hold of his eldest son. From Dakar to Kinshasa, via the small town of Makak in Cameroon, the spirits of the city lead fatally to an erosion of patriarchal power and respect for the ancestors, which for so long provided the basis of upbringing for young Africans.

As everywhere else on the planet, the city is also the place where the individual becomes autonomous. Certainly not immediately: as the Chicago School sociologists showed in the 1920s, the first steps of the exodus to the city are marked by withdrawal into the community.[5] The new urbanites in Africa have the same reflexes as the Jewish immigrants in the northeastern United States: ethnic solidarity plays a major part in the arrival of families from the village. The community remains the first port of entry to the city. But these traditional solidarities, made up of a chain of customary obligations within the community, are rapidly challenged when individuals start to climb the social ladder, thanks to the urban economy.

In the absence of any other form of social insurance, the solidarity of the rural community continued for a long time to respond to the need for security of a group particularly exposed to the hazards of its environment. These norms provided a common foundation for many African peoples. The legendary 'African solidarity' has often been described as inherent to African identity. But as ways of life are overturned by the urban phenomenon, we have to reconsider the evidence for this. The cracks that appear in periods of crisis show that, like many other elements associated with African identity, this mode of solidarity has nothing unchangeable or eternally African about it.

These changes also transform habits in the African countryside, far more rapidly than in the town. Sociologists detected, in the violence that bloodied a rural community in northeast Rwanda at the time of the 1994 genocide, one of the symptoms of this transformation in forms of solidarity.[6] The context of increasing shortages of land, and the gradual transition from customary rules of inheritance to market mechanisms, contributed to weakening traditional networks of mutual aid. While the customary system encouraged a regular redistribution of small plots of land to the most disinherited members of the Hutu community, the transition to a system of purchase and sale of land made possible an accumulation of property by the most favoured individuals, and had the effect of a growing marginalization of the less well-off. The most vulnerable members of the community quickly fell into situations of extreme precariousness. The sociologists who conducted this study showed how the breach in the traditional social contract, without the associated emergence of mechanisms of formal solidarity, contributed to unleashing the worst violence within this northeast Rwandan community.

'Colombians' in Africa

In several African big cities, the rupture of solidarities when the demographic and economic crises were at their worst gave rise to 'street children'. It was long believed that, thanks to the mechanisms of family and community, African social organization took care of children. This was mistaken: unknown in Africa before the 1980s,[7] there are today nearly 1,000 street children in Yaoundé, and probably more than twice that number in Kinshasa and N'Djamena.[8] Though pursued by the authorities who police the streets of their capitals, they are quite at home there, living off all kinds of trafficking – including their own bodies, marked by the city violence. As in Ceausescu's Romania, they are a daily reminder of the state's impotence to provide them with training. Icons – despite themselves – of societies whose structure is decomposing, these children of the urban crisis are to be found in all street-based movements.

In N'Djamena they are called 'Colombians': whether orphans or not, they live off drug traffic and petty theft. On the margins of society, their sociability and security come from their gang, particularly in time of war. In autumn 2007, when the Chadian army, facing difficulties in the rest of the country, had lost too many men, they were recruited to fight. It is impossible to say how many were killed: no one knows their original number. In the swarming masses of the city they are a negligible quantity. They also have nothing to lose; they are intrepid little soldiers. The young Colombians say they are ready to die for a small chance of promotion through arms.[9] If this does not happen, wielding power of life and death with the Kalashnikov they are entrusted with, they ransom the population in the east of the country, terrorizing the most respected old people. The tale of these Colombians is sadly notorious, repeated on four corners of the continent each time that violence breaks out. The characters are the same. In Congo-Brazzaville, the child-soldier militias are known as Cobras, Ninjas, Zulus, like in the Nintendo games that their young European equivalents learn to play on. The stories of their exactions remain untold.[10]

The cities will be the theatre of tomorrow's disturbances. Marginalized, since they are deprived of any constructive role in society and have no prospect of acquiring one in a context of double-digit unemployment, out-of-work youth are a sword of Damocles hanging over African societies. They are also the symptom of a social disintegration that is under way on a large scale: a ferment that leads them to fall through the net of traditional systems, without being sufficiently supported by 'modern' national solidarities torn between contradictory norms.

A century after Durkheim, anomie has reached these African societies that are changing so fast. This is the only way of explaining behaviour that is otherwise hard to understand: the epidemic of rape, for example, in Ituri and the Kivus, two regions in the east of the Democratic Republic of Congo.[11] Though it is impossible to get exact figures on violence against women, local, humanitarian and UN organizations agree that around 100,000 women have been raped in the east of the DR Congo since 1996. How can we understand the spread of such acts of barbarism? Is Congolese society vicious, sadistic and barbaric? It is certainly struggling to emerge from a long civil war – there is no better school of violence and barbarism. As in other conflicts with an ethnic dimension, rape was used on a massive scale as a weapon, sowing hatred within communities that were permanently shaken. But only one victim in five says that she was attacked by fighters. Many women in the towns were raped by neighbours, passers-by or street children. Rape went beyond a weapon of war and became a form of everyday 'civilian' violence.

The loss of bearings by entire societies offers a convincing framework for explaining this generalization of sexual violence in the Congo. No matter how real, this violence is also symbolic – almost political – insofar as it expresses a social stance. The act of possessing a woman is in fact a sign of respectability, of integration into society. But the *maïbobos*, the young men on the street, see themselves deprived of even this outward sign of dignity. Some of them, accustomed to the practice of violence after years of fighting, seize this privilege for themselves. In the words of a street kid at Goma: 'We don't have a right to anything, money or shelter or women. If I'm refused my right, I take it for myself!'[12] In a country where all prospect of progress is blocked by an interminable civil war, commonplace rape is a form of revenge against a stifled destiny. By accelerating social ruptures of all kinds, war is both the producer and revealer of anomie.

10

Crescent and Cross

Just like nature, human societies abhor a vacuum; the crisis of legitimacy that shook African customary and legal authorities during the 1990s triggered the emergence of replacement structures. Substituting for the absence of state institutions of regulation and support, civil society organizations grew up in this decade to provide sites of sociability and frameworks of regulation. In the town, where demand was strongest, these foci were centred less and less on ethnic identities. They were much more commonly the work of religious denominations.

Responding to the needs of populations in the full grip of the transition crisis, Islam and Christianity, each in their wide range of forms, steadily assumed a determining role in African societies.[1] They transformed the way they operated – a major event, which is hard for our secular societies to grasp. Let us dwell for a moment on this Africa of ritual and wonder.

Re-enchanting the world

Confronted with these tremendous needs, Christian churches and Islamic organizations initially occupied the social field, rapidly moving in where the African state had been compelled to abdicate under the weight of structural adjustment programmes. The 1990s saw the work of Christian and Islamic charitable associations proliferate, both local and national. Alms and *zakat*[2] made possible the emergence of religious solidarities where traditional ones had given way. 'Social security', which at one time had been based on the clan, became a religious function in many African societies lacking public insurance systems. Contrary to the traditional mechanisms of mutual aid, this new solidarity goes far beyond the family or clan. Often very strong within the community of faith, it may act on a national, regional or international scale. Islamic Relief, the major British humanitarian NGO present in several African countries, is typical of this new pan-Islamic solidarity.

The mushrooming of faith schools in Africa over the last twenty years also illustrates this new role of religious personnel. The Somali example is symptomatic: since the start of the civil war in 1990, the state has been invisible in the eyes of the Somali population. Pupils and teachers have been expelled, classrooms destroyed, and no public network still provides teaching in the country. Of all the educational structures, the traditional Koranic schools – the *dugsi*, and their Arabized equivalents the *medersas* – are alone in having kept their instruction going.[3] Under shellfire in Mogadishu, you can hear children's voices reciting the Koran. In the state of permanent civil war that the country has experienced, the faith schools today have a monopoly on education for a whole new generation of young Somalis. But their success is not simply confined to countries at war. In the countries of the Sahel, where these structures compete with state education, they are often preferred by parents disappointed with the public system, which lacks both human and financial resources. The last twenty years have seen *medersas* proliferate across the Sahel and Sudan, in the cities as well as in the countryside. Not subject to any clerical control, and largely independent of the official educational curriculum, their teaching is a mixed bag. From the transmission of basic skills and rules of social life to a rigorous and radical instruction, the world of the Koranic schools offers both the best and the worst. Whatever the nature and quality of its teaching, the provision of education is also necessarily that of a system of norms and values. The leverage that Islam has in Africa today is thus considerable. But the Catholic and Protestant churches are not lagging behind; from Cameroon to Côte d'Ivoire, via Burundi and Uganda, their private schools have also benefited largely from the withdrawal of incapable governments. In Africa, public service has dissolved into religious service.

Strengthened by their growing responsibility for the instruction of African youth, the continent's two monotheisms have been able to implant themselves in new soil, steadily abandoned by traditional religions and customs. Like these latter, they provide a set of norms for life in society, and help to make sense of the world. Contrary to them, they offer an entry into a certain form of modernity.

Islam and Christianity, in their new and eminently plural forms, are thus influencing the customs of Africans ever more, starting with clothing, diet and family practices. This increasingly strong social penetration is obvious in many towns of the Sahel and the Horn of Africa, where each year finds more women hidden behind black veils. But the Protestant churches are also involved in this powerful return of standards in upturned societies. Désiré, a young Chadian graduate who works as a guard in N'Djamena, tells us that he recently joined one of the new Pentecostal churches that are springing up in the outlying districts of the capital. Désiré's family are Catholic. But for him, Catholics do not respect their own rules, they have no community feeling. He explains to us, with the faith of the new convert, that it is all very different in the evangelical communities, where moral rules about alcohol, family and wealth are particularly strict and observed to the letter. To break them is not only seen as an affront to God; it means breaking the moral contract with the community. A genuine solidarity is present here: a community chest for helping the sick and widowed is topped up each Sunday by the faithful. 'When you are a member of an [evangelical] community, you cannot fall into destitution.'

In the face of the needs so vigorously expressed by African civil society, the religious field does not confine itself to these social, economic or normative functions. As in other regions of the world, African Islam and Christianity steadily outgrow their spiritual and social functions to claim societal and thus highly political preferences. Temples, churches and mosques have in fact long counted among the rare spaces of expression in these controlled societies. Given the weakness of opposition parties, either bought over or suppressed by the state, religion, spread by missionary groups that are often fundamentalist, has become the mouthpiece of an ever-present social unease. The role of tribune has now fallen to it: denouncing deviant political practices, stigmatizing modes of development that have failed, it confronts ruling elites with their defeats, and is transformed into an opposition voice. Calling for a break with African traditions, both sub-Saharan monotheisms offer a critical view of 'modernity' as it is embodied by the post-colonial state. They propose to their followers a kind of third way, an 'alter-modernity'. This movement into the societal sphere is particularly striking in Nigeria. Islamic groups here, speaking for a deeply Islamicized society, have obtained the application of sharia law in twelve of the northern states. The development of the Maghreb societies over the last thirty years suggests that the two religions have not come to the end of their movement from the spiritual into the political in sub-Saharan Africa.

'The twenty-first century will be religious or nothing', André Malraux supposedly said.[4] Africa will be no exception here, simply that everything happens more quickly in this continent set on catching-up. The 're-enchantment' of societies proceeds in parallel with a violent crisis of 'disenchantment'. A flying leap is taken from abandonment of traditional religious forms (whether traditional African cults or traditional forms of Islam and Christianity) into the adoption of new forms of religion. African societies, as they change, are experiencing a process of accelerated 'disenchantment/re-enchantment'.

We can thus see a second major rupture in relation to the 'African identity' described in old anthropology books: this Africa, which can no longer be qualified as rural, is also not a continent of the cult of ancestors and forces of nature. Whether in Nigeria or Kenya, Cameroon, Ghana, Congo, Uganda or Côte d'Ivoire, the ground of African 'animism' is rapidly dissolving, to the benefit of the militant monotheisms that are rising apace. The respective successes of Islam and the evangelical churches in the race for followers are the culmination of a new communitarianism of the urban space, the creation of new solidarities and the standardizing of norms – once more made consistent. 'In the town, it is better to be Christian or Muslim than animist', one of our interviewees in Burkina Faso explained. Religion thus facilitates entry into a mediated and 'domesticated'[5] modernity. It represents, after the erosion of traditional systems of values and social life, a return to a normative system. What is new is that these norms are perceived as more compatible with the urban condition. The two monotheisms, far more holistic than their European counterparts as they carry with them a whole series of social, economic and political functions, offer a ready-made response to the new urbanites in search of bearings.

In the name of the Father, the Son and the Holy Spirits

Neither Islam nor Christianity emerges unchanged from their African success. Both become more complex and are transformed as their new followers are incorporated. Africa is thus not just faced with their lightning expansion, expressed in recent years by the proliferation of religious buildings across the continent. It is also the location for deep mutations in both religions – which have little to do with their origins on the continent in the ninth and seventeenth centuries respectively.

It is a usual phenomenon in the spread of religions in a particular cultural epoch that old beliefs survive and are incorporated into the new practices.[6] Nowhere did this blending strike us more than at a Catholic Christmas mass celebrated a few years ago in a remote region of northern Cameroon.

On this morning of 25 December, the communities of the adjacent hillsides come down in procession under the observant eyes of the town's Muslim shopkeepers seated outside their stores. Traditional dress alternates with football shirts: the atmosphere is festive, everyone in their Sunday best. Accompanied by songs in as many tongues as there are hills (each mountain village, perched on its hill, forms a distinct community with its own dialect), these processions converge towards the site of the celebration, where young people from the town have set up several rows of benches made of tree trunks. The mass is celebrated by several Cameroon priests and one French priest, who has lived for many decades in this remote township. The traditional chiefs of each village, elderly men carrying various accessories of earthly and spiritual power, sit in a row facing the ceremony. If they plainly do not understand this curious celebration (none of them speak French, or understand the Catholic ritual), it is clear from their faces that they are honoured to be there, invited by the white priest and doctor – whose roles are somewhat similar to their own. Their rather distant looks light up when one of their villages is invited to start a song. A section of the congregation rises and stands in the middle, before the altar.

We hear a mixture of songs, traditional percussion and string instruments. Then – surprise – a portable radio, carried in the hand by a young dancer, starts making a powerful sound, emitting music broadcast from a Cameroon station. This clamour leads into a kind of mystic dance that, as it gets louder, is rapidly transformed into a collective trance. The children of other communities rush into the throng. The little group of French people, now disoriented in their turn, clap their hands and seek in vain a rhythm to latch on to. Curious to see how the celebration will develop, we are aware of living a magical moment. A shamanic trance? A celebration of the mass? Each person seems to live this moment of spiritual communion in their own way: from the most fervent Catholic to the most ardent animist, the Cameroonians present in the assembly probably cover the whole spectrum. At the end of about ten minutes the priest makes a sign, then raises his voice to put an end to the music and ask the group to return to their seats. The next community is then invited to the altar. Its chief understands that it is his turn to lead the dance. After four hours of celebration, the mass comes to an end. A few purchases at the town market, and each community makes its way back up the mountain in joyous procession. The young girls, beating the ground in a rhythm, raise a cloud of dust that gradually veils them from sight.

Is the new religion taking hold, or are the old and the new simply existing side by side? As foreign observers we did not have the keys to understand all the changes under way in this ceremony. But we did have the feeling of living a fleeting moment in the history of these communities. Islam and Christianity, religions of the plains, are steadily climbing up the hills of north Cameroon. Despite this survival of traditional elements within the new monotheisms, and despite the presence of sorcerers and witchdoctors on Africa's soil, the gradual disappearance of traditional religions in favour of Islam and Christianity is manifest throughout the continent.

One of the most striking changes that the two monotheisms are experiencing in the course of their spread through Africa is a certain atomization. From one place to another, the spirituality on offer displays a whole diversity of new churches, new currents, new preachers competing in the quest for followers. So much so that young converts often espouse religions very different from those that African Christians or Muslims practised at the time of independence.

N'Djamena counts increasing numbers of both monotheisms. Animist practices are on the retreat, nibbled away from both sides. The Catholic church, however, attracts few new followers. It even loses some, seduced by the evangelical Protestant communities. This quiet evolution of African Christianity seemed confirmed to us one Sunday morning when we attended a ceremony at a church in an outlying part of town. We counted close to 1,000 faithful piled up inside the building, brand new but already too small. Despite being destroyed when rebellion flared up a few months earlier, it had already been rebuilt thanks to Canadian finance. What surprised us right away was the calm of the celebration, in contrast to evangelical cults elsewhere in Africa or in the United States. The Chadian pastor, who had returned from Toronto, tried his best to inject a bit of atmosphere, encouraging his congregation to stand up, sing and clap their hands. A partial success. He addressed himself to a number of them in his sermon, but they only responded in a low voice and with their heads bowed, visibly embarrassed. A few women who had to be carried out unconscious and shaking in spasm had not been suddenly struck by the Holy Spirit, like some of their North American fellow religionists, but rather by crises of malaria. Only the songs of the choir, formed by a group of young people touring round the communities of the region, recalled evangelical services in New York or Washington. How to explain this? The assembly consisted of quite new converts, probably former Catholics or animists, and was still unaccustomed to the dynamic of an evangelical service.

However anecdotal, this story does illustrate a much wider and structural phenomenon: the radical diversification of supply on the religious market, and the conquest of ground by new reforming currents. On the Christian side, the Anglican, Methodist, Presbyterian, Baptist, Seventh-Day Adventist, Pentecostal and Roman Catholic churches are only part of a spectrum that is now far wider than young people like Désiré perceive. There is a whole series of specifically 'African' churches (the Bethel Church of Christ, Salem;[7] the Global Frontiers Church; the Assemblies of God), as well as new churches appealing to evangelical Protestantism that have come from the United States: the Gospel Church of Christ, Message of Truth Universal Mission, Healing Sabbath Church, Deeper Life Bible Church, Redeemed Church of God, to give only a small sample. We are thus witnessing an explosion on the market for spiritual goods. And it is indeed a market, in which each has the duty to save souls, win followers, expand the congregation. In this wide religious catalogue, Africans vote with their feet: the tours of big American tele-evangelists play to full houses and make considerable profits. Africa in change is a rich seam, arousing vocations: whether in Nigeria, Kenya or the RD Congo, founding a church can be a speedy path to riches or social ascent. The pastors of the new Pentecostal churches, some of whom cross the country in their Mercedes, thus emerge as new models of social success: they symbolize wealth, social prestige, connections with international networks and political power.[8] Certain of the continent's heads of state who have joined these new cults have in fact been able to make use of these networks as a power base. African Islam is equally plural: traditional Islam – Sufi and non-hierarchical – is supplemented and partly displaced by reforming currents upholding Salafi[9] and Shiite traditions – each divided in turn by widely varied tendencies.

In the land of the (un)believers

Both monotheisms have long and deep roots in Africa. The Islam that developed there, particularly in the countries of the Sahel, had for a long time a collegiate structure. Christianity, imported from Europe in the age of colonization, was likewise 'classic' and conservative in both its Protestant and Catholic versions. Today influences are changing, and the new forms of both Islam and Christianity that now flourish south of the Sahara are revolutionizing the traditional African forms of these religions. Thus, despite their diverse proliferation, these modern avatars of Islam and Christianity have a curious resemblance, like mirror images. Responding to the same need for belonging and framework in atomized urban societies, these twin religions that are now on the rise share three main characteristics, as well as a number of paradoxes.

The first point in common is their strictness. Both are equally concerned to distance themselves from the old order characterized by violence, poverty and decay. This implies a break with the compromises made over the years by traditional forms of Islam and Christianity, and the establishing of a new normative framework.

This is a double break, affecting both rules and teachings. In Salafist Islam, which is expanding particularly swiftly, strict adherence is embodied above all in customs that set out to be incorruptible: the project of a new moralization of society involves the application of a clear and strict moral code.[10] This new religious sociability, particularly popular with young people in the towns, is thus one of an often ostentatious discipline. The five pillars of Islam, backed up by a series of obligations and prohibitions that cover diet, clothing and morals, bring the faithful together in a unifying self-denial. Respect for this ritual orthodoxy defines the perimeter of the community of believers; those who do not conform to it are considered impious. This lack of compromise is particularly striking in sub-Saharan Africa, insofar as it contrasts here with the traditional African practice of Islam, known for its tolerance and diversity. It also involves belief, which has to be purged of animist traditions. Like its counterparts across the world, rigorist Islam in black Africa displays a relentless hostility to the cult of saints, the combination of mystical Islam and traditional Koranic teaching. From Senegal to Sudan, via northern Nigeria and Cameroon, the apostles of orthodoxy wage an unremitting war against Sufi Islam, still very present in Africa.

There is a paradox here that is hard for our usual conceptual framework to deal with: no matter how puritanical, this piety is neither 'traditional' nor 'conservative', since it seeks emancipation from traditional Islam and its framing structures. At the root of this emancipation is the opening to any believer of the individual capacity to hear the words of the Prophet: there is no need to have any special 'qualification' to access directly the sources of faith and right. By returning to a more literal interpretation of the word of God, as expressed in the Koran, and to the prophetic tradition (the *sunna*), Salafism places the believer alone before the religious text – thus rejecting the long tradition of Islamic interpretation, the *ijthâd*. This new form of popular piety, with a marked anti-intellectual flavour, is thus part of a specifically 'reactionary' or 'neo-conservative' Islam. It has freed itself from traditional customs, from accepted interpretations of sacred texts, in order to 'return' to traditions in force in the Arabian peninsula in the seventh century – deemed more 'authentic'. It is to this reinvention of authenticity and tradition that we owe the rapid spread in the towns of Islamic Africa of clothing styles from the Arab heartland. Archaic in a number of ways, this 'neo-traditionalism'[11] is no less modern inasmuch as it makes possible a break with tradition. Judging by the proliferation of Wahabi mosques across the continent, it is perceived by Africans as more appropriate to the twenty-first century than traditional Islam. For this reactionary and puritanical Arab Islam is also modern and globalized: as witness its Internet sites, DVDs of sermons, religious broadcasts of all kinds transmitted from Saudi Arabia or Qatar and available throughout the Sahel.

These theological differences over ritual and teaching provide the backcloth to a bitter inter-generational conflict. Seduced by a religion that combines puritanism and modernity, young Africans reject 'old people's Islam', that of the confraternal sheiks.[12] The opening of new places of worship by young Arabizers who have returned from studying abroad can unleash a fierce competition for followers, as we were told by a scholar who had visited northern Cameroon, in relation to the duplication of traditional confraternal mosques by new Sunni ones:

> In the space of a few months, a glaring new building grows up close to the old mosque, often endowed with a minaret and in an architecture modelled on that of the Gulf states, which is where the finance generally comes from... The enterprise follows a logic of renewal of Cameroon's Islamic cadres, and the new mosque is always governed by imams and preachers selected among the Arabizers and fundamentalists trained in Sudan or the Gulf. These then compete with the old imam for the faithful in the local quarter.[13]

'Duplications' of this kind, common in Cameroon, are symptomatic of an increased competition on the religious market, from which the traditional sheiks and marabouts are the first to suffer. This new religiosity thus enables an educated youth, trained abroad and in search of modernity, to take over spiritual power. For these young self-proclaimed imams, this seizure of power offers the prospect of rapid social ascent: a further reason to replace 'Dad's Islam' by 'God's Islam'.

There is a striking resemblance here with the Pentecostal wave that has been so visible on the African continent for several decades. The new evangelical churches also insist on the strictest respect for moral rules – often playing on the opposition between a Catholicism corrupted by money and power and a Protestant-

ism supposedly ascetic and puritanical.[14] It is also important for
them to purify teachings, and remove the faithful from confused
religious practices they term 'witchcraft'. Strict moral codes and
purified doctrine provide societies experiencing daily upheavals
with an interpretative framework that enables them to see things
in terms of 'good' and 'evil'. We could see this in the case of Désiré:
this Manichaeism serves as a compass in confronting a modernity that is often disconcerting. But this hunt for evil spirits by the
puritanical churches is not without its ambiguities.[15] First among
these is that of strongly reintroducing magic into religion. In point
of fact, the discourse of these new churches explains the failures
of the past (individual and collective) in terms of straying from
God and practising spirit worship. Choosing the 'way of God' thus
implies freeing oneself from evil powers by conversion. But the
believer always risks falling back into superstition, so great is the
power of Satan. This leads many Christian pastors to adopt, both
in their preaching and in ceremonies of 'deliverance', language
and gestures akin to the magic that they claim to expel. A further
paradox arises here – and not the least: by struggling against forces
of bewitchment, the Pentecostal pastor actually reproduces the
system of sorcery.[16]

By placing the believer alone before God and his word, the evangelical sects parallel the Salafi tradition, which privileges the direct
relationship between God and the convert without any intermedi-
ary.[17] Any person who commands the ears of the believers has the
right to make himself the mouthpiece of 'God's call' (the *da'wa*[18] in
Islam, and cornerstone of the Salafi creed). This democratization
of spiritual power contributes to the fragmentation of religious
authority and the multiplication of preachers. This particular
mutation of African Christianity then explains the real social phenomenon presented by the rise of tele-evangelists on the continent.
'Self-made men' wielding a considerable influence over both citizens and their rulers, their only qualification lies in their ability
to attract a crowd. Like Salafi Islam, this charismatic Christianity
is fundamentally modern and 'neo-conservative', inasmuch as it
makes possible a break with classical religious forms. This modernity is often both claimed and proclaimed: in Nigeria a number
of temples are air-conditioned and equipped with the latest sound
systems – something that does not fail to have a certain fascination
for young people from the 'adjusted generation'.[19] Emancipation

from family and clan structures for these young people thus takes place by submission to God. If each believer is supposed to donate a considerable share of their income to the church and its evangelical work, they are free from the obligation to redistribute it to their family and clan when these do not belong to the community. The church thus makes up for the erosion of traditional solidarities, while at the same time itself accelerating their dissolution. Religion emancipates: so it is urgent to subject yourself to it.

Because they rest on an opposition between pure and impure, these modern religions, beneath their radical forms, bear within themselves a new exclusiveness. Withdrawal into the community of believers in fact offers protection from the outside. Islam and Christianity are conceived not just as a spirituality and way of life, but also as a way of organizing society, which does not tolerate any exception. The puritanical logic forbids any compromise with the impious and unbelievers. Coexistence between these twin religions becomes hard, once the conversion of others is made into necessity.

Beyond their rigorousness and its many paradoxes, the second major characteristic shared by these movements of renewal is precisely their missionary zeal. Salafi Islam and evangelical Christianity match one another in their desire to redeem African souls. The motto of the Nigerian Pentecostalists – that 'we are winning' – well reflects the logic of conquest in which these two fundamentalisms situate themselves. Africa still has many lambs to lead onto the right path. The prophets on both sides focus initially on this easy prey, increasingly seduced by the offer of renewal. Followers of the traditional African religions thus remain their privileged target: in northern Cameroon, the Société Internationale de Linguistique (SIL), American in origin, is involved in translating the Bible into several local languages. But souls for conversion are also to be found among the believers of the classic Christian churches (i.e. not evangelical or charismatic), or, for Muslims, among followers of the Sufi tradition. It is perhaps more disturbing that this frenzied race for believers implies, sooner or later, a clash between the two militant movements. The SIL, for example, in its missionary work, is translating the sacred texts into Kotoko, a language spoken by an exclusively Muslim group.[20] This encounter between two religious movements has begun to produce extreme tension in recent years. In fact, far from cancelling one another out, these two forces are being strengthened and radicalized. When they rub shoulders, Muslim and Christian fundamentalists construct themselves in opposition to one another. Nigeria, for centuries a site of coexistence between Islam, traditional religions and Christianity, constitutes a living laboratory of the complex relationships between these two radical movements – which are now in full swing. Initial results are disquieting.[21] The urban territory is in fact ever more marked by religious buildings: the ostentatious display of churches and crosses by those resisting Muslim domination is destined to counteract the spread of a demonized Islam. The provocations of the new Pentecostal churches wanting to convert Muslims are answered by calls for *jihad*. The 'clash of civilizations'[22] may be a myth, but will Africa be the continent of a clash of missionaries? On either side, this polarization of religion between its extremes serves the careers of the most radical politico-religious entrepreneurs – who do everything they can to make it worse.

A third meeting-point between the twin religions is that both are strongly influenced from abroad. We were surprised, on a visit to eastern Chad, to see a brick building, new and gleaming, close to a bush village with houses of dried mud and straw. The local population, hard-pressed to meet their basic nutritional needs, were clearly incapable of funding such a building. Our young guide explained to us that 'the Arabs' (from the Gulf) regularly visited the Ouddaï countryside, offering to build mosques for the Muslim villages that wanted them. They also offer to train a young man from the village for several years in order for him to return to the country strengthened by knowledge. If the village accepts, the mosque is financed, and supplied to its inhabitants ready for use. Many young Chadians go and study in Khartoum, we were told. But the most fortunate leave for Cairo, Jeddah or Medina. In sub-Saharan Africa, as elsewhere, this is how uncompromising Saudi Islam spreads – and with it the international influence of the oil kingdom.

But if this is its most noticeable form, the renewal of strict Islam is not just the result of these Salafi tendencies imported from Saudi Arabia. The 'revolutionary' Shiite movement of Imam Zaki Zaki in Nigeria, inspired by the teachings of Ayatollah Khomeini, is characteristic of the penetration of an Iranian influence in sub-Saharan Africa. Believers in these Shiite sects do not look towards Medina or Jeddah, but rather Teheran, Najaf and southern Lebanon. The

Lebanese Hizbollah or 'party of God', financed by Iran, is now said to have a Nigerian branch.[23] Though still anecdotal, the yellow and green processions in the Nigerian countryside in support of Sheikh Yassin and Hassan Nasrallah illustrate the importing, by way of religion, of controversies that are quite foreign to Africa. The tensions between Shiite and Sunni Islam are already a reality on the continent – as witness the clashes that took place following the building of a Shiite mosque in Douala in 1999. These foreign influences on the new African piety are not specific to Islam: the Christian renewal is deeply marked by the 'born again' tendency in the United States – well established in Washington through the neo-conservative movement.

This growing foreign influence, at the junction of religion and politics, is also the work of charitable organizations. Subtly mingling missionary work and charity, their social action enables them to get to the heart of the societies that they wish to evangelize. Once again, there is a striking similarity between certain Islamic NGOs from the Gulf States or Great Britain and their Christian counterparts from North America. While some of them clearly distinguish their humanitarian aim from the religious one (active or passive conversion), others deliberately maintain a confusion between the two. In the Sudan, a country where coexistence between Islam and Christianity is always delicate, the outbreak of wars in the south and Darfur saw the flourishing of a multitude of religious organizations within the humanitarian community. Is their presence intended to save lives or souls? For a number of them, these two actions go together – never mind how the fragile balance between local religious forces might be upset.

The religious transformations south of the Sahara, made up of multiple and contradictory movements, display a rare complexity, to which these few pages clearly are insufficient to do justice.[24] Scattered and changing, African religious practice comes in many different guises – which argues for fine-grained sociological studies at the levels of the individual, the community and the country. But in the chaos of these transformations, and despite contrary currents, it is possible to discern an underlying movement: that of the rise of two twin forms of 'neo-conservative' religious sensibility in response to a destructuring modernity. More puritanical and exclusive than African Islamic and Christian traditions, more eager for converts and more openly subject to foreign influences, these offer a seductive alternative to the modernity proposed in recent decades by the post-colonial state. High-tech and globalized, the two monotheisms are part of Africa's entry into globalization.[25] After all, people pray in the same way now in Toronto and N'Djamena, in Medina and Abuja.

11

Switched-on Africa

If Africa is in the front line of religious globalization, it is also rapidly making its way into the age of globalized media.

From *Big Brother* to Nollywood

A reality TV show which appeared on the continent's screens in summer 2003 illustrates the way that Africa is plugged into the world and its networks. Following a script now well-worn in the US, Asia and Europe, twelve competitors from the same number of sub-Saharan countries (Ghana, Kenya, Uganda, Tanzania, Malawi, Zambia, Angola, Namibia, Botswana, Zimbabwe, Nigeria and South Africa) were selected to take part in *Big Brother Africa*.[1] Shut up for three months in a Johannesburg suburban house christened 'Home of Africa', their life was tracked by dozens of cameras and microphones – and scrutinized by the whole of Africa. The public voted by SMS, each week eliminating one competitor until the winner was selected. The Zambian woman who won went off with a prize of $100,000, and full honours from her country's government. The programme, a real media phenomenon, was followed each night by 30 million viewers in forty-six countries. The 'final' broke all audience records: in town and country, in bars and homes, young and old pressed in front of their sets, just like with the biggest football matches. This popular success led a South African newspaper to say that '*Big Brother Africa* has succeeded where the Organization of African Unity has failed, in unifying the ordinary citizens of Africa.'[2]

To claim that the *Big Brother* effect was a unifying one is a bit exaggerated. It would be fairer to say that it left no one indifferent. Triggering an outcry of praise and indignation, it violently cast modern Africa against traditional Africa – both now connected to television. Rapidly accused of a dumbing-down by way of Western culture – certainly embodied by the house's interior, bedecked with kitsch accessories of the colonial age – *Big Brother* aroused impassioned debate in the African press:

> Why are we so quick to accept rubbish that comes from the West? Why are we not equally aggressive in promoting our own ways of life and values to the world outside? I support the leaders of Malawi and Namibia, and the Ugandan religious community, in censoring the broadcast of the reality TV show *Big Brother Africa*. What do our children learn from this show, watching the occupants bathe nude and vomit after hours of debauchery?

Replying to this indignation on the part of a Kenyan intellectual, an Angolan lawyer remarked:

> Africans have become cosmopolitan. The behaviour of the occupants and their sexual habits are representative of the lives and ways of seeing of this new globalized Africa. They have no affinity, or very little, with traditional values, norms and institutions...The immorality, drinking and smoking in the *Big Brother* apartment cannot be characterized as European or American. So it can't be said that this is 'un-African' behaviour. The Western clothes that we wear are 'un-African'. Even our religion isn't African. Where do these preachers see the frontier?

The Africa plugged into *Big Brother* is an Africa moving full speed ahead in a global media universe. But does that make it less African or more 'Western'? It is hard to see in what way reality TV is something specifically 'Western'. As the Angolan lawyer maintains, it is rather the symbol of the contemporary world with all its ambiguities, in which 21st-century Africa certainly counts on participating. Whether it speaks of Africa's 'Westernization' or 'modernization', the social phenomenon that *Big Brother Africa* represents has questioned African identities, and confirmed the power of television in the construction of role models. By way of this popular competition, in fact, ethnic divisions were set aside in favour of a popularity contest between twelve young African nations caught up for a moment in the game of patriotism.

Just as controversial as the South African reality TV shows, Nigerian films share their popularity. Like their counterparts made in Bombay, they capture and display everyday life in societies that are rapidly changing. In *Who Killed Okomfo Anonkye?*, a well-heeled 'born-again' tracks down his brother, a voodoo priest living in a shanty-town: 'You're no longer my brother', he says in English, a Bible in his hand. 'Nollywood' now produces some 2,000 films a year, more than either Hollywood or Bollywood. A rich producer often puts up the money for the film, which is rarely much more than $20,000. Mixing love stories with the social advance of young Nigerians, the screenplay typically presents, with a large dose of emotion, the clash between village tradition (languages, sorcery) and the modernity of the city (monotheist religion, urban ano-nymity). Genital mutilation, polygamy, traditional sorcery and religion, adultery, the hypocrisy of religious leaders, relations between tenants and rich landlords, drug traffic and urban violence, prostitution, AIDS[3] ... all the themes of everyday life in urban Africa find their place here. Shooting is completed in a week, and the product is then dispatched to the copying workshops that abound in Lagos. The Video Compact Disks (local equivalent of the DVD) or video cassettes are printed in an edition of 50,000, then distributed in video shops throughout Nigeria and surrounding countries. They are sold at less than US$3 a piece, and shown in restaurants and informal video centres. The greatest successes are exported and acclaimed in African shops in the Bronx, north London and the 18th arrondissement of Paris. These films are a way for the African diaspora to keep in touch with the life of their relatives back home. The film industry, with a turnover estimated at US$300 million per year, employs close to a million people, making it the second-largest employer in the country after agriculture.

This Africa, absorbing the cult programmes of global culture and possessing its own film industry, is also directly plugged into the world networks of information. Canal+ counts more than 100,000 subscribers in Africa: from Dakar to Yaoundé, via the small villages of Central Africa, dealers have started offering customers programmes from the encrypted French station. TV5

Monde and France 24 are also readily available, and popular across French-speaking Africa, just as CNN, the BBC and Voice of America are throughout the continent. Making a stop in Abéché, a small town in eastern Chad, more than 1,000 kilometres from the coast and far from any major centre, we were surprised to see the house security guard eagerly listening to the news on Radio France Internationale (RFI) while he prepared his mint tea. Dressed in traditional costume, he followed the same programme as the French expatriate working in Shanghai, the ambassador at his desk in the capital, or a Paris student. This recent penetration of the Northern media right to the heart of Africa, and the proliferation of available news sources, is a cause of accelerated transformation in ways of being and thinking. It offers not just an open window onto the world and its developments, but also a mirror for African societies, who see themselves through the prism of reports devoted to them by the BBC, CNN or TV5.

The 'Zoe's ark' affair in 2007 brought to light the activities of a French charity in eastern Chad. Profiting from the humanitarian wave then breaking over Chad and Sudan, this association was preparing to smuggle out to France Chadian and Sudanese children depicted as orphans – against all ethics and law. The association's staff were arrested and detained by the Chad authorities, under the inquisitive gaze of the French media. The statements of the French head of state, who announced after a first group were released his intention to 'go and find those remaining, no matter what they did', provoked a wave of indignation in Chad. Designed to reassure the French public, these words broadcast directly to N'Djamena were interpreted there as major interference by France in the Chadian judicial process, and immediately set off anti-French demonstrations. Treated as simply an object of news, Chadian society vigorously showed that it was also an actor. The international media, in their treatment of African news, now address themselves also to African societies. This transition of Africa from the status of 'object' to 'subject' is accompanied by effects that we have probably not completely taken stock of.

In particular, it may influence the dynamic of certain conflicts, both for the better and for the worse. The Abéché security guard, for example, lives in a country experiencing deep political crisis: on several occasions in recent years columns of the rebels' pick-up trucks have arrived in his town, heading towards the capital.

Apart from a window towards France, the world and pan-African affairs, RFI represents for him access to news and external analysis of the situation that his country is undergoing. He and those like him are that much less prisoners of the rumours that abound in any society at war, and of the propaganda of one or other of the warring factions. Would the Rwandan genocide have reached the level of violence that it did if Rwandan radio sets had been more tuned to the BBC or RFI than to the infamous Radiotélévision des Mille Collines – which for months became a mouthpiece of anti-Tutsi propaganda and incitement to murder? By helping to diversify the sources of information available, the growth in the audience of international media in sub-Saharan Africa may constitute a major factor of stabilization.

But this mirror image can sometimes have the opposite effect, when external perceptions contribute to deepening local divisions. Presenting complex conflicts in summary format to an international audience little acquainted with African questions necessarily leads to certain simplifications of the issues involved. When the mirror becomes excessively distorting, it may contribute to freezing an oversimplified interpretative grid – and thus influence the perception of the actors in the conflict themselves. This phenomenon played a particular role in the Côte d'Ivoire crisis, largely presented in the European and US media as a conflict 'between Muslim north and Christian and animist south'. This summary, however, was deceptive in many respects.[4] Not only did its representation reduce a whole series of social, economic and political tensions to an imagined religious conflict (thus avoiding the far more complex question of *ivoirité*), it was even mistaken on the country's religious landscape. The overall distribution of the Ivorian population (concentrated on the coast) actually shows more Muslims living in the south of the country than in the north. The myth of the 'Muslim north' in conflict with a 'Christian and animist south' was thus quite simply false. Such mistakes would be no more than regrettable if they simply contributed to poor information on the part of the European and North American public. But they bear far weightier consequences in the age of globalized media: simplified conceptual categories broadcast by the international media can be seized and manipulated by the actors in the conflict themselves.

This impact of outside representations on local reality is especially striking in the violence raging in Darfur, presented in the European and American press as the act of the *janjawid*[5] Arab (and Muslim) militias against African tribes (Christian and animist). The communal and political reality of the Darfur conflict is far more complex,[6] but the actors of the anti-government rebellion rapidly learned how to play on this stereotype, presenting their 'African' tribes as victims of the Arab *janjawid* in the pay of the government in power in Khartoum. By redefining themselves in this way, these local actors to some extent created the 'reality' that Western media were looking out for. The term *janjawid* was then taken up by the population of the villages in this zone to denote any group of brigands on camel-back, who were thus equated with dangerous Islamists. The same phenomenon is at work in Nigeria and Somalia: readings of the conflicts in terms of the 'clash of civilizations', no matter how simplified, are taken up and exploited by local political actors seeking outside financial support.[7] Africa's connection to world information networks thus places the international media under a new responsibility. The stories that they tell are not blameless.

Beyond this 'mirror effect', sometimes pacifying and sometimes poisoning, the media manufacture African perceptions of the societies of the North. The TV series and films that young sub-Saharans devour so eagerly display a prosperous Western consumer society that contrasts sharply with the conditions of life that the great majority of them know. This clash between poverty and wealth, daily rubbed home by images broadcast from elsewhere, can only be disquieting for the 'adjusted generation' that experienced the worst of the economic crisis at the same time as it discovered images made in Hollywood. The gulf between the desire to share this prosperity, and the inertia of great poverty, generates among many an ambiguous sense of both fascination with and rejection of Western society – perceived as uniformly rich and happy. It also arouses yearnings to emigrate. Switzerland and Spain both financed publicity spots broadcast in Cameroon and Senegal designed to present a less idyllic image of the life of illegal immigrants in Europe and warn against the dangers of irregular arrival. But it is hard for these video clips to match the continuous flow of images of prosperity that are paraded day and night on African screens. In the long term, at least, the greater inter-connection between African and Western societies should allow African perceptions of ways of life currently idolized to become more complex.

But even here things are changing. New voices have recently emerged in the sub-Saharan media landscape, challenging the monopoly of the Western media. Several Arab satellite channels broadcasting from the Gulf are attracting a growing African audience. The very real risks of a spread of fundamentalist ideology in religious broadcasts should not blind us to the advance that this change is bringing. International channels such as Al-Jazeera also contribute to the diversification of news and analysis sources for Africa, the 'West' and the world as a whole. By providing alternative models, they enable both Africa and Europe to escape from an outmoded confrontation.

Cyber@frica

The arrival of sub-Saharan Africa on the Internet is more recent than the exposure of African societies to international radio and television. But Internet access is already expanding rapidly. Major fibre-optic cables, running under the oceans for thousands of kilo-metres, now connect Africa with Europe, India and the United States. By releasing capacity on telecommunications satellites, this new infrastructure makes it possible to multiply the amount of information exchanged, the speed of downloading and the number of users alike. The hourly connection charge in an Internet café has fallen to a fifth of its previous level since the installation of the first big fibre-optic cable along the West African coast in 2002, opening the way to the democratization of the Internet throughout the continent.

This digital revolution has inaugurated a new age in Africa. It brings with it extensive gains in productivity, which the industrial-ized countries experienced at the turn of the century: in Africa as elsewhere, free and rapid access to information, work via email and Internet banking will lead to substantial gains in both time and costs. But this advance represents a much greater leap forward in developing countries than in our own societies that are already equipped with efficient networks and public services: a leapfrogging by which a country can skip stages of development by acquiring the latest technologies without going through the earlier generation, often more costly and less effective. In many parts of Africa, the Internet arrived while there was still no proper postal service. The population of these regions will therefore move in less than a generation from an almost total isolation from the world and its networks to connection to the Web – making possible a whole series of economic activities and exchanges that were inconceivable a short time ago. The digital unlocking of Africa thus enables it to overcome several of the handicaps that hindered the continent's development for so long.

Health care, which suffers right across Africa both from a lack of skilled personnel and from its concentration in the capital cities, has already benefited from this. The arrival of broadband Internet in Mali along with the African Cup in 2002 made possible a small revolution – that of telemedicine. The health care project *keneya blown*[8] ('health waiting-room') links together three hospitals in the capital Bamako and two regional ones at Ségou and Timbuktu, the whole network being connected to the Geneva university hospital in Switzerland. Besides the continuous training of Malian doctors by way of online lectures, this system permits the organization of teleconsultations. When staff at the provincial health centres are faced with complex cases, they can consult specialists in neurosurgery, dermatology, radiology, etc., at the larger hospitals. X-rays taken in the provinces can be transmitted electronically to Bamako (and, if need be, to Geneva) for analysis and advice. Consultations even take place directly at a distance of thousands of kilometres, by means of webcams. 'I had the impression of touching him', a Swiss doctor explained about a Malian patient. Conditions that were incurable only a few years ago are now diagnosed and treated. Proud that medical advice can move in both directions, the founder of the project explains that, in a case of leprosy, a disease very rare in Switzerland, a Geneva dermatologist called on the expertise of a Malian specialist – the disease still being common there. Telemedicine networks are now proliferating across Africa.

The connection of Africa to the world by fibre-optic highways is also revolutionizing the field of teaching, particularly in higher education which was greatly affected by structural adjustment. How can valuable library collections be rebuilt, after being pillaged in the course of political disturbances or run down for want of maintenance? The number of academic books and papers available throughout the world in electronic format is now considerable, while the Internet connection of the major university libraries of the main African cities offers African students an access to knowledge that is incomparable with what their predecessors had only ten years ago. Whether in Paris, Dakar or Johannesburg, every Web surfer today has access to the online resources of the Library of Congress in the US, can download podcasts of classes given at the Collège de France, or can follow on video dozens of lectures on political science from the University of California at Berkeley. Access to leading specialists is no longer reserved just for students at the great universities of the North.

Even a virtual university has been set up for African students. Founded by the World Bank and supported by Microsoft, the African Virtual University (AVU) offers young Africans in a dozen countries degree courses up to doctoral level with a Canadian university. In specially equipped centres at African universities, students follow video conferences on the big screen, work on CD-Roms, and interact with their teachers by email and phone. Without leaving their own country, they can thus obtain a Canadian degree in languages, renewable energy, journalism or information technology. The award ceremonies for the Canadian degrees are held at the universities of Niamey, Cotonou, Noukachott and Bujumbura. The AVU now plans to set up in societies emerging from crisis, with a view to making up for the lack of any higher education structure or professional training. With support from the United Nations, it has opened learning centres in Somalia, the RD Congo, Gambia and Sudan. No doubt 'cyber@frique' is still in the course of development: the rate of Internet penetration remains weaker in sub-Saharan Africa than on other continents. The 'digital divide' is a reality, and the cost of Internet access remains too high for the majority of sub-Saharans. But nearly 7 per cent of Africans already use the Internet regularly (10 per cent of Nigerians), and the rate of use has increased thirteen times on the continent as a whole between 2000 and 2009.[9]

This steady democratization of access to information and means of expression is changing the balance of forces between political authority and civil society. As in other controlled societies, the Internet has become the privileged voice of expression for political opposition, enabling it to side-step the censorship of the media. Political blogs that are hosted abroad attract expatriates, domestic political opponents and international human rights activists. Spotlighting cases of corruption in forums or online magazines sometimes forces the judicial authorities to deal with them.

Africa's connection to the Web is also generating more harmful secondary effects: by virtual linkage of people at such vastly different standards of living, the Internet promotes a rise in crime. Africa has rapidly been plugged into cybercrime networks. Profiting from the absence of national regulatory structures, cybercriminals outbid one another in their ingenuity. 'Phishing', i.e. sending electronic messages to thousands of surfers with a view to obtaining banking information and siphoning their accounts, is a rapidly growing practice, particularly in West Africa. Often operating from Nigeria, 'phishers' no longer hesitate to attack major banks in the North, using their logos and sometimes their customer files. They put advertisements on French property sites offering apartments to let in the heart of Paris, backed up by photos, and asking for a few hundred euros as a preliminary deposit. Isn't this pathological form of integration the best evidence of Africa's participation in globalization? The continent is certainly in no way outdated and cut off from the world.

12

The End of Ethnicity

The identity market

For a long time, ethnicity summed up our representation of African identity. In this changing Africa, is it still as important as we like to believe? There are good reasons for answering in the affirmative.

It is clear enough that attempts to explain African social and political phenomena in terms of an ethnic framework have always been quite inadequate. Whenever people are unable to account for the complexity of a sub-Saharan conflict, ethnicity is called into play and essentialized: it's Hutus against Tutsis, Kikuyus against Luos and Kalenjins... But as many Africanists showed back in the 1980s,[1] this false evidence blinds us to the specifically political, economic and social dimensions of such conflicts: power, interests, the interplay of leading actors, etc. Once it is opened up, the black box of ethnicity reveals a far more complex reality, starting with the fact that the African continent is not made up of a 'mosaic of tribes'. To use a Marxist distinction, ethnic groups and tribes have never formed classes 'in themselves'. Historians and anthropologists who study black Africa have shown in fact how colonization froze a complex and changing reality by its construction of ethnic types. In a classificatory mania inherited from the natural sciences, the colonizers labelled peoples and often arbitrarily associated a certain 'race' with a territory, a language and a kinship system – regardless of the extreme fluidity of all three components of ethnic identity.

The history of the Bétés of Côte d'Ivoire is a telling example of the arbitrariness of the colonial construction of races:[2] this ethnolinguistic group actually arose from combining a whole set of peoples living on a certain territory – conveniently defined by three main roads! The name they were given, for its part, came from the expression '*Bete o bete!*' meaning 'Peace!' or 'Gently!', used by these people when they were victimized by the colonizers and their allies. But the colonizing ethnographers were not content just to group neighbouring peoples into 'races'; they also ethnicized economic and social realities. When the German, and later Belgian, administrations sought to classify the inhabitants of the colonies of Burundi and Rwanda into races, the criterion for distinguishing a Hutu from a Tutsi was simply the number of cattle they possessed. In brief, ethnic groups have a history;[3] to take them as fixed and settled amounts to succumbing to a dangerous 'identitarian illusion'.

Yet however artificial this may be, it has to be noted that ethnic identity continues to be mobilized in sub-Saharan Africa, with very concrete consequences. We all remember the traumatic images of the Rwandan genocide of 1994. That moment of collective violence illustrates how, if an ethnic group is not a class 'in itself', it has often been successfully mobilized as a class 'for itself'. Ideological constructions, no matter how artificial, can become a reality if enough people act accordingly. After Rwandan independence, for example, the distinction between Hutus and Tutsis was taken up and manipulated both by the 'dominant' seeking to naturalize their domination and by the 'dominated' seeking to overthrow it. In Côte d'Ivoire, the Bétés themselves have claimed their Bété identity in a strategy of struggle against the Baoulés in power – going as far as to play on some of the stereotypes associated with it. The election of Laurent Gbagbo, of Bété origin, expresses in a certain Ivorian political imagination the revenge of minority communities after a long period of submission to the Baoulés.

Ethnic consciousness may be manipulated to cause illusions, but there is nothing inherently illusory about it. It is not enough to demonstrate the inconsistency of reductionist conceptions of ethnicity; we still have to try to explain how this collective imagination structures political reality, and understand why ethnic consciousness is mobilized by a given actor at a given moment, in place of other markers of identity. The 1990s marked the high point of this tendency to (re)tribalize African society. From Rwanda and Burundi to the RD Congo and Côte d'Ivoire, ethnic identity went on to serve as a pretext for phenomena from mass violence through to genocide. And this mobilizing power of ethnicity seems to have extended into the twenty-first century: in Kenya in 2008, the electoral competition between two candidates from different communities led to the death of over 1,000 people in intercommunal violence.[4] The importance of the ethnic phenomenon, moreover, does not just find expression in violence: a logic of patronage continues to hinder the operation of political and economic systems in many African countries. Is it possible that this ethnic phenomenon, still so powerful today, will some day disappear?

We believe that it will. The use of ethnicity as a pillar of African identity is characteristic of a particular period in sub-Saharan history, the last hours of which we are probably living through today. Just as Europe had its 'nationalist moment',[5] so sub-Saharan Africa is coming to the end of its 'ethnic moment'. Ethnicity fulfilled certain definite functions. As we have seen, it responded to the need of the colonizers to 'know' (and thus classify) the peoples that they governed. At the time of independence, ethnic identity also served the formerly colonized in taking over the state and negotiating its fragile social contract. In the years of economic crisis, ethnic solidarity was both a way of mobilizing communal solidarity and a way of appropriating the scarce resources available. Whether for the dominant concerned to base their power, or the dominated seeking to challenge this, ethnicity proved in the end a powerful instrument of social struggle. But the mobilization of this marker of identity can only succeed as long as there is a certain real similarity – linguistic, cultural and social – between people of the same group.

This similarity, however, is rapidly evaporating as a result of the economic and social upheavals described in these pages. A Bété may be rich or poor, urban or rural, Protestant or animist, a company boss or an unemployed worker. A poor Bété, rural and animist, has far more in common with his Baoulé counterpart than with the rich Protestant company boss in Abidjan. Idriss would find it hard to join with people in his native village, whose language he no longer speaks, in order to oppose members of a rival ethnic group – perhaps one from which his girlfriend originates.

Désiré will spontaneously be more likely to come to the aid of one of the young people of his church than to that of a distant cousin. Joseph, for his part, makes it a point of honour never to make use of his ethnic group in business – and his children do not speak its language. Under competition from other identitarian markers, ethnicity is diluted. And the African identity market is rapidly diversifying.

From one exclusiveness to another

The city, melting-pot of these new African identities, is the site of encounters of all kinds – once the first phase of community-based withdrawal is passed. What is true of lifestyles is also true of beliefs or languages. Issa explains to us that his father is Muslim and his mother Christian. He himself is atheist, but knows the traditions of the village where his mother grew up. He can speak six languages. His children do not speak the dialects of their native region, and do not understand its customs. They intend to learn French, Arabic and English, and see this as enough. Inter-ethnic marriage is now very common, particularly in the towns. Why should this be surprising? Young urbanites from different communities speak the same language, listen to the same music, have the same idols and attend the same schools, universities and football matches. It is also striking to note how rapidly the practice of ethnic scarring is disappearing – along with the rites of passage that are often associated with it. We are probably seeing the last generation of Africans with cheeks marked by the indelible imprint of their ethnic group. Freed from the weight of their community, young city-dwellers are now free to choose their affiliations as a function of personal affinities.

This is the paradox of life in Africa's big cities: like everywhere else in the world, their size makes each of their inhabitants anonymous – opening a new field in which to exist as an individual. There is nothing new in this: the great nineteenth-century novelists wonderfully described the new freedom that Paris or London offered young people arriving from the countryside. But this movement towards individualism coexists in Africa with a strong demand for membership. Ethnicity, often bound up with the extended family, the native region and group pressure, is no longer necessarily best equipped to respond to this. It is rapidly being replaced by communities of choice.

As we have seen, the religious community is the foremost of these. In the churches, chapels and mosques of African cities, 'brothers' and 'sisters' of different ethnic groups pray side by side. Ethnic rivalries are clearly not absent from religious communities, but they unavoidably collide with the universal calling of Islam and Christianity. This debate between religion and ethnicity has been at work in a striking manner in recent years within the African Pentecostal church.[6] With its origins in the Ashanti community of Ghana in the 1950s, this church long remained bound up with a particular ethnic group: services were conducted in its language, the preachers and officials were recruited among Ghanaian Ashantis, and its headquarters were in Accra. But the success of the church, helped by the migrations of Ghanaians in different directions and present today in fifty countries, has faced this church with the contradiction between its evangelical vocation and its roots in one ethnic group. The recruitment of officials and preachers, and the language of services, have thus become objects of keen controversy. Faced with threats of a split on the part of the Ivorian branch, the traditionalists were forced to give way and agree that services could be held in French and English, as international and therefore 'modern' languages. By so doing they accepted its 'de-ethnicizing', thus marking a step in the retreat of the ethnic marker for these communities of Pentecostal Christians. For the same reasons, this process has also occurred within Islam, where African ethnicity is steadily being dissolved in the global *umma* – if not without introducing its own cleavages. For many young African Muslims, this phenomenon also involves learning the language of the Koran. As God and Allah do not discriminate between peoples, the rise in power of universal religions in Africa contributes to the erosion of ethnicity as the main marker of identity.

The emergence of the African middle classes means the rise of men and women concerned with their social advance and participation in global networks. If they have an occasional interest in mobilizing family or clan connections so as to obtain employment or develop their business activity, there is no advantage for them, in terms of economic or professional opportunities, in permanently enclosing themselves in their communities. Besides, their 'modern' values, oriented to the outside world, do not lead them to define themselves in ethnic terms. They are the first to favour national languages in the education of their children, so as to give them the chance to prosper in a national and international context far richer in opportunities. The life assurance policies they take out likewise replace the 'traditional life assurance' of the family, clan or ethnic group. Whether in the religious community, with colleagues at work or with members of a tennis club, their investment in elective communities is made at the expense of their involvement in their ethnic ones.

As with religion, this dilution of ethnicity in no way heralds the end of community exclusiveness. Communities are reinvented, with social class gradually taking over from ethnic group. The black Africans who settle in gated communities[7] in Cape Town or Johannesburg in effect leave an ethnic ghetto to join a social one. The new well-to-do classes of Nairobi or Kampala also take refuge behind barbed wire. But there is a difference of scope between these two ghettos: for Africans, ethnic membership counts less than social status.

Nationalism is also nibbling away at the roots of ethnicity. With more than 200 spoken languages, Cameroon is among the African countries most marked by the ethnic phenomenon. Yet nothing can break the national communion when the 'unbeatable Lions' hit the turf. The national selection of Cameroonian football, with its exceptional success, gives the country its self-image. Mixing English and French speakers, it draws on players from different communities and regions, and a wealth of talent. Each player is a national icon. In spring 1990, street battles between supporters of Paul Biya (mostly Béti and French-speaking) and those of John Fru (mainly Bamiléké and English-speaking) left several hundred dead. A few months later, the Lions took part in their second World Cup. They faced Argentina, the incumbent champions, in the opening game. For an hour and a half the whole of Cameroon held its breath, as one man. To general surprise, the Lions won against Diego Maradona's team. The young people who had violently fought one another three months earlier now invaded the streets where they had battled and celebrated together the victory of the national team.[8] Certainly a contradiction, but perhaps also symbolic: communal tension had persisted in Cameroon for a whole decade. But symbolism is the stuff of national sentiment, and the symbol of the Lions gives meaning to the Cameroon flag.

During the years of crisis, African states with their tottering national institutions lived off symbolism. This is now less and less the case, to the extent that the state wins back margins for public investment and gradually reassumes the unifying role that it had for a long time abandoned. Studies show that educational progress tends to reduce ethnic identification in favour of other markers – social and national in particular. Now rates of school attendance have begun to rise sharply again in Africa, after two decades of stagnation. The return of national means of communication in countries that were long devoid of these also makes its contribution to strengthening national consciousness. 'We need roads, education and health care, so that people live better and stop going back in time and clinging to their microcultures', a Chadian academic explained. His state still has a great deal to do. In other African countries, roads, education and health care are making rapid headway. Even if national allegiance is only one of the many identities that an African can claim, it is in general more widely shared than was the case ten or twenty years ago. Surveys demonstrate that when the inhabitants of the big cities are asked whether they identify with their nation above their ethnic group, between 65 and 85 per cent opt for the nation as against 18 to 34 per cent for an ethnic group.[9] Now nothing will halt the juggernaut of African urbanization.

Ethnicity, therefore, no longer systematically forms the basis of identity that it long did for many Africans. Africa is not a patchwork of ethnic groups; it is a patchwork of ethno-linguistic communities, of languages, nations, social classes, religions, etc. These different poles of identity coexist, and Africans switch between them in defining themselves. Identity, in fact, responds to needs. A person may choose to mobilize their community network one morning in the search for a job, present their religious belief at lunchtime to solicit charity, define themselves as a city-dweller in the afternoon as against a new arrival from the country, before feeling deeply Zambian or Nigerian when the moment comes to vote for the elimination of a competitor on the *Big Brother* programme – all this without denying for a moment what they are. This identity 'market' displays its whole strategic character at the points where people switch from one position to another: there are moments of ethnicization, of an individual or a whole society, but there are also moments of national identification and religious polarization.[10] This is particularly the case at election times, when politicians seek to mobilize electorates by all means available.[11]

Let us be clear: noting the inevitable advance of alternative identities that compete with ethnicity does not mean pronouncing the end of ethnic consciousness. Europe may well have emerged from its national moment, but it is not protected from national-ist impulses. In the same way, Africa is starting to emerge from its ethnic moment, while remaining prey to periodic and violent resurgences of ethnicity. More fundamentally, this structural ten-dency to the dilution of ethnicity is not the same as any weakening of African collective identities – or with community-based mobi-lization. In Africa, identities will continue to create illusions, and yet they will remain anything but illusory.

13

African Democracy

How can one write about Africa and its changes without tackling the thorny subject of democracy? For many observers, the failure to establish democracy on the continent in the wake of independence is a puzzle that arouses unease. Is twenty-first century Africa ready for democracy?

After a phase of enthusiasm for democratic revolutions on the continent, repeated coups d'état, electoral farces and a new wave of dictatorships sowed doubt among the most convinced humanists, fuelling an already stubborn cynicism regarding the capacity of Africans to adopt the principles of popular participation. This occurred to such an extent that people with great knowledge of the continent, on both sides of the Mediterranean, hold opposing views as to the prospects for democracy in Africa. For some of them, the history of the last twenty years shows that African societies are not made for democracy – a political system imported from Europe. For others, such a claim only excuses a blameworthy complacency towards abuses that are no more tolerable south of the tropic of Cancer than they are to the north, a complacency that was not without impact on the democratic failures of the 1990s.

What then is the situation with African democracy? Is it compatible with the moment that the continent is going through? Let us take the time to trace its recent history, starting from the ruins of the Berlin wall.

The end of a history

We should remember that the early 1990s were marked across the world by an unprecedented faith in this form of government. The 'end of history' was proclaimed, embodied in the unstoppable triumph of free markets and liberal democracy.[1] Indeed, the great wave of democratization born in the 1970s with the fall of the Iberian dictatorships, then echoed in Latin America in the 1980s, seemed to shatter the most tenacious regimes. The wind of change, after blowing down the Berlin wall and dissolving the Soviet bloc, was now announced for Africa.[2]

The African continent did indeed change in its turn into a terrain of sometimes violent confrontation between democratic and repressive forces. The liberation of Nelson Mandela in February 1990, signalling the end of apartheid in South Africa, seemed to confirm the strength of this irresistible movement towards self-determination. The French president of the time, despite having been little concerned with democratic struggles in Africa in the course of the previous decade, now decided to rank himself on the side of history. François Mitterrand proclaimed, in a speech at La Baule in June 1990, that 'France will do all that it can to contribute to the efforts being made in the direction of greater freedom': French aid to African states would in future be dependent on the advancing process of democratization.

But if this historic speech encouraged the process of 'national conferences'[3] and promoted the appearance of multiparty systems in West Africa, elections rapidly changed into a ritual for the legitimization of incumbent regimes – emptying the democratic process of any content. Still worse, the unlikelihood of these electoral masquerades leading to a change of government helped to discredit them.[4] So much so that two decades after La Baule, the purchase of votes and stuffing of ballot boxes are still par for the course south of the Sahara, the protection of the most basic civil and political liberties is hazardous at best, while coups d'état still seem less unusual than democratic changes. The wind that blew across the continent seems to have well and truly abated.

How should we explain the fact that Africa and Asia have both resisted the democratic tide that was not so long ago deemed inevitable? These two major parts of the world underwent opposite developments in the 1990s, but each of these was unfavourable to democratic advance: from China to Indonesia, via Taiwan, Singapore and the Philippines, the economic performance of 'development states' geared to the conquest of Western markets contributed to legitimizing authoritarian regimes. Parties opposing the established order had a hard time making their case in the face of a rise of 5 to 10 per cent each year in standards of living, the effectiveness of state action being one of the most powerful sources of legitimacy.

In sub-Saharan Africa, on the other hand, established regimes were challenged in a context of deep economic and social crisis, when governments experienced with full force the pangs of structural adjustment. Popular discontent was real enough, but the breakdown of society into a tangle of interest groups and an economy of improvisation made the construction of alternative political platforms difficult – all the more so as large swaths of the electorate, particularly in the countryside, lacked the rudiments of a national democratic culture. The advent of multiparty systems and elections at a time of an accelerating breakdown of economy and government structures[5] meant that democracy was associated with economic chaos in the mind of many Africans. Besides, when democratic parties did manage to take over the reins of power, they discovered an emasculated state, unable to pay its employees and lacking means of intervention in the social field as well as in matters of sovereignty. The 'democratic dividends' promised by the Western powers, which might have helped to support the democratic experiment in Africa, were now reoriented to rescuing the economies of Eastern Europe: as we saw above, economic assistance to Africa fell by a third in the course of the 1990s. Though it is a matter for concern, the difficult transplantation of democracy in Africa in this decade is no more mysterious than the period of stagnation that the continent's economies experienced at the end of the century. We might rather be surprised that so many African societies have managed to make the headway they have in the direction of political pluralism in a context of generalized economic regression, recurring political disturbance and devastating civil warfare.

African politics today presents a picture of great contrasts.[6] The African Union contains, living happily side by side, a bloody dictatorship that hunts down opponents and journalists; a number of young democracies whose institutions are being sharpened and their powers refined; a whole spectrum of single-party regimes, allowing varying degrees of space for opposition between people and currents of ideas; cosmetic democracies that combine a democratic[7] façade with domestic nepotism – not forgetting a fashionable model launched in the Arab world in the twentieth century, that of a life presidency inherited from father to son. It is amazing that such 'children of La Baule' as Bénin and Mali should coexist today with the horror of the Mugabe regime. This is the politically disjointed nature of the continent.

Barefoot democrats

Did a Western double game nip the sub-Saharan democratic revolution in the bud? Did the African struggle for participation die under the blows of reborn dictatorship or succumb to the temptation of dynastic succession? Accepting such ideas would mean deafening oneself to the desire to participate that is rumbling in Africa's streets, universities and countryside. This appetite, expressed in harsh and often bloody combat, throws up emblematic figures of struggle, but also a political practice made up of mobilization, the forming of interest groups, local participation – in other words, the very stuff of democracy, just what was lacking in the sub-Saharan societies at the time of the fall of the Berlin wall. The failed democratization of the 1990s gave rise to a long process whose fruits Africa is now beginning to harvest, behind the disturbing veil of authoritarian restoration.

Though not completely unreal, Africa's democratic retreat is partly an optical illusion: in the same way that the first expressions of 'democratic transition' in the 1990s subsequently proved to be superficial, so the retreat of external democratic signs should not make us forget the weighty tendencies at work on the continent today. The strength of African democracy, in fact, is not to be found where we generally look for it, as the 'indicators of democracy' elaborated by North American political foundations and Nordic universities do not measure democratic processes at work, but rather their results – free elections, political liberty, etc.

The processes currently under way, to which indicators such as these are blind, are made up of struggles that are shaping the future of Africa in the same way as the Spanish republican resistance, the great European trade-union struggles or the Solidarnosc movement shaped the history of the old continent. The general strikes that paralysed Lansana Conté's Guinea, and the massacre of 100 opposition supporters by his successor in a Conakry stadium in autumn 2009, quite understandably suggest the idea of democratic failure. Genuine failure, however, consists in the resignation of a people, not their struggle. We have to note that the resilient potential for mobilization of Guinean, Kenyan or Zimbabwean youth contrasts with the apathy of a West European generation that may well be heir to long traditions of struggle, but is too confident in the permanence of the democratic gains it has inherited.

The strength of these struggles, moreover, is not just a result of the commitment of their actors. They are steadily more effective to the extent that they take up the international vocabulary of democracy, human rights and freedom, relayed to them by modern means of communication (local radio, mobile phones, Internet...), and that they are involved in the multiple networks of international non-governmental solidarity (Reporters Sans Frontières, Amnesty International, Transparency International, etc.) – being therefore less prey to the complacency of realpolitik. The return of dictatorship that marks certain parts of the continent can in this respect be interpreted as a sign of regimes digging in as they are besieged by increasingly demanding populations.

The political liberalization of the 1990s triggered a second time-bomb by allowing a real explosion in the number of voluntary associations. The effects of this are now beginning to be felt right across the continent. In several countries, this fabric of civil society is now so dense and well rooted that it is assuming its role as a sentinel of democracy.[8] This is particularly the case in Senegal. The 'national assizes' held there are evidence of the maturity of political and social forces in this country. This broad popular process – whose proclaimed objective is 'by deepening democratic gains, strengthening rights and liberties, consolidating political and social dialogue, and improving the conditions of life of the citizens, to recreate the immense hope aroused by the change of government of 2000' – illustrates the powerful moral wellspring of the Senegalese people.

The struggles of these associations often start out from the everyday lives of African people. Both their roots and their strength lie in poverty, disease and hunger. They make possible the emergence of new men and women onto the political stage. Wangari Maathai, the first African woman to receive the Nobel peace prize, symbolizes the local struggles that are one of the most fertile grounds for African democracy. After studying in Kenya, the United States and Germany, this Kenyan biologist founded in 1977 the Green Belt Movement, a broad popular movement against deforestation and soil erosion. Imprisoned several times under the presidency of Daniel Arap Moi, she campaigned for multiparty elections, the end of corruption and community-based politics. This environmentalist, feminist and champion of non-violence led the National Women's Council in Kenya and contributed to the founding of Mazingira, the Kenyan ecological party. Her association, which has the planting of several tens of millions of trees to its credit, has also planted the seeds of women's political involvement in East Africa.

The weakness of national political culture in the African countryside was for a long time an obstacle to democratic progress, with the established authorities playing on the poor mobilization of this part of the electorate. But the emergence of peasant organizations is also changing the facts on the ground, by associating citizens who were historically only little politicized with local issues – and the international factors that influence them. The struggle of the West African cotton growers and their emblematic leader François Traoré is representative of the dynamism of West African civil society.[9] The son of a small Burkina Faso farmer, Traoré found himself head of a large family at the age of sixteen. With some education in a largely illiterate peasant world, he became secretary of a village association in 1982. Along with his friends, he campaigned for small producers to take part in the management of the national cotton industry – and successfully: the Burkina Faso state allowed the Union Nationale des Producteurs de Coton de Burkina to invest in the capital and participate in the management of the companies created from the privatization of Sofitex – companies responsible for the entire production process from seeds to exports. With this successful struggle behind him, François Traoré was one of the representatives of Southern farmers who joined the debate on globalization: at the WTO negotiations in Cancún in 2003, then the head of the Union Nationale des Producteurs de Coton Africains, he questioned the industrialized countries in front of the whole world's cameras, demanding an end to subsidies for their farm products – accused of slowly killing off sub-Saharan agriculture.

Behind such emblematic figures as Wangari Maathai and François Traoré are the thousands of workers for professional associations, trade unions and NGOs who, strengthened by their experience of local struggle, are daily playing the mediating role that European labour leaders played in the early twentieth century. Like the character Étienne Lantier in Zola's *Germinal*, they facilitate the expression of popular demands as a first step towards the establishment of a social contract between government and governed. The process of decentralization that has marked the last decade has transferred substantial powers to the local level, where it is easier to begin a process of involving people. The democratic culture that was largely lacking at the start of the democratic transition is thus now in the course of construction. Twenty years after the illusion of a democratization 'from above', this is now being forged, slowly but surely, by way of struggles 'from below'.

These underlying trends are coupled with the increased demands of the African middle classes on states in which they feel stakeholders, as well as the demands of their respective diasporas. The Sudanese 'Mo' (Mohammed) Ibrahim is one of the icons of the new African transnational elite, as well as a leader of the struggle for democracy at the continental level. An outstanding academic and businessman, Dr Ibrahim had repeated success in the telecommunications sector. Operating in sixteen African countries, his company Celtel made a substantial contribution to launching the telecom wave across the continent. Selling this to a Kuwaiti group in 2005 for the modest sum of $3.4 billion, Dr Ibrahim joined the exclusive club of big international philanthropists. Today he uses his wealth to improve public governance in Africa. His foundation, established in 2007, celebrates African leaders who have shown excellence in governing their countries. Each year it presents an award to a democratically elected former head of state or government who completed their term in the limits fixed by their country's constitution. By offering a prize of $5 million each year and a further $200,000 for life, as well as an additional investment in activities of public interest that the politician in question supports, this foundation reduces the temptation of illegally extending terms of office – while providing a rewarding status of 'former president' in societies where abandoning a power dearly acquired was long synonymous with dethronement or even danger.

Origins

Two decades after the fall of the Berlin wall, an initial balance-sheet of African democratization will clarify debate. It teaches us that neither Francis Fukuyama's age of inevitable democracy nor George Bush's messianism produced the effects expected: democracy does not come about of itself, nor thanks to forceps. It also teaches patience and humility: if we may regret that the embryonic democracies of the 1990s were not given better support, no one can believe today that support from outside could have carried through an imported democratic revolution. There is no democracy without democrats, and there are no democrats without democratic struggle. These lessons are nothing new; they are the very words used by the British philosopher John Stuart Mill in 1859.[10]

What matters today is to avoid reproducing the mistakes of the past, and to identify the real decisive factors for change. Just as it was illusory to believe, in 1990, that an Africa in full structural adjustment could swing over to liberal democracy like a single individual, clarity demands today that we are attentive to the underlying forces that are moving the continent. This authorizes hope. The discreet but undeniable emergence of a political culture 'from below' shows the existence of internal processes – the essential ingredients of a genuine democracy. Local struggles are coming together to weave the mesh of alternative political projects and a new social contract. An army of democrats is working in this direction, expressing a deeply modern struggle. While its outcome is still uncertain, its course will shape the Africa of tomorrow.

Part Six

Three Lines of March

The structuring of peoples and spaces, the appearance of the first signs of internally generated growth, new foundations of identity, democratic struggles: if these great transformations are affecting the whole of the continent, they are not doing so in a uniform fashion. And there is no more an average state than there is a typical African.

Beyond each particular case, however, three major trajectories seem to stand out, marking out a space that was considered too long in a crudely uniform fashion. 'Africa', as we have said, no longer exists. Let us look at its successors.

14

The Dangers of Rent

The continent's image is ambiguous. Sometimes Africa is seen as sunk in poverty; sometimes it is a land of cockaigne, rich in gold, diamonds, oil and coltan.[1]

It is indeed true that certain African countries count among the world's most richly endowed. Africa[2] is the second-largest exporter of oil after the Middle East, it possesses a third of the planet's mineral reserves, and its forests constitute one of the largest reserves of tropical woods. The growth in world needs and the rapid exhaustion of many stocks promise a steady rise in the price of raw materials in the course of the coming decades, whether energy-related (oil, gas, uranium), mineral (gold, magnesium, bauxite, cobalt) or 'natural' (tropical woods). The scarcity of arable land on the planet also makes African territory desirable. The combination of the 'price effect' and the 'stock effect' thus gives Africa a considerable legacy, whose value is set to rise. This bonanza offers an obvious opportunity for the future: the record growth rates that sub-Saharan Africa has notched up in the last ten years were partly derived from the rise in value of the continent's exports. Estimated at some thousands of billions of dollars, this natural manna would be able to finance the transformations needed for the continent's increasing population. One study assesses sub-Saharan Africa's anticipated oil revenue from 2002 to 2019 at $1,000 billion, or $60 billion per year.[3]

But history teaches a deep distrust for this gift of nature. Rent from raw materials brings with it considerable risks for the states that draw it. Why should one Congolese in two live on less than

$1 a day when the country's daily oil revenue is close to $2.50 per inhabitant? Why is life expectancy here stuck at an average of fifty-two years, hardly above that of Mali or Burkina Faso? This is the enigma of these rich countries populated by paupers – the 'curse of natural resources'. It also deserves our attention here, since the challenge of rent will affect more than half of all sub-Saharan countries in the decades to come.

The curse of rent

Natural wealth brings unhappiness. The long list of victims of uranium, oil, gold, copper and aluminium, the war and famine that follow in the wake of the mining bonanzas, the hungry stomachs at the foot of the oil derricks – all this is evident enough. Yet there is nothing mysterious in this 'curse':[4] these riches enclose whole societies in a political economy of capture or predation rather than production. The demystification of the rent disease involves analysing its three main symptoms.

The first of these is the Dutch syndrome. This well-known macroeconomic phenomenon, also known as the 'Dutch disease', is named after the loss of competitiveness of manufacturing industry in the Netherlands in the 1960s, following the discovery of large quantities of natural gas off the country's shores. The income drawn from a high-value natural resource damaged the competitivity of other export industries by driving up the real exchange rate.

On top of these monetary effects, the highly profitable extractive sector also siphons off factors of production or drives up their price, and weighs down the ability of other sectors to attract workers and finance. Mauritania likewise experienced the full effects of the Dutch disease: agriculture was abandoned as the country's mineral exports rose, and rapid urbanization did not translate into the emergence of a modern manufacturing sector, due to the over-valuation of the national currency. Nigerian agricultural exports also suffered much from the growth in the country's oil industry in the 1970s. These economic phenomena explain why a number of countries exporting minerals and hydrocarbons experience an extreme concentration of their economies that is unfavourable to a balanced economic development. The wealth of

Gabon or Congo, since it derives from an industry that needs only little labour, is very poor as a generator of employment. This is the paradox of economic growth without development, i.e. without structural transformations of the economy and society.

The second sickness of rent-drawing states is financial manic depression. This syndrome involves an extreme volatility of public revenues, which depend on the changing prices of raw materials, both erratic and externally controlled. The vigorous economic growth of these states is thus highly fragile. After having largely benefited from the oil shock of 1973, the economies of oil-exporting states experienced head-on the counter-shock of 1986. The Gabon budget tripled in 1975, before being halved again in 1986.[5] In that same year, Congolese oil receipts did not even cover the state's current expenditure, leading to the country's political destabilization. For an exporting country like Nigeria, though its economy is far more diversified than those of its neighbours on the Gulf of Guinea, the impact of the fall in the price of oil from $140 to $40 per barrel affected almost half of its GDP.[6] A similar unexpected collapse in the price of this 'black gold' occurred again in 2008, in the course of six months. The management of the national budget and the drawing up of investment programmes become risky indeed in a context of extreme fluctuation in public finances. On top of this, the financial sector reinforces these cycles: it lends and invests when it anticipates high yields. Suddenly public expenditure that was not a problem when times were good leads to over-indebtedness, followed by painful adjustment when prices fall. The Congo, one of the richest countries in Africa, held for a time the record as the most indebted country in the world: its national debt reached 247 per cent of GDP in 1997.[7]

A third sickness is institutional cholesterol. This final key to the enigma bears on the relationship of the citizen to the state, as the origin of state resources deeply influences the nature of relationships between governments and the societies for which they are responsible. In the majority of our societies, in fact, state receipts, drawn for the most part in the form of compulsory charges (taxes, national insurance, etc.), come from the work of their citizens. This makes the taxpayers stakeholders in the state, which is accountable to them, its capacity to act depending in the last resort on consent to taxation – itself subject to the government's respecting the political contract renewed with each election. Democracy in a certain sense is the organization of this relationship between tax-paying citizens and governments, to whom resources are entrusted for the sake of carrying out policies serving the general interest. It was in the name of this principle of the accountability of the state towards its citizens and taxpayers that the North American colonies of the British crown formed themselves into independent republics in the late eighteenth century.

In the case of the rent-drawing state, however, this relationship is reversed, because the oil bonanza assures it a large financial autonomy in relation to its citizens. Experienced as a gift of nature, and controlled by the holders of power, it generates a political economy that is described as 'patrimonial' or 'neo-patrimonial', rich in tempting public expenditures that are useless and overcharged.[8] Since it redistributes to its citizens in a more or less generous and equitable fashion the bonanza that it collects, the neo-patrimonial state positions itself in a relationship of patronage towards its population, simultaneously buying the support of its citizens and escaping their control. The dependence relationship, and thus that of loyalty, is reversed. The citizen-beneficiary in fact proves less concerned with the utilization of public resources than does the taxpaying citizen; citizens who are bought cannot protest against their employer and benefactor for fear of seeing their share of the rent confiscated. During the thirty-two years of Mobutu's reign in Zaire, this clientelist political economy lay at the root of a system completely geared to capturing rent, its partial privatization and its distribution – all by way of unofficial patronage networks and a swollen civil service. State employment in such cases becomes a way of redistributing state resources as an end in itself – to the detriment of considerations of competence or efficiency.

But the redistribution of rent by the holders of power also takes place in more exotic ways. This is, for example, the very serious function of 'moving festivals' and the tradition of 'municipalization'. Both consist in focusing luxury expenses (renovation of public buildings, organization of festivities, sometimes even the distribution of cash to citizens or their representatives) in one region of the national territory at a particular moment, then in another, and so on. It is often when this redistributive mechanism seizes up that things turn bad.

The political economy of predation, which characterizes mining states in time of war, is in a way the diseased expression of an economy of capture, privatization and redistribution of rent. While the switch from one to the other can occur very rapidly, the war situation that ensues can display a rare violence and long duration – not being restricted by any limit in terms of resources. Biafra, Guinea, Sierra Leone, Angola, Sudan, Congo-Brazzaville, RD Congo – how can we avoid noting that it is the regions of Africa most rich in natural resources that have generally experienced the most ravaging wars? It is this fact that leads the economist Paul Collier to see rent as one of the ingredients of the 'conflictuality trap'.[9] Sometimes its sharing out is deemed insufficient and arouses protest, or even separatist demands on the part of the producer regions. That is the story behind the long struggles of the delta peoples of Nigeria for a greater share of the oil resources drawn from their region, the unhappy attempt at secession by Biafra in 1967, and the more successful South Sudanese struggle for independence.

If they cannot simply be reduced to a single factor, other conflicts around rent are still closer to the pure model of predation. Thus the RD Congo (formerly Zaire) has seen since 1998 a succession of wars that are among the most murderous in modern history, against the background of the pillaging of the country's resources by neighbouring states.[10] Originating at the end of Mobutu's predatory rule, against the background of the Rwandan genocide, these conflicts rapidly acquired their own dynamic – in particular, the battle for control of the country's mines. At the turn of the century, the armies of six African countries faced each other on Congolese territory, backed by mercenaries from the four corners of the world and financed by lucrative contracts from mining companies quoted on the leading international stock exchanges. Laurent Désiré Kabila, after his bloody itinerary across the country in 1996, signed futures contracts for mining extraction to a value of $500 million.[11] Despite large-scale rape, pillaging and massacre, often perpetrated by child soldiers, the coltan mines of the RD Congo did not for a moment stop fuelling the mobile phone boom across the world. That is the war economy in a rentier state. It prospers, fuelled by violence and plugged into the world. The RD Congo, which the Belgian geologist Jules Conret describes as a 'geological scandal', and which has still not managed to emerge from a decade of civil war despite the largest peacekeeping operation in the history of the UN, is thus the sad laboratory of a rentier state in decomposition.

Democracy: remedy or magic spell?

Diagnosing these three evils, which combine to make rent such a curse, is not the same as treating them. How is it possible to overcome this insidious political economy, which fetters the development of more than one African country and continues to fuel several wars on the continent? If the relationship between citizen and state is at issue, does the solution to the curse of natural resources lie in seeking greater democracy?

Unfortunately, matters are more complicated: what served as a rallying cry for the international community in the 1990s is in no way the Holy Grail of an effective and responsible governance. The promotion of national elections and multiparty systems is not enough to establish a democratic practice, based on strong countervailing powers. Worse, the experience of these years shows that, in the absence of a solidly anchored democratic culture and powerful institutions, a rent-drawing democracy has a still greater tendency to press in the direction of dispensing patronage and gangrenous favouritism than one of an authoritarian type.[12]

In Africa, as elsewhere, competition between would-be governments by way of election has in fact increased the incitement of ruling classes towards clientelistic practices, with a view to winning the support of the population – without necessarily permitting the productive use of public resources. In those countries that passed suddenly from the status of mining colony to that of single-party dictatorship, there could be no question of democratic culture. When winning an election was at stake, the advance purchase of votes often proved more profitable than the launching of public investment projects. The impact of the latter is only visible, in the best of cases, after a number of years. That leads Paul Collier and Anke Hoeffler to say that 'electoral competition only transforms this form of stagnation into a still more widespread waste of resources'.[13] What is more, formal democratization, by reducing the time spent in charge of the state, places the holders of power in a more fragile position, and paradoxically incites them to draw still more on rent yields. This was particularly the case in Congo-Brazzaville, where the single party, which had formalized stable (though quite unsustainable) practices of redistributing the oil revenue in the course of its thirteen years in power, faced difficulties in the early 1990s due to the process of democratization. Drawing still more on oil income for fear of a change of government, and wrongfooted by the sudden fall in prices, it upset the subtle redistributive mechanism that had been established, triggering popular resentment. The political change that followed was accompanied by three civil wars that were particularly costly in human lives, the basic issue at stake being simply control of the 'black gold'. More than elections, which are wrongly equated with democracy, what matters is therefore the existence of strong and stable institutions, able to act as a check throughout the governmental term. These are the first steps in a slow process of democratization, which can ultimately be driven only from inside the country.

Is it, nonetheless, possible to promote the emergence of such institutions? This is the key issue for the mining countries of Africa. But the sad outcome of the experiment that the World Bank attempted in order to prevent Chad from succumbing to the curse of natural resources teaches us to view this lengthy task pragmatically, patiently and humbly. It shows in fact the extreme difficulty of creating from scratch the institutions of a virtuous rentier state.

On paper, the system seemed robust enough. In exchange for aid in financing the Doba–Kribi pipeline, running for 1,000 kilometres from the extraction zone to the oil terminal on the Cameroon coast, Chad agreed to put into practice the complex arrangements 'made in Washington' for the allocation of oil revenues. The Chadian law to this effect was passed in 1999, following prolonged negotiations and several delays. In order to combat any risk of wastage and to forestall the effects of the Dutch disease, 10 per cent of oil income would be placed in a 'savings account for future generations', located abroad and blocked. Out of the remaining 90 per cent of resources available each year, 80 per cent of these would be allocated in advance to programmes to combat poverty. These funds were to be paid to the ministries in charge of five sectors that the National Strategy for Poverty Reduction deemed priorities: health care, education, infrastructure, rural development, environment and water. To prevent any feeling of the oil region's population that injustice was being done to them, 5 per cent would be allocated to decentralized local authorities in the producing region. And finally, the reality principle required that the remaining 15 per cent flowed to the government for current state expenditure. As a finishing touch, a Collège de Contrôle et de Surveillance des Revenus Pétroliers (CCSRP) was established, in order to act as a protection and a democratic check. Self-governing and distinct from the state, this was composed of prominent members of civil society, drawn from religious groups, trade unions and local NGOs.

The experiment didn't work. In 2006, less than three years after the opening of the pipeline, an armed rebellion threatened the east of the country – the native region of the president, who had himself taken power by armed force some fifteen years before. The Chadian parliament passed an exceptional law that unilaterally doubled the quota of the oil revenue allocated to the government, and this was immediately used to finance a large-scale arms purchase. The 'fund for future generations' was also abolished. Protests from the Collège de Contrôle were to no avail; and though the new share-out of the rent was reluctantly accepted after the fact by the World Bank, this again broke down in early 2008 when a new rebel offensive brought the insurgents to the gates of the presidential palace. Invoking *force majeure*, the president proceeded to new arms purchases – thus signing the death warrant of the ailing agreement. The early repayment of the finance provided by the World Bank in summer 2008 sealed the failure of this well-thought-out arrangement, and the end of a praiseworthy attempt to turn a new rentier state into a development state.

Is the struggle to manage rent income properly, then, lost in advance? Are African political systems incompatible with the structures of the virtuous rentier state? The history of Botswana proves not.[14] A landlocked country of less than 2 million people, Botswana experienced Africa's highest growth rate in per capita income during the thirty years that followed its independence.[15] When the British left in 1966, this country the size of France had a total of 12 kilometres of paved roads, 22 university graduates and 100 or so high-school graduates, but the investment of revenue from the diamond industry in economic and social development enabled it to lift itself into the category of so-called 'middle-income countries'. Today its GDP per capita is eight times the average for sub-Saharan Africa. Though diamonds continue to represent three-quarters of the country's exports and half of government income, Botswana has been able to limit the effects of the Dutch disease by wise macroeconomic management. A policy of zero tolerance has also borne fruit: annual figures regularly place the country among the least corrupt in Africa. The government has chosen to spend around 20 per cent of its budget on education. And on the difficult question of price volatility, Botswana is one of the few sub-Saharan countries to have escaped the pains of structural adjustment, thanks to a reserve fund built up early on from the diamond revenue. In the early 1980s, when the price of diamonds fell, the government could even let six months pass without a single sale, while maintaining the level of expenditure on programmes of public expenditure. With a view to the situation when income from diamonds comes to an end (the country's seams are expected to run out by 2030), it is practising a vigorous strategy of economic diversification, with the development of tourism, a textile industry, agriculture and financial services. It is also with an eye firmly on the future that a commission appointed by the president has been charged with planning the country's path of development. The commission's report, titled 'Long-term vision for Botswana – towards prosperity for all', represents the culmination of a long process of consultation of civil society.[16]

Botswana is certainly not unfamiliar with major socio-economic problems: inequality and unemployment remain high, half of the active population are engaged in the public sector, and it has suffered the ravages of AIDS. It remains true, however, that this small landlocked country in southern Africa presents an object lesson in good management of mining rent. How else can one explain that mineral extraction has produced 'blood diamonds' in Sierra Leone but 'development diamonds' in Botswana? Comparing the trajectories of these two countries confirms the fundamental role of institutions. Those of Botswana, in some cases going back to the pre-colonial period, preceded the discovery of diamond wealth. The state, relatively strong and centralized, was likewise able to avoid all centrifugal temptations by imposing itself right from independence as the sole proprietor of the country's mineral resources, while basing its legitimacy on a 'house of chiefs' endowed with real influence over the country's affairs. Finally, we have to recognize the role of individuals and the political choices they make: by anchoring his country in the long process of development, the father of the Botswana nation, Seretse Khama, and his successor, Quett Masire, were able to protect their country from the curse of natural resources.

Savings and investment

As we can see, what is at stake for Africa is the long-term management of a non-renewable legacy. A recent and promising generation of economic theorists, analysing the development of national wealth over time, gives us new tools for understanding the conditions of a sustainable management of this legacy.[17]

It is interesting to view the development of a country in terms of managing the portfolio of assets (natural resources, physical and human capital, etc.) at its disposal. According to this mode of analysis, a path of sustainable development requires the present generation to transmit to its successor a capital at least equivalent to that which it disposes of today. Is this possible when the great bulk of an economy's legacy is made up of mineral and oil resources, which are by nature non-renewable? Theoretically yes, if the income derived from the natural capital exploited by the present generation is invested in the creation of physical or human capital, in such a way as to enable it to hand down to following generations capacities for the production of wealth that are at least equivalent. This implies that the whole amount of income derived from non-renewable raw materials should be invested in the production of other forms of capital.[18] This is certainly far from being the case with the rentier states of Africa, certain of which are heading on the contrary towards the accelerated exhaustion of their wealth. Economic studies conducted in recent years on the development of African capital show in fact that the majority of these states are actually in a phase of de-capitalization, i.e. that the loss of natural capital is not compensated by equivalent gains in economic or human capital. The oil-producing countries of Africa, for example, are seeing each year the disappearance of the equivalent of between 30 and 50 per cent of their national income. Behind flattering growth rates, Gabon, Congo, Nigeria and Equatorial Guinea are growing poorer.

This leads to a distinction between three models of rentier state, marked by three different political economies.[19] The model of the 'virtuous rentier state' involves the sustainable management of a natural capital, expressed in the investment of its rent in the formation of other kinds of capital (human or material). If Norway is the most perfect example of this model, Botswana, despite the difficulties that still beset this country, approaches it fairly well. In the 'stable rentier states', the clientelist political economy is geared not to the production of these different forms of capital, but rather to the privatization and distribution of rent – without this being invested in the development of sectors of the economy other than the extractive. Macroeconomic figures seem to indicate that Congo and Gabon, both archetypes of the rentier state, have not yet managed to extricate themselves from this model. Finally, the political economy of 'decomposing rentier states' is completely geared to predation and seizure of rent. If Angola and the RD Congo were for a long time the most striking illustrations of this conflict trap, the Chad experience shows that new rentier states also risk getting caught in it.

15

The Vanguard of Development

The story of Botswana reminds us that, alongside RD Congo, Gabon and Congo-Brazzaville there are states that, though still poor, are each year beating a path out of destitution. The long spell of growth that this group of countries, seemingly quite different from each other, has experienced now for a decade is perhaps the best sign that sub-Saharan Africa is not stuck in an inescapable 'poverty trap'.

In 2008 and 2009, in a shaky global economic environment and with the engine of raw material demand spluttering, these countries continued to drive sub-Saharan growth. Since the turn of the century, average growth rates have been 5 per cent in Ghana, 5.4 per cent in Burkina Faso, 6.4 per cent in Tanzania and 7.4 per cent in Mozambique,[1] all in countries that have not up till now had copious mineral or oil reserves. This rediscovered and sustained economic dynamism has enabled them not only to finance their population growth, but also to take a further step each year in the long march towards catching-up with middle-income countries.

Along with a few other African 'stars' (Mauritius, Cap Verde and Botswana, already mentioned), these nations are the pioneers of development. 'Aid darlings' of the international community, they obtain the lion's share of development aid received by the continent. They likewise attract a growing share of foreign investment. A number of them have experienced very major political crises, but have managed to resolve them. How can this success be explained? Is there a lesson to be learnt from their practices?

A 'brighter future'

The Ghanaian nation, child of the charismatic leader Nkrumah and homeland of the first African secretary-general of the United Nations, Kofi Annan, is one of the symbols of this new departure.[2] Turning the page on a long economic agony punctuated by repeated coups d'état and marked by plunging prices for raw materials, debt crisis and structural adjustment, the democratic transition of December 2000 inaugurated a decade of vigorous growth. Driven by a popular desire for participation, and supported by strong institutions, it now enables Ghanaians to dream once more of prosperity, a dream that the father of the nation shared with the first European colonists – who christened this blessed land the Gold Coast. A journalist for the http://allAfrica.com website could even write recently that 'today is perhaps the best time to live if you are Ghanaian'.[3]

The national budget for 2008 had a title that bears witness to this optimism: the 'Brighter Future budget' was oriented around a national project steered by a developmental state. The aim is to reach the Millennium Development Goal of poverty reduction by the end of 2010, and the status of a 'middle-income country' by 2015. This was achieved well ahead of schedule: Ghana graduated to middle-income status on 1 July 2011. Good macroeconomic management has in fact enabled Ghana to take advantage of successive waves of relief on the national debt, which has fallen from 160 per cent of GDP in 2001 to less than 40 per cent in 2006. Once debt relief had been put in place, international aid began to flow rapidly to Ghana: its status as a good pupil brought the equivalent of 10 per cent of its national income in development aid in 2007. Massive investment from the Ghanaian diaspora, moreover, came to nearly four times that amount. But these external resources were not to the detriment of Ghanaian citizens' own contribution to the national effort: tax revenues range between a quarter and a third of GDP, i.e. far above the average for sub-Saharan Africa.

The Ghanaian government has been able to put these margins of recovered public expenditure to good use: investment makes up a third of GDP, around ten points above the sub-Saharan average, and close to that of the Asian tigers at the time of their economic take-off. It is massively oriented to infrastructure (energy, transport) – whose backwardness is one of the major factors holding back the economy – as well as education – primary, secondary and higher. A new system of health insurance is also on track, with over a third of the population covered, as of 2007. A stabilization fund has been created to protect the economy from outside shocks. The recent discovery of oilfields off the Ghanaian coast is thus coming as a cherry on the cake. It raises a legitimate concern about the potentially destructive effects of rent – but also a legitimate hope, insofar as the institutions needed for the good management of future oil revenues seem now to be well anchored in Ghana.

This is because economic success is coming on the basis of a rediscovered political stability. After twenty-five years of a military regime (in fifty years of independence), the army, engaged in peacekeeping operations across the world, is no longer the sword of Damocles hanging over the democratic process that it was for so long. The steady strengthening of the state and institutions has not been to the detriment of a civil society that is itself increasingly organized: in the last twenty years, professional associations, trade unions, farmers' and women's organizations have all proliferated and become more effective. Traditional chiefly authorities also remain powerful and recognized. By their everyday mediation activity, they act as a relay between local communities and the state.

This broad undertaking to put the country back on its feet is producing the results that were promised. Sustained growth has made it possible to reduce the proportion of the population living below the poverty line from 40 per cent in 1999 to 28 per cent in 2006. Equally spectacular results have been achieved in basic education: Ghana is en route towards universal education in a few years' time, and the struggle for equal enrolment of girls is already won. The country boasts five public universities, which attract students from across the continent. Certainly the risks bound up with rapid growth cannot be ignored: the take-off of the Ghanaian economy is accompanied by growing inequality between individuals and regions. The energy market is experiencing major tension. The capital, Accra, has one of the highest growth rates in Africa, and the country's natural resources are rapidly degrading. The fragile civil service, whose lack of efficiency and competence is pointed out by many Ghanaians, finds itself in the firing line in the struggle for the good management of this rediscovered growth. But it is true nonetheless that Ghana is confidently advancing today on the track of economic catching-up. It serves as a model for several of its neighbours.

The recent history of Mozambique, often cited as an example of successful transition from war to peace, is another African 'success story'. Like its Angolan cousin on the west coast, this East African state passed in 1974 from the status of Portuguese colony to that of a pawn in the Cold War, serving as the battle-ground for a particularly murderous civil conflict. Following the agreement of 1992 that put an end to sixteen years of fighting between Frelimo (a socialist party long aligned with Soviet interests) and Renamo (an anti-communist group supported by apartheid South Africa), Mozambique found its way to a process of accelerated economic catching-up. With an annual growth rate of more than 7 per cent over the last fifteen years, it boasts the best economic performance on the continent, with the exception of a handful of oil-exporting states, placing the country on a trajectory comparable to that of its Asian forerunners at the time of their take-off. Twenty years after the end of its conflict and the abandonment of a socialist economy, Mozambique is continuing to draw the dividends of peace and the major macroeconomic reforms made in the early 1990s.

This catching-up process presents opportunities for rapid profit, which are attracting investors. Each year the country receives several billion dollars of foreign investment, oriented towards mineral extraction, tourism, agribusiness and big industrial projects. This private finance is accompanied by substantial foreign government investment in infrastructure – enthusiastically supported by the international community. As with Ghana, development aid makes a major contribution in this country favoured by the big lenders: Mozambique receives over $1.5 billion each year in international aid, a sum equivalent to over half of its public expenditure and a quarter of its GDP (against an average of 6 per cent of GDP for sub-Saharan Africa as a whole).

But if these flattering growth rates remain largely drawn from foreign aid, domestic demand is beginning to take up the baton. The service sector in Mozambique now accounts for more than 40 per cent of GDP. Tax revenue is rising from year to year, allowing the government to invest in priority social sectors. Over 2 million mosquito nets were distributed in a national campaign against malaria between 2004 and 2007, making an evident contribution to the rapid fall in infant mortality recorded in recent years. The rate of school attendance, which was disastrous at the end of the war, has begun to supply the growing economy with more and better-trained high-school graduates. The 'green revolution', involving in particular the distribution of fertilizer and seeds to the country's farmers, led to substantial progress in the agricultural sector, which continues to employ the majority of Mozambicans despite the steady transition towards industry and services. Formerly a leading beneficiary of food aid, Mozambique has had one of the most rapid periods of poverty reduction in the world. The proportion of its people living below the poverty line fell by fifteen points in six years (from 69 per cent in 1997 to 54 per cent in 2003). Liberia, which emerged more recently from a long civil war, is likewise well on the road to reconstruction, and counts on following the path traced by Mozambique, led by its president Ellen Johnson-Sirleaf.

If the successes of Ghana and Mozambique are remarkable, they are scarcely surprising. Trapped for so long in situations of chronic instability, these two coastal countries embarked after the return of political stability on a catching-up process that was almost automatic. Far more astonishing – but also encouraging – is the performance of countries that, despite all structural shortcomings, have also shown unprecedented growth rates in recent years. These demonstrate that this is possible even in conditions that are seemingly difficult.

Few countries on the planet are as handicapped as Burkina Faso. Landlocked, lacking natural resources and subject to the most extreme vagaries of climate, this Sahel country remains one of the poorest in the world, classified among the lowest in terms of human development ever since this index was established. Yet, judging from the rapid increase in the number of bicycles and motorbikes on the streets of Ougadougou, for the last decade economic activity here has been increasingly strong. Statistics confirm this: despite its strong dependence on cotton production, and fluctuations depending on both rainfall and raw material prices, the growth of the Burkina economy has stood at more than 6 per cent on average since 1995. Appropriate macroeconomic management, combined with the political stability of this country known as 'the land of whole men'[4] (a somewhat flattering name), has enabled it to make substantial progress each year. There is growth in handicraft activity and the processing of agricultural products, as well as a strong rise in sectors that accompany the urbanization process – property, construction materials, etc. Spurred by the mobile phone boom, services now make up over a half of national income, the sign of an economic transition under way.

Achievements in the social sector have followed the rhythm of economic activity, supported by an international community that has been particularly generous towards a state that cultivates its image as a good pupil. Burkina Faso in fact receives development aid each year to the tune of 15 per cent of its GDP. Thanks to a national public-health programme developed in 2000, the country has experienced a sharp fall in maternal and infant mortality, as also in the incidence of AIDS – which fell from 7 per cent of the population to 2 per cent between 1997 and 2006. Substantial advances have also been made in primary education, with the rate of school attendance leaping from 30 per cent to 68 per cent between 1990 and 2007. A broad national effort in vocational training has been put in place, to provide the Burkina economy with skills that are still in short supply. Despite a population growth that continues to be high, the proportion of its people living below the poverty line, though still around 45 per cent, is falling from year to year. If it is impossible to prove this, it is at least probable that this steady progress has helped to protect Burkina from the side-effects of the Ivorian crisis.

From model student to studying a model

Can a model be extracted from these African success stories? The experiences of Ghana, Mozambique and Burkina Faso allow us to review certain of the explanations put forward to account for the period of sharp growth that Africa has experienced since the turn of the century, as well as the recommendations habitually put forward as supporting it.

Much has been written, for example, to the effect that the continent's economic take-off can be explained by the sudden rise in raw materials prices – itself triggered by the rise in demand from the emerging countries. The growth of mineral- and oil-exporting states has certainly helped the whole of sub-Saharan Africa – if not without certain ambiguities, as we have seen. But the three examples discussed above show that good performance of this kind, in economies poorly endowed with natural resources, cannot be reduced to the prices of raw materials. The sub-Saharan countries with the highest growth rates include only six that are rich in natural resources, whereas a further eleven do not share this benefit – five of these also being landlocked, which counters the arguments of certain geographers that we discussed in chapter 5.[5] States such as Ethiopia and Ghana were able to increase their rate of growth even when their terms of trade deteriorated, with export prices falling in relation to imports. As we have seen, increasing population density and structuring of space automatically create economic activity, on which the 'pioneers of development', once free from the burden of debt, were able to capitalize in order to generate socio-economic development. After such long dependence on exports, the continent thus has new sources of growth at its disposal, the first among these being a rapidly expanding domestic market. A new growth model seems to have established itself in Africa, embodied by states as different as Mozambique, Ghana and Burkina Faso.

What policies enabled these countries to take such a path? Can they be reproduced elsewhere on the continent? A brief survey will supply a preliminary diagnosis.

First of all, each of these countries is a pioneer, and has avoided the mistakes of the 1960s and 1970s by combining a number of ingredients necessary for take-off: renewed political stability, healthy macroeconomic management (control of inflation, sustainable public debt), market economy combined with targeted state intervention, reasonably efficient public administration – and all this despite substantial corruption, a widespread characteristic of poverty. This is no small success, if we consider the two decades of painful adjustments that enabled them to rediscover this path, and the number of countries that are still seeking it. It is also to a large extent the progress of these indicators that opened access for them to the manna of international aid – no small factor in a catching-up process that is very demanding in terms of investment.

Furthermore, and despite the above, none of these countries corresponds to the 'good pupil' model inasmuch as none has followed the Washington consensus[6] package to the letter, with its triptych of 'democracy', 'human rights' and 'good governance'. This is something we shall come back to later.

Finally, these development states share three points in common, which the standardized recommendations of a superficial liberalism have long neglected. First, their tax rates, significantly higher than those of their neighbours and rising from one year to the next, give the governments of these countries crucial margins for investment in a period of heavy needs. This investment, whose public component also gives an impetus to private resources, indicates a commitment to the future. Second, each of these countries is moving in the direction of a diversification of its economy, thus reducing its vulnerability to externally provoked crises. Third, and contrary to the opinion that long prevailed in the global development bodies, the economies that have had an economic take-off in the last decade have been able to count on a proactive state, capable of making strategic choices and steering public investment.

Yet, from this minimum basis of certain correct policies that are common to the pioneers of African development – and on which the take-off of the Asian tigers was also based – there is no single winning model that emerges, no straight path to salvation. Ghana, Mozambique, Burkina Faso, Cap Verde, Mauritius and Botswana made very different choices in public policy, whether in terms of state involvement in the economy, or of modes of regulation, organization of the legal system, the size of public services, etc. Botswana's growth model, for example, is based on a system of relatively precise rules and a very active state, whereas the growth of Burkina Faso has arisen in a landscape where the informal sector is prevalent and the presence of the state is relatively weak.[7] To the dismay of certain economists, the standard theoretical models of the major development institutions find it hard to account for sub-Saharan economic take-off. While it is easy to identify practices that have damaging results on development (generalized corruption, price controls, a bloated public sector...), the quest for the Grail, or a foolproof growth potion, is in vain: there is no best recipe, only good cooks.

This is what is indicated by our brief overview of the economies of some good examples of African development. But it is also the conclusion reached by some twenty experts led by the Nobel economics laureate Michael Spence,[8] who were charged by the World Bank with exploring the policies applied by this small group of countries that have had both rapid and sustained economic growth. Two years of work, and evidence from 300 consultants, enabled them to conclude that, apart from this minimum foundation of good practices that are essential for economic growth, it is impossible to establish a formula that will automatically generate development. Though certain commentators were disappointed by the vagueness of the findings,[9] this ambitious undertaking will be valuable if it makes it possible to escape once and for all from the search for the 'right' model, universal and everywhere reproducible. How many times, in fact, has blind application of foreign economic models led to disaster, for the simple (and good) reason that they were foreign? The rock of local circumstances is far more solidly anchored than the fragile bark of international decrees – led on by the sirens of ideology and the hit-and-miss steering of its captains. The subtle potion of development can only be home-brewed.[10] In Africa, as elsewhere, the time has come to focus on the brakes to growth specific to each particular society, as well as on the conditions that promote emergence of institutions that kick-start – and individuals that drive – development.

This procedure will call into question certain ideas that are still taken as evident today.

The chicken or the egg?

As we have seen, these pioneers of development have been able to make room, in their national strategies, for substantial public investment in priority sectors, such as improved access to education and health care. But when they are examined closely, these histories of growth force us to qualify the thesis, commonly accepted in the new development gospel, according to which education and health care are preconditions for economic development[11] – a thesis which would mean that absolute priority must be given to the social sector in the allocation of aid finance to Africa. Mali and Burkina Faso actually have the lowest rates of literacy on the continent, with less than a quarter of adults being able to read and write. Yet they are both in the group of countries at the head of African development, and have been for a whole decade. Botswana, which is one of only thirteen countries on the planet that can boast a growth rate higher than 7 per cent over a period of twenty-five years, has the lowest life expectancy in the world (thirty-five years), as a result of the ravages of AIDS.

These facts force us to question the direction of the causal connection that is often presented as proved: is it the expansion in
primary education and the provision of health care in these countries that has made possible their economic take-off, or, on the
contrary, is it the economic growth they have discovered that
enables the state to invest at last in the education and health of its
citizens – and, at the microeconomic level, enables these citizens to
devote a greater share of their expenditure to covering these essential needs? There is no doubt that the causal connection acts in
both directions, and it would be foolish to weigh economic growth
against access to basic services. But to the extent that budgetary
constraints automatically imply prioritization of investments, it is
crucial to study their impact in the short, medium and long terms.

Isn't investment in infrastructures (energy, transport, etc.) that
makes it possible to remove certain obstacles to growth more effective in the end in reaching these objectives of access to health care
and education than an overinvestment in education and health
systems that are bound to depend on international resources unless
the country's economic growth provides the budget revenue to
cover them? We can see how economic take-off in China, Malaysia and Korea, three models of twentieth-century development,
did not wait for universal primary education; rather, these states
were able to invest massively in the education of their people once
their national income was rising at 8 or 10 per cent a year. Given
that the effect of economic growth on access to basic services is
more notable and immediate than vice versa, the choice of massive
investment in primary education and health care, which has too
often been made at the cost of investment in economic growth,
needs to be reconsidered. The African success stories are those
of countries that have managed to invest in their social systems
because they did not forget their agriculture, energy supply and
transport infrastructure – three powerful brakes on growth in an
Africa with an expanding population.

In search of lost governance

Study of the recent history of those sub-Saharan states that have
been able to sustain a strong growth also leads to reflecting on
the relationships between democracy, 'good governance' and

development. Dissecting the political and institutional models of
the industrialized countries, regiments of right-minded intellectuals have been busy in recent decades establishing a relationship
of direct causality between these three variables. A democratic
regime, according to their studies, is better placed to steer a society
onto a path of lasting economic growth.

Nothing could be less certain. The economic take-off in China,
Malaysia and Vietnam, which have managed to raise hundreds of
millions of their citizens out of poverty over the last few decades,
did not wait for the arrival of multiparty democracy. Even the first
shoots of this are scarcely visible in many such countries. Why
should it be different in Africa? If Ghana, Burkina Faso, Uganda
and Mozambique have in common a stable political situation,
their political regimes are still very different. The fact that the pioneers of development on the African continent are not all such
models of democracy has not prevented them from experiencing
periods of rapid and sustained growth.

Does this mean that African democrats are asked to wait until
later, when a prosperous Africa will finally be 'ripe for democracy'?
As we have seen, this is not the opinion of activists for freedom,
who are ever more numerous on the continent despite repression
and a cynical view of democracy. Most of them are unconcerned
about the relationship between growth and democracy: freedom
for them is a good in itself, and does not tolerate compromise. In
this sense, the broad project of interweaving economic and political liberalism that has been at work since the fall of the Berlin wall,
and reached fever pitch in George W. Bush's 'transformational
diplomacy', has paradoxically weakened the position of African
democrats. The subprime crisis (born in New York and London,
but with very definite effects in Bamako and Cape Town in the late
2000s) succeeded in undermining the credibility of Europe and
the United States as lecturers in political economy. But as political
and economic liberalism had long been presented as both inseparable and indispensable for economic progress, the undermining
of neoliberal orthodoxy in the wake of the financial crisis of 2008
seriously affected the legitimacy of the teachings of political liberalism. It is time to recognize that democratization in Africa will
result from an internal struggle, the eminently legitimate one of
constructing a state run by and for its citizens.

How then do things stand with 'good governance', which in
recent years was presented as the right development strategy by

the lending community?[12] Language is no help here in clarifying things.[13] Who would think of questioning the idea that a country should be 'well governed'? It remains hard to define, however, what exactly this prescription means. The concept of 'good governance' refers to transparency in state actions, control of corruption, the free operation of markets, democracy and the rule of law – in other words, a set of characteristics that more or less describe the mode of organization of the so-called 'developed' countries. This is now part of all national strategies of poverty reduction, and is even the key to the releasing of finance by the largest lenders.[14] But this hides a dangerous ambiguity: is good governance an end in itself, or a means in the service of development? Can it be legitimately presented as a factor accelerating development, or even a preliminary condition for economic growth? This is the nub of the matter.

It is certainly not surprising that the 'good governance' of a country – in other words, the existence of formal and impersonal institutions – should be correlated with the country's *level* of development. This is even somewhat tautological, inasmuch as the model of 'good governance' in its accepted use is patterned on the modes of regulation characteristic of developed societies. But the three African cases we have examined force us to modify the idea of a link between 'good governance' and the *pace* of economic development. Mozambique and Madagascar, for example, states that both have 'poor' levels of governance (high level of corruption, embezzlement, favouritism, etc.), have seen very different growth rates over the last ten years, whereas the Asian development stars of China and Vietnam, like their African counterparts Ghana and Uganda, are not the best performers in terms of good governance. Foreign businesses, however, are little bothered by developmentalist teachings, and they are not mistaken in this: they orient their finance not towards the model countries of 'good governance', but towards dynamic economies where systems of regulation are in force – whether formal or informal – that enable them to operate without excessive harassment.[15] Some of these countries have chosen to follow the recommendations of the World Bank to the letter (Mauritius being a star pupil); others are very far from this. The vast project of drawing-up rules and depersonalizing economic relations that lies behind the injunctions of 'good governance' is thus neither necessary nor sufficient for growth.

Doesn't the legendary 'African corruption' – the very archetype of 'bad governance' – despite everything, place a brake on the continent's economic growth? There no doubt exists an extreme and destructive form of corruption. We have seen this in the case of the rentier states, and will return to it in that of 'fragile' states. But in the countries of rapid growth, 'petty corruption'[16] often performs a social function of keeping economic relations fluid, when formal systems of economic relations and exchange prove slow or ineffective. This is typically the case when, in a phase of economic take-off, administrative bureaucracies are not in a position to respond efficiently to the 'demand for administration'. The difference is not so much a matter of degree as one of kind.[17] Vigorous economic growth is compatible with a high level of 'benign' or at least 'stable' corruption, its products being broadly redistributed or reinvested in the country itself. How can we otherwise explain that particularly high levels of corruption in Mali, Tanzania, Mozambique and Uganda[18] have not prevented these countries from growing at such high rates for more than ten years?

If neither 'democracy' nor 'good governance', nor even the absence of corruption, provides the discriminating factor between countries in a phase of take-off and the others, what then does? The development process, oriented as it is towards the future, requires a reliable institutional framework that makes it possible to reduce the uncertainties of economic actors, and thus extend their time horizon. This is what makes investment decisions possible, dependent as they are on the possibility of anticipating future profits. But these frameworks can vary considerably from one country to another, particularly in their degree of formalization. Mozambique, Burkina Faso and Ghana, despite not being great models of 'good governance', each possess public institutions capable of coordinating economic actors and bringing their individual choices to converge around the same national project. One of the keys to development then seems to consist in the always unique fashion in which societies manage to structure interactions between actors so as to reduce uncertainty – while preserving a vital space for individual initiative. Rather than seeking this in the choice of this or that particular policy, we have to look further upstream, at the junction of the political and economic orders, in the quality of their institutions and the ability of these to ensure the provision of the essential public goods that are political stability, human security, the rights of property and a clear economic direction.

The difficulty in demonstrating an unambiguous link between 'good governance', democracy and economic growth should thus suggest questioning the priority given to the (forced) march of African societies towards institutional and political models that are imported ready-made from our own societies. Pious injunctions about 'democratic governance' loudly pressed by the international community on societies that are not ready for this only end up rendering national political and economic systems increasingly fragile. They can also bring about the coexistence of internal systems of regulation alongside complex legal systems imported to satisfy the conditions of international lenders. This is what led Nicolas Meisel and Jacques Ould Aoudia to explain that 'the countries of the South are not countries that would be "rich if they were not sick". They are structurally different in the mode of operation of their systems of social regulation.'[19]

The history of industrialized and emerging societies shows that development propels a society towards a greater formalization of rules along with the depersonalization of social relations, and also towards a gradual opening of both the economic and political fields to competition. But it equally shows that these deep transformations do not all take place at the same time, and that there can sometimes be a gap of several decades from economic take-off. Adopting institutions of 'good governance' only comes about, in fact, when a society comes up against the limits of informal or unorthodox modes of regulation. Taking on the same modes of operation as institutions of the developed countries can thus only come at the end of a long process of transformation – which it would be absurd to try and do away with.

16

Fragile Africa: One Crisis after Another

Movement invariably means imbalance. In this great march of African repopulation there are many stumbling-blocks – with consequences that are potentially formidable for the continent and its neighbours. Will a changing Africa manage to avoid the violence that continues to paralyse some of its members?

Contemporary Africa also has its share of fragile states, in a condition of permanent tension or repeated conflict. When they are not suffering open warfare, under transfusion from disaster-relief NGOs or in the spotlight of the international media, they are hard pressed to overcome their last crisis or are moving towards another. Half of the countries emerging from civil war fall back into it again in the five years that follow,[1] which makes the academic distinction between situations of 'crisis' and 'post-crisis' often quite theoretical.

Somalia, Chad, the Central African Republic, Guinea-Bissau and Guinea-Conakry, the RD Congo and Zimbabwe all share in this early part of the century an erratic economic situation, whose performance fluctuates as a result of the periodic return of civil peace. While an agreement between warring factions can sometimes usher in a period of rapid growth (these countries, among the poorest in the world, are starting from a very low basis), the plunge into violence, political or military, inevitably brings with it a far more lasting impoverishment. This is why GDP per capita in the Central African Republic (CAR) has fallen by a third since its independence, why that of the RD Congo has been divided by four in twenty years of troubles, and why the standard of living of the Zimbabwean population fell by half in ten years of acute political crisis. These bloodlettings take decades to heal – for those states that manage to escape from the cycle of violence. Paradoxically, in fact, the state of crisis has a dreadful stability. In a context of stagnant national wealth, any profit is made at the expense of someone else – whether an individual, a group (social, ethnic, religious) or a country. Predation and violence then make up a system. And the all-embracing 'conflict trap' combines with the poverty trap to create the conditions for a stable equilibrium of violence.

The politics of empty stomachs

The crisis of structures of governance can take two very different forms in fragile countries: that of a phantom state or that of a predator state.

Phantom states possess only the external trappings of a state: flag, national anthem, ambassador to the United Nations. Outside the capital, the absence of the state is striking; it controls neither its territory nor its population. How can it administer a population that it doesn't know? In these states that have melted away, there is no reliable information about the population, its whereabouts and its needs. The latest statistical data go back twenty or thirty years, if not right to the colonial era. Demographers, economists and humanitarian organizations compete in ingeniousness to estimate roughly the size and distribution of the population, changes in GDP or prices. This is how a recent demographic study conducted on the basis of satellite photos revised the population estimates of several African countries. From one day to the next the populations of certain countries lost or gained several million individuals.

Phantom states, tapped at source by their most powerful – and least scrupulous – ministers, experience permanent financial difficulties. In the absence of transfusion from the international community, it is often impossible for them to pay their officials. 'The state pretends to pay us, and we pretend to work', a Central African civil servant explains to us; his arrears of pay now amount to thirty-six months. Deprived of their pay, civil servants have no other choice but to make the population pay. From top to bottom of the administrative pyramid, abuse of power is the rule of the game: 'I have to feed my family', explains a Central African midwife when questioned about the 'top-up' she demands from her patients. At least this is fixed; other people, she tells us, increase the tariff when the patient is already in labour. Anti-AIDS kits distributed by NGOs are also reused for several successive childbirths – the surplus being sold off on the black market. At least in Bangui the services of a doctor are available. The rest of the country, as large as France and Benelux combined, is a real administrative desert. Out of the country's 17,000 civil servants, over 10,000 live in the capital, leaving only something like 450 officials per prefecture – some of these being as large as Slovakia.[2] Teachers appointed to jobs in the provinces prefer to remain in Bangui. Why should they brave the bandits known as *coupeurs de route* and get isolated in the place to which they are assigned, when their salary, even if it is paid, can only be cashed at the counter of the Trésor Publique in Bangui? This explains the mushrooming in the countryside of schools where 'parent-teachers', who can sometimes themselves scarcely read or write, teach overcrowded classes the rudiments of French or mathematics. It also explains the Somali *madrassas* where the Koran serves as textbook, for better or worse.

It is this cycle of under-administration that seals the breaking of the social contract: once the state can no longer fulfil the basic functions of sovereignty (starting with controlling its territory and protecting its population), it loses its prerogatives, starting with 'the monopoly of legitimate violence'.[3] In a village in the north of the Central African Republic, the head of an insurgent group explained to one of our interpreters the reason for his rebellion in terms of the absence of the state. What would happen if the prefects again occupied their prefectures, the teachers their classes and the doctors their surgeries, she asked him rather provocatively. 'Then we would be policemen, not rebels', he confidently replied. In Somalia, too, the power vacuum that has lasted for decades has provoked a forceful return of clanism, proof less of an identity backlash than of a security vacuum: people are not fighting for an ethnic group or ideology, but for the survival of their families[4] – or, more prosaically, for a piece of the cake. 'All rebellions are initially about food', a French soldier tells us; 'People shoot in order to get something: power, if they have the means of going that far, but at least a good job when they have to start negotiating with the government.'⁵

The lack of any border control aids the formation of systems of conflict: between eastern Chad, southwestern Sudan (Darfur) and the north of the Central African Republic, armed groups made up of young uprooted men alternately fight on the side of one government then another, join up with the rebellion or become *zaragouinas*⁶ in times of truce between the warring factions. Some of these *coupeurs de route* that paralyse Central Africa move around today in jeeps and communicate by walkie-talkie. Armed with sophisticated materiel imported from Sudan, their main source of income is kidnapping the children of nomadic herders. The system of war in the no-man's land between the RD Congo, Rwanda and Uganda, though it operates along somewhat different lines, is just as well oiled. The Congolese rebel leader Laurent N'Kunda, who has long played on the rivalry between Kigali and Kinshasa, contributed to their temporary reconciliation early in 2009. The Lord's Resistance Army, a bloody Ugandan rebel group, is also a past master at exploiting the porous borders between the Central African Republic and the Congo. Like the child-soldiers of Liberia, Sierra Leone and Guinea in the 1980s and 1990s, these fighters, often mingling with refugees, keep the spiral of violence going. Hardly has one state in the region managed to reach a fragile peace than these paramilitaries are recruited the other side of the border – embarking once more on their sinister enterprise of destabilization. Uprooted and often rejected by their own people, they are at home wherever violence prevails and booty is easy to obtain.

Trapped between rebels, government forces and *coupeurs de route*, the population faces a state of permanent insecurity. In such a precarious situation, it is impossible to make plans for the future. When a village burned down first by the rebels, then by the presidential guards, risks the same fate when the next clash comes, any investment is pointless. While we were crossing northeast Central Africa in 2008, we saw inhabitants return to their villages after two seasons spent camping in their fields – away from the road and from military violence. Humanitarian workers found these men and women suffering from diseases that had previously been eradicated: though the village had a well, the water in the field was infested by parasites. They also detected psychological effects of violence: in a phantom state people are forced to live in the present

– but also in the past; the civilian population are at the heart of the
fighting,[7] and bear the scars of the violence they have experienced.
They organize themselves as best they can. Safety can only come
from the group itself, often formed on an ethnic basis. Self-defence
collectives, sometimes armed with simple lances, bows and arrows,
are created as protection from bandits. A parallel system of justice
is established: when the Islamic courts do not replace the absent
courts of the state (as in Somalia), it is often those of the street that
step in, and they are rarely any more merciful.

If phantom states are states without an administration, predator states are administrations without a state: the omnipotent
representatives of power drain the life from both the economy
and society. The head of state is the head of the budget, which is
applied without any legal procedure. Presidential decrees, emergency measures, exceptional financial laws: an international official posted to N'Djamena explained to us that making economic
forecasts in such conditions was no more than 'mental exercises'.
The same goes for Zimbabwe, whose economy, in the hands of
a fallen national hero, has experienced a decade of unmatched
chaos. Formerly the breadbasket of Central Africa, Zimbabwe
depends today on international food aid. Grain production has
fallen by half since the application, amid chaos and violence, of
an agricultural reform that was arbitrary to say the least – consist-
ing in expelling white farmers from the land they cultivated. The
descent into hell can then be striking, even for those countries with
the most promising economic potential. The educated population
of Zimbabwe and the wealth of its soil did not prevent its falling
in a few years to the bottom rungs of international classifications.
Inflation in early 2009 was running at several thousand-fold per
year. The rate of unemployment (theoretical, at least) was close to
95 per cent.

The corruption and arbitrariness of predator states has nothing
in common with small-scale everyday corruption. It paralyses the
economy: unless protected (by payment) at a high level of authority, the least accumulation of capital is prey to extortion and harassment by anyone who holds power. It is hard in such conditions
to attract foreign investment. No matter what the potential profitability of the activity in question, its gains are subject to the arbi-

trary whim of the state. This corruption also destroys the slightest economic fabric. In a predator state it is not only useless to get rich, but even dangerous. This is what we were told by a woman at a market on the edge of the Chari when we asked her why, in a context of chronic food shortage, she was content just to sell eggs rather than trying to produce them. 'Why should I do that?' she asked us, both surprised and amused by the naivety of the question. 'The peasant who I used to buy my eggs from has had his chickens seized by the authorities. When he protested, they threatened to imprison his son. Today he has nothing left. I've had to change producers.'

The economy of predation is the 'politics of the stomach'[8] taken to a logical conclusion: contrary to the situation in systems of taxation–accumulation–redistribution that are common to many developing countries, the holders of power in this sickly configuration are like parasites who prey on their host until they kill it off. This is the sad story of cotton production in Chad. Cotonchad was the semi-public company around which the national cotton industry was built up. While its initial purpose was to buy cotton from the producers, gin it and sell it, it also maintained for many years the roads taken by its trucks, the distribution of seed and fertilizer to farmers, as well as a credit system which allowed farmers to delay until the end of the season repayment of the sums they had borrowed to buy seed. For a long time Cotonchad was one of the pillars of agricultural development in the country's cotton zones, and a whole series of other crops that were sown alternately also depended on it.

But now this company with its antiquated equipment is burdened with debt and close to bankruptcy. Tapped for years on end by its managers, people close to the regime, it owes its survival today to being bailed out by the state and international investors – worried about the impact of its closing on the millions of peasants who depend on this branch of agriculture. While lenders question the refloating of this semi-public company, and Chadian parliamentarians deplore the opaqueness of its accounts, the peasants who have not been paid for several harvests on end have begun to abandon cotton. Deprived of the goose that lays the golden eggs, the gravediggers of Cotonchad will look for another animal to feed on. Where the citizens of a phantom state yearn for a more visible state, those of a predator state would often prefer to see its extinction. In both cases, people are forced to live from day to day. And in such a context, violence – whose means are everywhere at hand – becomes a rational individual response[9] and an instrument of social advance – hazardous but accessible to all.[10]

These fragile African states, destined by their very structure to be poor pupils, are development-aid orphans. While aid donors have rushed to assist their growing neighbours (no less than fifteen European countries are involved with Mozambique in terms of development aid, not counting the many multilateral lenders, foundations and NGOs), they leave these countries in the hands of emergency helpers. Thus, while growing Africa is being equipped and constructed, fragile Africa sees its weak infrastructure deteriorate further each year. For these populations, whether they suffer from too much state or not enough, desertion by the development community has come as a double penalty.

'To know the meaning of things'

We can now understand the full importance of the state in the development process. The aid programmes of the Reagan and Thatcher years, marked by the philosophy of the minimal state, deeply underestimated this. It was only after the implosion of the state in several African countries during the 1990s that its role was again recognized. But the broad programmes of 'nation building' then undertaken by the international community to relaunch so-called 'failed' states sinned in the opposite direction – following the balancing movement characteristic of prevailing thinking. Seeing the fragility of the state, they remained blind to the underlying socio-economic vulnerabilities. Treating the symptoms of the disease, they failed to attack the causes. The study of fragile Africa, however, emerging or struggling to emerge from warfare, reveals a series of structural weaknesses that bear the seeds of further violence in the future.

Growing pressure on agricultural land has played a decisive role in several African conflicts of the past twenty years. This was the case in Côte d'Ivoire, whose population leapt from 3 million to 17 million in less than half a century – the combination of a high birth rate and massive immigration from neighbouring countries. The number of inhabitants per square kilometre rose 550 per cent in forty years, proportionately reducing the average size of agricultural plots.[11] This greatly increasing density, an ingredient of the 'Ivorian miracle' under Houphouët-Boigny and an age of high export prices, was transformed into a factor of tension with the sudden fall in the price of cocoa, when the country also came up against the limit of its cultivable space. Competition for land between native Ivorians and immigrants, in a country where over a quarter of the population were foreigners in 1998, rapidly brought an end to the Houphouët model ('the land belongs to those who farm it'), fuelling the emergence of the ominous concept of *ivoirité* in political life. The escalation of tensions led to massacres of Burkinese immigrants by groups of 'young patriots', then to the civil war that is so notorious.

Côte d'Ivoire is not an isolated case. Everyone knows of the descent into hell that Rwanda experienced in the mid 1990s. Competition for land was also one of the major causes of the violence that gripped this small Central African country, where eight people out of ten then lived in the countryside. The Rwandan conflict is still presented as the expression of an ancestral hatred between two peoples, Hutus and Tutsis. But research conducted by two anthropologists in the northeast of the country in the years preceding the genocide of 1994 established a striking link between growing pressure on agricultural land and the social tensions that led to this genocidal madness[12] – quite apart from the racist discourse that exploited this pressure. Catherine André and Jean-Philippe Plateau have shown how massacres also took place among Hutus in a highly uniform ethnic community, and in proportions similar to those in other regions. As in the rest of the country, the growing shortage of land (divided into ever smaller plots each generation) threw the most vulnerable members of the community into an extremely precarious situation: forced to sell their holdings in order to survive, they fell below the subsistence level. Where the ethnic marker did not play a role, generational or economic divisions served as a dividing line for a bloody settling of accounts among neighbours. Study of the list of victims of the butcheries of spring 1994 within this Hutu community led these two observers of Rwandan society to write – in a paper with the revealing title 'Rwanda caught in a Malthusian trap' – that 'the 1994 events provided a unique opportunity to settle scores, or to reshuffle landed properties, even among Hutu villagers'.[13] In less than three months, 800,000 men, women and children died by the bullets and machetes of genocide across the country, or 11 per cent of the population of Rwanda, and three-quarters of the Tutsis.

People like to believe that the episodes of crisis in Ivorian and Rwandan society represent sad exceptions, produced by an unfortunate combination of circumstances specific to the 1990s. This is perhaps why the recent electoral crisis in Kenya made such a strong impression. In late 2007, journalists from across the world arrived in this country to cover a model election campaign. Millions of citizens took part, sometimes lining up for hours to put their voting slip in the ballot box. Kenya, perceived at this time as a new candidate for 'good pupil' status in development after so many years of mistakes, was cited as the very symbol of African renaissance. The 'Kenya Vision 2030' plan, an ambitious combination of macroeconomic, legal and constitutional reforms, was developed in close cooperation with the World Bank. As the new poster child of donors, the country received close to $1 billion in development aid in 2006 – an increase of 250 per cent since 2002. Its flourishing tourist industry and market gardening were put forward as an example for other African states, models of successful integration into world trade. Economic growth had reached an average of 5.5 per cent over the previous four years, drawing the other countries of East Africa in its wake. It seemed to prove that vigorous growth was possible in Africa, even for a country poorly endowed in minerals and hydrocarbons.

The sudden eruption of post-election violence, however, led to the death of over 1,000 people and the flight of several hundred thousand others, compromising an economic miracle that was seen as already achieved.

As in Côte d'Ivoire and Rwanda, there were a multitude of factors hidden behind this sudden outbreak of violence, including the manipulation of markers of identity by politicians in search of power. But the context of anarchy that reigned for weeks at a stretch was also the occasion here for a vast redistribution of land by force of arms. International news channels greedy for images showed young Kikuyus drunk on violence and alcohol, chasing out their Luo neighbours with machete blows and cudgels with the avowed aim of taking over their houses and lands. From districts with a Luo majority came Kikuyu families who had been expelled from their lands by young Luos armed with bows and arrows. More detailed analyses of Kenyan society preceding the massacres of winter 2008 show here, too, increased pressure on agricultural land and growing inequality, which threatened social peace even in a context of firm economic growth. 'Land is getting scarce, but there are more and more people depending on it as their main source of income. Many families have fought because of lands. Last night a woman and her children killed a man over land. Most conflicts take place over land', observed a deputy chief of Bungoma district in the west of the country in 2007.[14] Substantial vulnerabilities were thus brewing beneath the Kenyan economic miracle. If there is nothing inevitable about the resort to violence, the using-up of agricultural space in certain localities can nonetheless go some way to explaining the seemingly inexplicable.

On top of this tension over available agricultural land, which affects ever more African regions, there is that of natural resources (water, wood, pasture). As well as their political causes, the crises that Darfur and Somalia are undergoing cannot be understood without considering the growing competition for scarce resources, overexploited in this arid zone. The phenomenon of desertification[15] fuels tension between Fur and Arab communities, which is opportunistically maintained and exacerbated by the Khartoum government. Deforestation is visible to the naked eye from the air. Between the scattered villages east of the town of Abéché in eastern Chad there used to be trees. But all that is visible today where they stood are faint circles in the sandy soil. Women sometimes have to go several kilometres to gather wood for cooking. Memories handed down by the elders confirm the facts noted by the geologists: underground water supplies built up over millennia are exhausted in a few decades under the combined effect of overexploitation and climate change.

Along with competition for access to agricultural land and natural resources, Africa will have to deal with several other factors of vulnerability in the course of its transformation. But the structural weaknesses of today are the breeding ground of violence tomorrow. It would take too long to go into a detailed analysis of each of these factors here. But we can mention the urban crisis, made up of uprooting, inequality and the large-scale unemployment of young people who have lost their bearings; the massive movements of population that, while necessary to reduce pressure on space in certain zones, can contribute to exacerbating urban and rural crises in others; socio-economic inequalities, particularly blatant in societies in the midst of economic take-off; and finally the effects of climate change, whose scale on the African continent will soon be revealed.

In sub-Saharan Africa as a whole, violent conflicts have declined. The number of states involved in war (civil or international) has halved from 1999 to 2009, distancing the continent from the peak of violence reached in the early 1990s.[16] It is too soon to claim that this is a lasting tendency. The question raised today, on the other hand, is whether we shall be able to devote the resources needed to tackle these fragilities in order to prevent the wars of tomorrow – or whether we shall wait for them to erupt before we act. This is a choice of public policy.

Dead aid?

This cursory portrait of three Africas reveals an image full of contrasts. If the continent is on the march, its forty-nine members are not advancing at the same pace or in a single direction. Each has its share of challenges.

Mining Africa, with a growing list of members, will have to manage its wealth for the long term in order to put it in the service of development. The experience of Botswana shows that this can be a path of rapid and sustained growth. The issue for fragile Africa will be to find its way out of violence – as Liberia, Sierra Leone and Angola have succeeded in doing in the last twenty years. The continent's economic changes are at last opening a path for these countries. Finally, the challenge for those countries that are doing best in terms of economic and human development will be to achieve those few points of extra growth that will anchor them permanently on the path of catching-up with the developed countries.

Nonetheless, the rapid transformation of economic and social structures in these three Africas cannot help but subject each of them to multiple tensions, calling for the greatest vigilance. In fact, if the promising stories of Mozambique or Burkina Faso show that rapid economic growth is within reach of states marked by several decades of war, or with a number of structural handicaps, the episodes of violence in Kenya and Côte d'Ivoire tell us that economies in take-off are not sheltered from sudden relapses of this kind. In an Africa that is rediscovering a dynamic of growth, instability will be a watershed: some countries have experienced repeated decline. The coming decades will therefore see the continent's societies swinging from one course to the other – or remaining wedged between the two.

But the contrasts between these three ideal types – rentier states, fragile states and pioneer states – should not make us forget the grey zones that several African countries inhabit. Certain West African countries have managed to guard against the most characteristic tendencies of fragile Africa without joining the pioneers of development. The African swamp is full of societies stuck halfway across, which manage with difficulty to maintain economic growth rates close to the rates of population increase, not allowing any improvement in their citizens' standard of living. To keep these states from falling into violence and propel them towards economic catching-up – this is the issue for the states of the African swamp.

What can international aid achieve in the face of these multiform challenges? The effectiveness of aid is a controversial subject, and has given rise to a long series of mistaken positions, falling prey in turn to excessive optimism or cynicism. For some people,[17] in whose eyes international aid represents the be-all and end-all of growth, the economic and social development that Africa can hope for in the coming decades will be proportional to the volume of finance that international solidarity succeeds in mobilizing. For others,[18] economic aid is a vast machine that has to be brought under control, as it damages the development of the recipient economies by a system of negative effects. For the more radical of their number, a pure and simple halt to this 'dead' aid is a preliminary condition for the continent's economic take-off.

The issues at stake south of the Sahara are too great for debates over aid to be monopolized by these rhetorical postures, whose excesses nourish one another in an unhealthy seesaw.

As we have seen, international aid has historically played a major role in the structuring of sub-Saharan economies – for better and for worse. Like any public policy it has suffered from mistaken choices, the lessons of which need to be drawn for the future. Like all other components of the foreign policy of the countries of the North, it has had to respond to objectives that have only little to do with those assigned it today, and that should not be repeated.[19] Like any public policy of redistribution, aid generates negative effects and risks of misuse, which it is important to minimize.

Those who expect public development aid to 'make Africa take off' – or any other region of the world – are bound to conclude that it is ineffective: it is not reasonable to demand of aid that it should generate growth by itself. The sums involved are not sufficient to meet this challenge alone. And those who expect that the stopping of aid would signal the emergence of internally generated growth, freed from the yoke of conditionalities, are bound to be similarly frustrated: Zimbabwe, Madagascar, Central African Republic – there is a long list of countries that are aid orphans, or have temporarily been deserted, but where the consequence is only a long descent into economic, social and political hell.

The truth is that development aid, if properly targeted, is in a position to swing the balance of risks and opportunities of the African transformation. It can do so by supporting the dynamics of development under way, steering public finance to investments which private flows are too timid to reach. It can do so by working to make this growth more sustainable (in other words, more 'green', i.e. less greedy in terms of natural resources, as well as better divided among the population). It can do so by rendering this economic growth less vulnerable to the great international shocks that have destroyed it in the past. It can do so by compensating for the absence of growth in zones where this is lacking by subsidizing access to services essential to human dignity. It can do so by working to reduce certain of the fragilities (environmental, economic, social, political) on which violence feeds. And it can finally do so by organizing the strengthening of talent by the transfer of know-how.

If they cannot generate development by themselves, these efforts by Africa's partners will count in the management of delicate transformations – helping to reduce the number of 'fragile' states and increase the number of 'pioneer' states. But they will be equally determinant in negotiating the difficult turn to a sustainable economic development. Though far from enough on its own, development aid will be a necessary part of the toolkit supporting the African renewal.

Part Seven

Invigorating the World

Beyond the extreme diversity of the issues that the various parts of sub-Saharan Africa have to tackle, a common challenge threatens – imperilling the growth that the continent has once more experienced since the turn of the century. Africa is embarking on its take-off at a time when humanity has discovered that there are limits to the planet's resources. This represents one of the most decisive issues for a continent midway in its repopulation process. It is taking time, though, to penetrate people's minds.

On the other hand, the form of growth that this Africa chooses will be one of the determinant variables in the future of the green planet – another factor that is often overlooked. We now offer some reflections on the singular place that sub-Saharan Africa occupies in the planetary ecological crisis.

17

The Limits to Growth

In the eighteenth, nineteenth and twentieth centuries, when they emerged as industrial powers, Europe, the United States and Japan still lived in a limitless world. The size of their labour-force, and the investment capacity of their bankers, were the only limits to the expansion of these countries' economies and the improvement of their standard of living. A generous nature provided whatever people needed. So much so that natural resources, at one time viewed as scarce, simply disappeared from economic models. Whereas the economists of the eighteenth and early nineteenth centuries saw land as a factor of production, for their neoclassical successors – who dominated economic thought from the late nineteenth century onward – the only cost of natural resources was that of their extraction, transport and processing.[1] There is nothing very surprising about this belief in abundance: the exhaustion of a mine, the disappearance of a forest or the pollution of a river only represented the inconvenience of having to mine, cut or dig a few kilometres further away. Once minerals were exhausted in Europe, it was in Africa, America and the Indian subcontinent that the fuel for world economic growth was gathered.

But the era of unlimited natural resources is coming to an end, and Africa has arrived at nature's mighty feast at a time of shortage. Since the start of the industrial age, our societies have entered a phase of accelerated de-capitalization, destroying in two centuries a natural capital built up over several million years. By exhausting non-renewable resources, threatening the disappearance of the genetic treasury of thousands of species, and disturbing major climatic balances, humanity is in the process of making a fearsome ecological trap for itself, something that it is hardly beginning to be aware of. In the early twenty-first century, it is at the level of the planet as a whole that water, air, soil, fossil fuels and food products are proving scarce – and expensive.

Green perils

This context, unprecedented in the experience of economic development, presents an additional burden for a continent launched full-pelt on the path of take-off; in the present state of knowledge and technology, we know that it will not have sufficient reserves to finish this race. None of the natural resources on which human societies have previously built up their economies is protected today from overconsumption and pollution, so that African societies are bound to come up against the global environmental crisis along their development path. This crisis will affect Africa in two ways.

First of all, because exploitation of the continent's raw materials is today one of the main engines of its growth. The economic models of many African states, as a legacy of the colonial era, still rely too much on the export of non-renewable mineral, fossil and plant resources – the increase in their prices in the early years of the century being largely responsible for the region's economic growth. The exports of African raw materials will be a substantial bonanza for a few decades more. But dependence on these will still prove damaging sooner or later. As we have seen, the rent economy rarely produces jobs and balanced economic growth. And the exhaustion of the rentier economic model with the erosion of African subsoils also risks undermining the fragile foundations of the continent's economic growth.

But the search for models of sustainable development in Africa is important above all because the continent's populations will be the first collateral victims of environmental degradation – whether local or planetary. A World Bank study shows that natural capital makes up on average 30 per cent of the wealth of low-income countries, as against only 2 per cent for the rich countries. And this differing dependence on natural capital also holds for each of their citizens. Everywhere, the poorest inhabitants are the first to suffer from the degradation of the natural resources around them,[2] since it is these that form their productive capital, providing irreplaceable environmental services and serving them as life assurance.[3] Some two-thirds of all Africans derive their incomes from the environment. This proportion is still higher in the poorest and most rural countries of Africa such as Burkina Faso, Niger and Ethiopia. The decline of natural systems in the wake of soil exhaustion, deforestation, over-fishing or the pollution of rivers thus directly threatens the poorest populations' means of production.

Industrial fishing off the West African coast, formerly a particularly rich zone, has already considerably reduced the stocks on which close to a million small-scale fishers depend: the Senegalese *piroguiers* who see European and Asian ships operate off their coast bring back less fish in their nets each year. The degradation of West African fishery, by industrial and urban pollution, offshore oil exploitation and the disappearance of mangroves, also threatens the reproduction of many species. By 2025, the 500 kilometres of coast between Accra and the Niger delta will form an uninterrupted chain of cities with a population of around 50 million, leaving little room for the coastal ecosystems on which young fish depend – and thus for the fishery resources of tomorrow.

This 'green peril' goes hand in hand with a brown one: the 320 million city-dwellers that Africa now counts are more and more exposed to an ever-present urban pollution. Owing to the lack of drainage systems, any rain transforms the informal residential quarters that surround the continent's big cities into vast open sewers.

We crossed the shanty-town of Mathare with Kenyan officials and a clutch of European diplomats, dressed in leather shoes and high heels, a day after heavy rain. The 'epic' dimension of the visit, punctuated by episodes of slipping into the mud to the laughter of local children, didn't remove the sense of amazement at the work that was needed. A few kilometres from here, the immense open refuse tip of Dandora, one of the largest in Africa, continues to offer a livelihood to hundreds of young people from the outskirts of Nairobi.[4] They sort plastic bags, bits of metal and other objects of value from the 2,000 or so tonnes of refuse produced each day by the 5 million inhabitants of the Kenyan capital. Before being resold, these finds are rinsed in the river that borders the site – and flows tranquilly on to the shanty-towns lower down the hill.

Their children have abnormally high levels of heavy metals in their blood, a slow poison for these youngsters, many of whom already suffer from chronic respiratory problems.

As if the challenge of refuse produced by the African mega-cities was not enough, some foreign companies profit from the absence of standards and weakness of controls to make these African cities the rubbish tip of the world. The *Probo Koala* affair shocked Africa in summer 2006, showing what's involved in one of the most sordid dimensions of globalization. Tens of tonnes of toxic mud, unloaded from a Greek ship carrying a Panamanian flag, with a Russian crew and chartered by a Dutch company, were dumped in an Abidjan suburb, leading to at least twenty deaths and many cases of poisoning.[5] The ship had set out from Amsterdam with the sole intention of offloading its mixture of diesel and caustic soda. The company that chartered it judged the treatment of this cargo according to European standards to be too costly. Beyond this particular unpleasant story, the fact is that Africa has become a privileged destination for the planet's toxic waste.

Collateral damage

As a victim of the degradation of natural ecosystems and urban pollution, Africa will be the first affected by the current upsetting of the global environment. Experts agree that this continent will undergo the most severe climatic developments, while African societies' capacities for response are among the weakest in the world. In August 2005, hurricane Katrina illustrated the vulnerability of coastal cities to natural disaster, flooding 80 per cent of the surface of New Orleans. The IPCC forecasts are quite clear: extreme climatic events will be both more frequent and more intense in Africa in the coming decades. The rise in sea level, which could be more than 50 centimetres by 2100, will affect African cities in full growth. Today, 250 million Africans already live along the coast. How many will do so at the end of the century?[6] One recent study estimates that, without appropriate adaptation plans, over 3 million people will be exposed to floods by 2070 in the cities of Lagos and Abidjan alone – essentially the inhabitants of their marginal districts, living at ground level in informal dwellings. Infrastructure close to the shoreline will experience severe erosion: damage to coastal infrastructure in Côte d'Ivoire could reach a quarter of the country's GDP, and 10 per cent in the Nigerian case. On top of this, the agricultural lands of the great African deltas will suffer water salination.

Water shortages will also grow more acute. In the last forty years, rainfall recorded in the Sahel has fallen by 30 per cent[7] – while the region's population has more than doubled. The surface of Lake Chad in flood has shrunk steadily due to this reduced rainfall, from 25,000 square kilometres in 1960 to less than 5,000 today. These figures conceal human dramas, such as that of the villagers we met in the east of Chad, close to the Sudanese border. We arrived after they had made a second unsuccessful attempt to dig a new well. 'These people are living on a pile of sand', the hydraulic engineer in charge told us. The villagers we had met earlier in the morning were luckier; the water had spouted. But for how long? 'Hard to say', he replied; 'Wells dug a few years ago are already dry, particularly around refugee camps.' There is no more doubt today that climate change will exacerbate underlying tensions. A few hours further along the track, in the north of Darfur, the desert has advanced by an average of 100 kilometres over the last four decades, pushing southward the populations settled there and stoking up tensions between communities.[8] The zone is ready to flare up at the slightest spark. Long viewed as subjects for science fiction, 'water wars' are now erupting into African reality.

It is this close tie between the environment and the quality of life of the poorest African populations that motivated the pioneering initiative of Wangara Maathai. By helping to plant more than 10 million trees in Africa with her Green Belt association, with the intention of struggling against soil erosion and providing wood for the use of local populations, this major figure in environmental protection laid down important markers on the path of durable development – proving by example the mutual dependence between human and natural capital.

Preservation of the environment is sometimes presented as a whim of the rich, a subject 'for later', opposed to the immediate imperative of economic growth. Nothing could be further from the truth. Energy shortage, climate peril, soil exhaustion, the return of hunger: the different components of the world environmental crisis are so many burdens on Africa's economic growth in this phase of repopulation. Whereas other societies are facing the environmental crisis at a time when they have resources available to tackle it, Africa is confronted with it while still poor. Adaptation to its effects will require substantial investment for the industrialized countries. The African continent, less well endowed with financial, human, technical and institutional resources, will have to pay a still higher price. Its inhabitants cannot allow it to slip further out of control. Protection of the environment and adaptation to the global environmental crisis are thus not the luxury of developed countries. In Africa, as elsewhere, this is fundamentally a matter of human development. Each year lost in the search for sustainable solutions carries a cost for African growth and the populations that depend on it.

An environmental bonanza

At a time of world ecological crisis, Africa's interest in finding a path of sustainable growth is equally that of the international community. For one thing is certain in the maze of predictions about the future of our planet: the African continent, though first victim of the planetary environmental crisis, holds some of the most powerful keys for springing the ecological trap that is in the process of formation.

This puts the African nations in a unique position, from which they have a great deal to gain. Anything that is scarce is always dear. And Africa hides a treasure of natural resources that are still unexploited, and coveted by others in this time of shortage. In a context of growing world tension over food, it is the African continent that contains the largest reserves of agricultural land. At a time when we are discovering the value of the genetic heritage of the planet's living species, and growing afraid at the pace of their extinction, it constitutes the largest reservoir of biodiversity. While carbon sinks are becoming scarce, Africa's equatorial forests are the planet's second-biggest lung. The world of the twenty-first century will be caught in such a vice that this unique natural heritage can yield Africans a substantial rent. If Africa manages to preserve this heritage and turn it to profit, it will form one of its major comparative advantages in the 21st-century economy.

At the time of the first industrial revolutions, how competitive an economy was depended largely on its command of technologies and its access to the major routes of world trade. Territories were uncompetitive if they did not manage to produce a sufficiently large quantity of goods for exchange on world markets, or if they were too remote to be able to find an outlet for their production. During the 'third industrial revolution',[9] that of the boom years of technological, economic and financial globalization, competitiveness was determined above all by access to information and world financial flows. Societies remained on the margins of globalization if they did not succeed in capturing the investment flows that moved by way of New York, London, Tokyo and Hong Kong, or in penetrating the world of knowledge and the global intelligentsia – academics, writers, political decision-makers. We may venture to say that in an age of world environmental crisis, with the scarcity of natural resources ever more apparent, sustainable access to natural capital will constitute one of the major determinants of a territory's competitiveness.

Africa is setting out on this race with a long lead. It will keep this lead as long as it is able to capitalize on its comparative advantage. But this scenario is not written in advance and, as we have seen, the window of opportunity is brief. There is nothing inevitable about the energy crisis, the urban peril, the food crisis or even the erosion of Africa's natural capital: there are only bad policies. In each of these fields, sub-Saharan Africa is today paying dearly for the choices of its colonial rulers, its first post-independence leaders and the gurus of structural adjustment. Beyond each of these stalemates of public policy lie the keys for the competitiveness of African economies on a path of sustainable growth.

18

Light against Darkness

The first stalemate that threatens Africa is the short-term choice of energy sources. The energy trap that is being formed is all the more sinister in that Africa has an energy capital at its disposal that surpasses anything else in the world.

Energy crisis

Human societies are like living bodies, in that all growth is inevitably accompanied by an increase in their energy consumption. Over the last fifteen years close to 80 per cent of the rise in world production of fossil fuels has gone to meet the growth in energy demand from the emerging economies.[1] In 2009, for the first time in history, their consumption overtook that of the developed countries.

Since the turn of the century, the return of economic growth in sub-Saharan Africa, the population explosion and accelerated urbanization have combined to increase the needs of the continent's economies. Senegal's energy demand has grown by 8 to 10 per cent each year, a pace at which it will double in less than eight years. Yet several decades of underinvestment have led to a run-down infrastructure, polluting and unreliable, across most of the continent. A quarter of the existing electricity-generating capacity is out of service. The tension between the upward spiral of energy needs and a lagging supply has plunged Africa into a state of permanent energy crisis – a bitter paradox for a continent that dispatches thousands of oil tankers each year to Asia, America and Europe. Sub-Saharan Africa counts something like 65 gigawatts of generating capacity for 770 million people, or more or less the same as Spain with its 45 million inhabitants.[2]

Two-thirds of all African countries face a chronic shortage of energy, revealed by frequent power cuts. From Burkina Faso via Ghana and Liberia to Kenya, these leave whole regions without electricity for several hours each day – the equivalent of fifty-six days per year for the continent as a whole.[3] When these happen at inconvenient moments, the better-off switch on their own generators, costly and polluting. Other people are forced to wait until the current comes on again: thousands of businesses interrupt their activity, some clinics can scarcely keep their stocks of vaccines refrigerated, and school students can no longer study after nightfall. Africa is often perceived as a continent with a health and education deficit. But this is above all an electricity deficit. While one child in three fails to complete primary school, three children in four have no access to electricity. This lack is often the greatest worry for the poorest section of the population, caught in a struggle for survival. The 124 kilowatt-hours that an average African consumes each year are scarcely enough to power a 100-watt bulb for three hours a day.[4]

The impact of this energy crisis, disastrous at the level of a family, a clinic or a business, weighs down the continent's economic progress as a whole. It is estimated that shortage of electricity cuts Africa's economic growth by two percentage points a year – two precious points that, as we have argued, would set several countries on the continent on a path towards catching up economically with the developed world. Post-apartheid South Africa, the only really emerging economic power on the continent at the turn of the century, saw its growth eroded by the energy crisis well before the problems of the global economy in 2008. But Africa's energy crisis is also a major factor in the political health of its societies. And in the same way as the health and education crises, this is experienced as a proof of public bankruptcy.

The United States alone consumes each year eighteen times more energy than the whole of sub-Saharan Africa apart from South Africa.[5] If it is inconceivable that Africa's energy consumption per capita will ever reach the extravagant levels of the land of the air-conditioner, the urban freeway and the SUV, there can be no doubt that energy supply will have to advance at a brisk pace in the course of the next few decades in order to fill the African energy gap. This imperative catching-up process, a sine qua non of sub-Saharan economic take-off, poses two distinct kinds of problem in this new age of scarcity.

There is, first, the problem of climate change. As we have seen, the first violent symptoms of climate change show that air, a 'free good' if ever there was one, is itself scarce. All indicators show that the earth cannot supply the 9 billion population that is predicted for forty years' time with the energy formulas of today. And so the exponential growth in energy consumption expected in these years in the developing countries, no matter how legitimate, raises an unprecedented environmental and ethical challenge: humanity will suffocate if the emerging countries follow the same path of industrialization as that taken by the societies of the North in the nineteenth century. Attention today is turned towards China, India and Brazil, and the policies of greenhouse gas reduction that these nations will agree to adopt. African emissions, which presently make up no more than 3 or 4 per cent of total man-made greenhouse gas, are of little concern. But they should be.

The carbon footprint of a society depends both on the average emission per head of population, closely tied to the level of economic development, and on the number of its inhabitants. Yet the tempo of both population and economic growth expected in sub-Saharan Africa is too rapid for the greenhouse gas emissions of these societies, almost negligible today on the world scale, to still be so in 50 or 100 years' time – a reasonable horizon for considering our planet's climate problems. A continent of close to 2 billion people, half of them living in towns, will be far more greedy for energy and far more productive of greenhouse gas than its ancestor at the end of the twentieth century, still largely rural and with only half this population. It is precisely because Africa is today the poorest and least-industrialized major region of the world that it will surpass any other in terms of the growth of its energy needs over the next 50 years. And so it is also in Africa that the battle against global warming will be played out.

The lifetime of an electric power station is a few decades, that of an urbanization plan several centuries: inertia in energy production and consumption choices is such that, no matter how urgent the need for change, the question of African greenhouse gas emissions arises already today. The way that industrialized societies have 'overdrawn' on global ecosystems stands along with slavery and colonization as one of the greatest injustices of human history. It poses a moral challenge of the highest order, and imposes a duty of compensation and assistance. But the environmental constraint will be unfairly imposed on everyone; to deny it can only increase the costs of inevitable adjustment.

Above all, however, and in the shorter term, the upward spiral of African energy demand raises the problem of the exhaustion of fossil fuels. Even in the most favourable scenario, it will take the continent a century to reach the living standards of the developed world. And whether experts predict the famous peak oil production for 2010, 2020 or 2050, they all agree that time is running out. On horizons that vary but are all quite close, the same goes for other carbon fuels. Mining Africa will not escape this law of nature: whereas the Middle East, North America, Latin America and the CIS[6] can count on an oil surplus through to 2050, the African continent as a whole will switch into the position of a net importer before that date.[7]

In the intervening period, the price per barrel is bound to pursue its erratic course, fuelled by Asian demand and the chronic political tensions in the producing zones. The age in which emerging economies could meet the needs of their industrialization process with cheap fossil fuel is well and truly over: the African countries will now have to pay a high price. Africa is facing an exploding demand at a time when the price per barrel swings feverishly between $40 and $140 – as against the equivalent of $10 to $15 during the second industrial revolution, or $20 to $25 during the take-off of the Asian tigers.[8] The sub-Saharan 'energy mix', in which fossil fuels make up more than 80 per cent, is thus becoming unaffordable for the African states. The exhaustion of hydrocarbon stocks will also give rise to increasingly severe geopolitical tensions, a sign of the failure of the present energy formula of our industrial societies. Africa, sitting on an envied treasure of natural resources, will find itself, regardless, at the heart of this struggle for raw materials. Too fast a growth in energy demand, and an energy mix too skewed towards carbon fuels, risks leading to an over-rapid rise in consumption.

The transformation of the world energy landscape will happen, whether voluntarily or by constraint. Africa will not escape this.

African states, however, still in a phase of equipping themselves, have the luxury of making a choice that will affect their prospects of economic progress: either to tie their energy future to resources that are increasingly costly and in the process of disappearing, or to anchor this in renewable energies.

The world's dynamo?

The steep rise in oil prices over recent years should have pushed the African countries to promoting the shift to renewable energy sources that are abundant on the continent. But its erratic course has not made this passage easy. When oil is dear, several states subsidize petrol or gas prices in order to stave off social unrest. However rational in the short term, these policies of putting the economy on a life-saving drip have their downside. By masking the real cost of fossil fuel from the consumer, they encourage the persistence of energy-guzzling activities and delay inevitable adjustments. When the oil price fell again, investment in sustainable energy was judged too costly in relation to fossil alternatives. Even though Africa only uses a minimal fraction of its potential for hydroelectric, geothermal, wind and solar power, the oil and coal solutions, less costly in the short term, continue to be privileged.

The imperative of energy transition faces African governments and their international partners with a conflict between love and duty. How can immediate energy needs be reconciled with sustainability of supplies? Increasing production while reducing dependence on fossil fuels is a risky business, as not all options are available in the short term: an extra thermal power plant leased at high cost in order to meet urgent needs can start production in a few months, where almost ten years are needed for a large dam or geothermal plant to produce a single watt.[9] African energy needs are so great that many countries cannot afford the luxury of waiting. This is why fossil fuels represent two-thirds of sub-Saharan electricity production today, the poorest African countries being those where the cost of this production is the highest in the world – and the carbon content likewise.[10]

Though there is no easy solution to the African energy crisis, there is still nothing inevitable about it. Africa in fact has a massive energy potential, cheap and relatively non-polluting, whose exploitation will form one of the necessary pathways in the world energy revolution.

Despite what is often maintained, the high level of sunshine in most of Africa does not make solar panels the miracle solution to the continent's energy crisis. A vast network of solar power plants is indeed being planned for the Sahara, but major technological advances are still required to make this kind of project workable and profitable. Yet solar energy holds a key place in the African energy mix, by virtue of being a 'distributed energy'. Just like wind turbines and micro-hydraulic power, solar panels, ever less expensive, make it possible to electrify zones hard to connect to national networks.

As well as photovoltaic, a number of other renewable energy solutions are also operational already on a large scale.

The foremost of these is hydroelectricity. Africa harnesses less than 10 per cent of its hydroelectric potential – a fuel that is virtually free, inexhaustible and non-polluting. For a long time, a whole range of difficulties hindered the large-scale exploitation of this energy source. Big dams have been the object of a long dispute between economists and environmentalists, the latter challenging both their environmental and their social impact. In a context where capital was scarce, and the big international institutions were particularly concerned for their reputations, this dispute restricted the opportunities for financing certain large projects. Moreover, 90 per cent of the continent's exploitable hydroelectric sites lie across international boundaries, requiring complex institutional arrangements that take time to set up. Finally, the hydroelectric potential is concentrated along the continent's major rivers, often far removed from the main zones of consumption. Reducing Africa's energy gap thus implies putting an end to the fragmentation of electricity markets and the formation of regional electricity networks. This change of direction is in sight: the considerable advances made in recent decades in reducing the social and environmental impact of big dams, in establishing international bodies for the management of cross-border waterways and constructing regional electricity networks will facilitate the future exploitation of the prodigious engine of the big rivers that cross the continent. Already today, almost all the electricity consumed in Ghana and the RD Congo is hydroelectrically generated. Hydroelectricity is set to be far more than a supplementary force, rather a crucial element in the energy spectrum that will illuminate and move tomorrow's Africa.

The world environmental crisis will also redraw the map of world trade. And Africa is set to play a major role in this new model of post-oil economy: the relocation of energy-greedy industries to sources of energy that are inexpensive and low polluting will enable a reduction in production costs while considerably reducing greenhouse gas emissions. Is this utopian? Cameroon is in the process of becoming one of the leading players in world aluminium production, with the establishment of a gigantic plant belonging to the Rio Tinto group close to the port of Kribi – and requiring major expansion in this port facility. By establishing itself in south Cameroon, and offering tens of thousands of jobs there, the Australian group is seeking to take advantage of the enormous energy capacity of the rivers that cross this territory.

Africa's geothermal potential is also considerable, and on course to be harnessed.[11] This energy source is certainly not exploitable everywhere: the 'hot' layers of the earth are closer to the surface in some regions of the globe than in others. But the countries of the Rift Valley, still highly dependent on imported fossil energy, happen to be sitting on one of the world's leading geothermal sources. For a long time, the huge start-up costs of developing geothermal power discouraged African governments and foreign investors: a single deep well costs 3 million euros, and such attempts are not always fruitful. But in the wake of the third oil crisis, which saw oil prices climb 320 per cent from the start of 2003 to the middle of 2008,[12] this form of energy has seen a return to favour. With the support of international lenders, Kenya has decided to set under way a spectacular programme of growth in its electricity production, 85 per cent of which will be based on geothermal power. The African continent has the possibility of producing 9 gigawatts of electricity from this source, only 1.5 per cent of which has so far been tapped. If they manage to exploit this amazing source of energy, Djibouti, Eritrea, Ethiopia, Kenya, Uganda and Tanzania will in due course be able to export electricity to the rest of East Africa, sparing precious hard currency without the slightest damage to the environment.

Africa can also *grow* a part of its energy needs. Vegetable biomass (wood, charcoal, etc.) has been used by people as a source of heat and light for several hundred thousand years. During the century when oil was king, it was perceived as the 'energy of the poor'. The sharp rise in oil prices in the first years of the twenty-first century has triggered a lively renewal of interest in biomass. Converted to this new kind of power, vehicles of all kinds can use soy, palm oil or cane sugar as fuel, and so too can electricity generating plants. Biofuels have also been presented as one of the great solutions for combating climate change, tackling the exhaustion of fossil fuels and revolutionizing world agriculture.

This enthusiasm is somewhat misplaced: the lukewarm impact of first-generation biofuels on greenhouse gas emissions, the risks of deforestation, excessive water consumption and unfair competition with food crops in the midst of a world food crisis – all these factors rapidly overtook the passion for this new exploitation of vegetable biomass. Now that the fuss over the first generation of biofuels has calmed down, it is possible to examine more calmly the merits and possible extent of their exploitation. On condition that it is managed in a balanced way, this 'energy of the poor' can indeed be a source of enrichment for Africa without upsetting the continent's food equilibrium. But for this we must wait for a new generation of biofuels, which use whole plants as raw material instead of just seed or root crops. Certain waste products from agriculture, forestry and agricultural processing, whose energy potential is not yet exploited, would then be recuperated and converted. It is estimated that from 10 to 15 per cent of sub-Saharan Africa's electricity demand could be met by co-generation on the basis of agro-industries such as sugar and wood. Biofuels from plants like jatropha, grown where food crops cannot be cultivated, also offer opportunities for a responsible 'energy agriculture'.

Technological advances in the field of alternative energy will also make it possible before long to capture and exploit the energy potential of urban waste. The city of Durban in South Africa now generates electricity from the conversion of its refuse into methane. Besides saving on the fossil fuel that would have been needed to produce the 10 megawatts supplied from this each year, the plant for treating refuse and generating electricity is expected to save the equivalent of 8 million tonnes of CO_2 in the course of its life, or the equivalent of 16 million trips from Lille to Marseille by car. Though costly, this technology can benefit from capital contributions in the context of the 'Clean Development Mechanisms' permitted by the Kyoto treaty. This system of transfer of

technology and finance from the countries of the North to those
of the South by way of projects for reducing greenhouse gas emissions is one of the key elements in Africa's urgent energy transition.
Repaying its borrowing out of the revenue from selling carbon
credits allowed the city of Durban to invest in this state-of-the-art
technology. And yet sub-Saharan Africa has so far largely failed
to take advantage of the Clean Development Mechanism (CDM)
bonanza: in 2009, only 2 per cent of projects under this heading
were in Africa, as against 75 per cent in Asia.[13] With over 3,000
clean energy projects eligible for the CDM programme, Africa is
the new frontier for the carbon market.

One other energy source is also often neglected: that of increasing energy efficiency. Complementary to the 'production' side,
action on demand is generally less costly and quicker to put into
practice than is action on supply. Africa does not have the inertia
of some industrialized societies that suffer from a vast and highly
inefficient urban infrastructure. African cities are being built at
a time when humanity has become aware of the ecological challenges it faces, and when technological advance makes it possible
to meet the challenge of expensive energy. By replacing electric
light bulbs with LEDs, which consume only 15 per cent of the
energy of traditional bulbs, Ghana has managed to do away with
power cuts without increasing its production capacity. Senegal, for
its part, sold a credit of 120,000 tonnes of CO_2 to a carbon fund
of the World Bank, this emission being avoided by the distribution
of 1.5 million LED bulbs in the context of a wide project of rural
electrification.[14]

It may seem an ambitious gamble to put an end to Africa's
precarious energy situation at the same time as embarking on an
energy revolution. But is this leap into the unknown any less dangerous than the status quo – with its certainty of scarcity in the
middle term?

The African mega-city

As well as the stalemate of short-term energy choices, in the early
twenty-first century Africa has also become stuck in an urban
impasse.

The planet is in the process of living through the final stage of its repopulation and densification. Africans are congregating at high speed, with some of the continent's cities growing by more than 10 per cent a year. Africa will have an urban population of 1.2 billion by 2050.[15] Town-planning choices can commit societies for the long term to radically different models of life and consumption. When the lifespan of urban structures is taken into account, the nature of the growth that African cities will experience in the course of their accelerated urbanization phase will determine their energy bills, and the ways in which their inhabitants get around and live, for a long time to come.

Depending on whether these conurbations follow the model of Los Angeles or of Hong Kong, their level of consumption and emission of greenhouse gases may vary by a factor of ten or more.[16] Whereas Barcelona has a larger population than Atlanta (2.9 million against 2.5 million), it produces only 0.7 tonnes of CO_2 per inhabitant in transport emissions against 7.5 tonnes for Atlanta.[17] The main difference between the two cities is that Barcelona occupies a space of 162 sq. km, whereas Atlanta spreads its tentacles over 4,280 sq. km.

Africa is thus in the process of shaping its geography. But how is it doing this? At the moment it is building 21st-century versions of Atlanta or Los Angeles: African mega-cities stretching beyond the horizon, generating uncontrollable transport costs, unsustainable energy bills and fearsome problems of access to water supplies, sanitation and electricity. Often established close to the most fertile lands of their countries, these trample on agricultural space, mortgaging food security for many years to come. This choice may well have been made not voluntarily but simply by default, a bit at a time, in the anarchy of rural exodus and as outlying districts steadily spread out. But other paths are possible: sustainable urban solutions do exist, learned from two centuries of tortuous urbanization in Europe, America and Asia. These are particularly hard to put into effect in poor cities with a rapid growth rate, but it is precisely here that they are most important.

How is a 'sustainable' urban environment constructed? By necessity, in the case of both Hong Kong and Barcelona: a town grows denser when its population is forced to occupy a confined space. In other cases, the same effect is achieved by the choices of public authorities. It is true that greenhouse gas emissions were of little concern to Baron Haussmann or the designers of the Paris Métro. But it is no less the case that the town planning and organization of transport networks undertaken in the nineteenth century still bears its fruit today. It proves that solutions combining planning, incentive policies and legal constraints can shape the urban space and orient the behaviour of its inhabitants over the long term. Three broad groups of solutions could enable African cities to overcome the urban trajectories in which their megalopolises have been trapped – the most polluted, congested and dangerous in the world.

The first of these is to design the city in a planned way rather than passively accepting the way it grows. In a context of urban explosion, the structuring of a sustainable city cannot result simply from the spontaneous organization of its inhabitants or from property developers. No one is unaware today of the extreme violence of the favelas of Rio de Janeiro or the townships of Johannesburg, nor of the social costs that these urban ghettos involve – real pockets of misery close to Copacabana and the most fashionable gated communities of 'Jo'burg'. Only by proper structuring can African cities combat tendencies to social, racial and religious concentration, and particularly by preserving existing spaces of mixing: markets, parks, public places. It is also by the structuring of viable urban spaces that it will be possible to plan their adaptation to the consequences of climate change. Only a fraction of African cities have investigated how they might be at risk, with the result that whole districts are still being constructed in zones susceptible to flooding or at risk of enormous landslides; brick by brick, the human tragedies of tomorrow are being built. Such proactive work on the city will also make it possible to design the networks required (transport and sanitation, but also energy and information) as a function of the needs of a growing city. To design the vital arteries of urban Africa simply based on the needs of today means condemning its inhabitants to suffocate tomorrow. The situation of anarchy and permanent emergency in which the majority of African mega-cities live could lead us to believe that any forward planning is simply a pious wish: in a race against the clock, considering the future is something of a luxury. But when they house a ninth of the planet, African cities will not have the leisure to pull everything down and rebuild. Unplanned urban sprawl is so costly to rebuild that financial efforts provided today for the sustainable improvement of African cities will be eminently profitable in the long run.

The second key to a viable urban environment in Africa is mobility. Pollution, noise, accidents, millions of hours wasted in traffic jams – the mega-cities of Jakarta and São Paulo today combine all the symptoms of urban suffocation – the result of galloping urbanization and the anarchic reign of individual transport. Following this model by default, the great African conurbations of Lagos, Nairobi and Abidjan are heading for strangulation in five, ten or fifteen years' time. Yet such paralysed cities are uncompetitive in the global race for economic attractiveness.

The third group of solutions for a sustainable African city concerns housing. The war on carbon emissions is a global one by definition. But whereas in the developed world some 90 per cent of urban building is already in place today, this is true of only 40 per cent of the housing, offices and infrastructures of the great African cities of the mid-century to come. One of the most substantial ways of reducing emissions on the planet is thus to be found in the construction of 'sustainable' buildings in the populating world. At a time when the first 'positive energy' buildings are being invented, a number of African cities are seeing the proliferation, in proportion to the growth of their middle classes, of badly insulated suburban houses equipped with air-conditioners powered by individual electric generators – genuine machines for maximizing carbon emissions.

These three fields represent a colossal challenge for the cities of the poor countries in the midst of their population explosion. But these options are unlikely to be the most costly over ten, twenty or thirty years. The cities that manage to grow on less energy-greedy and polluting paths will be the most competitive ones in an age of costly energy. Those that succeed in developing sustainable mobility networks and combating spatial segregation will avoid decades of struggle against urban sprawl and pockets of poverty and criminality. The great African metropolises are fortunate to be in the process of construction at a time when the lessons from the world's existing cities are already available, as well as practical solutions that have been developed for these. But there is only a brief window of opportunity for applying the fruits of this experience. This is one of the great issues at stake for Africa, and for the whole world. Cities emit 70 per cent of all greenhouse gases. It would be unsustainable for both Africa and the world if the hundreds of millions of new city-dwellers expected on the continent in the coming decades lived in cities like Los Angeles. The time has come to construct Africa's Barcelonas, Parises and Tokyos.

19

The Hunger for Land

After the energy crisis and the urban crisis, the third awkward crossroads on the path of sustainable growth relates to the question of food security.

A new era

The first years of the twenty-first century have also been the time that humanity has come up against the end of available land and the return of hunger.

For a long time we lived in a context of agricultural overproduction. If the global food supply was badly distributed, it had at least been abundant for a number of decades. The continued rise in yields in Asia, Europe and Latin America, along with the clearing of new agricultural land, allowed supply to increase more rapidly than demand, maintaining the illusion of an inevitable fall in the prices of the principal food products. In this context, the Common Agricultural Policy, established in the late 1950s in order to increase European production, was led to subsidize taking land out of cultivation in order not to aggravate the overproduction crisis. The African countries, undergoing structural adjustment, were invited to purchase the surpluses of the North to feed the population of their rapidly expanding cities. Their imports of wheat rose more than tenfold in a few decades.[1] This policy of food provision, based on the assumptions of a sharply rising world supply and of prices remaining low in the long term, was deemed to be far less troublesome than investment in national agriculture with low productivity.

The food crisis of 2008 brutally revealed a new era. We discovered first of all a strongly growing demand. World population growth, and that of Africa in particular, continued to swell overall needs, while the improvement in the living standards of millions of Chinese and Indians pushed them towards foods richer in protein – leading to grain prices spiralling upward.[2] The energy and climate crises also played a part in this tricky food equation: the oil shock and the growing awareness of climate change provoked a strong resurgence of interest in biofuels, spurring major agricultural producers to switch from food crops towards biodiesel.

But this crisis also made us realize that agricultural supply cannot simply be extended at will. For the first time in more than thirty years, the rise in world production was outstripped in several successive years by the growth of demand. Exceptional climatic events in Australia and Ukraine reduced world production of wheat, affecting an international market that was already tight. World grain stocks, after falling for a number of years, reached in 2008 their lowest level since 1974 – the time of the last great world food crisis. In this context, agricultural raw materials became real objects of speculation. Between winter 2003 and summer 2008 the price of food commodities on the international market rose by 138 per cent. This price explosion threatened the purchasing power of European consumers. In Italy it triggered demonstrations against the increase in pasta prices. In sub-Saharan Africa, chronically short of grain, and where half the population live on less than a dollar a day, it was expressed in the return of hunger to homes that had escaped this some time before. Echoing the riots in Mexico and Port-au-Prince, African streets rumbled during winter and spring 2008: Dakar, Douala and Abidjan saw repeated demonstrations against high food prices. The 'return of hunger' was a leading news item in the press and on television. A world food shortage was proclaimed. Then came the financial crisis. Newspapers found other headlines and forgot the food disaster they had been so full of.

What conclusion should we draw from this episode? Was it a media frenzy or a justified cry of alarm? Are African capitals at risk from further food riots?

Despite the steadying of international prices in the context of the world economic crisis, the underlying causes of an upward pressure on the price of agricultural products remain, on both the supply and demand sides. We know now that the world will have to double agricultural production by 2050 in order to feed a population of 9 billion.[3] Both Europe and Asia, however, seem to be approaching limits to both cultivable land and productivity, thus reducing the scope for adjustment on a global scale. In Latin America, the extension of agricultural land comes up against the concern to preserve the Amazonian forest. Climatic hazards, which threaten to become more common across the world due to global warming, also contribute to increasing the volatility of prices. In this context of scarcity of arable soil, unprecedented on a planetary scale, the African continent must remedy its lack of agricultural production. On the one hand, international market prices will be permanently higher than in previous decades, while on the other hand, the availability of food commodities can no longer be guaranteed. The first signs of the 2008 food crisis, in fact, prompted the producer countries to take protectionist measures. There can be little doubt that, in future, the main producing regions will again reduce their exports in times of crisis, in order to ensure the food security of their own populations. An Africa suffering chronic food shortage would once more be the first affected. The model of food provision from global markets is thus no longer appropriate for an Africa that is catching up in population.

In order to ensure its food security, Africa will have to increase its production five times by 2050 – starting right away.[4] Such an increase will demand a real leap forward, akin to the 'green revolution' – born in Mexico in the 1950s – that enabled India to escape famine in the following decade. But Africa cannot be satisfied simply with reproducing an identical sharp take-off in productivity. Despite the size of the leap in productivity required, the strictly productivist choices that enabled European, American and Asian farmers to increase their yields cannot serve as a model for their African counterparts. The agronomist Michel Griffon is right therefore to emphasize that Africans will have to conduct a 'doubly green' revolution in agricultural productivity – based on two pillars, one strictly productivist and the other ecological. By having arrived too late at nature's mighty feast, Africa has no other choice but to combine economic and demographic catching-up with a transition in energy policy that has no equivalent in developmental history and with a 'doubly green revolution' that is equally unprecedented.

The problem is that, just as the fluctuating price of oil impedes the energy transition, so the swings in food prices that have marked recent years do not give African agriculture an incentive to take this turn. The upward spiral of prices on international markets may have been violent for a continent suffering a chronic shortage of food, but it offered the hope that a change in direction was at last in sight, drawing Africa away from the shores of dependence. African food products, which had long been subject to the unfair competition of subsidized exports from the countries of the North, suddenly became once again competitive. Local production prices followed the rise in those of imports, and investment that was unthinkable a few years earlier became profitable. Massive irrigation programmes were envisaged by governments concerned about their citizens' food security. Still more encouraging, the farmers we met in the Senegal River valley at the height of the food crisis were beginning to invest in their holdings with a view to benefiting from the rise in prices, as a sign of better days to come.

Then came the world economic crisis and the bursting of the 'food bubble'. The relative – and undoubtedly temporary – fall in the prices of basic food products was a welcome respite for the countries most severely affected by the food crisis. But this easing delayed many structural changes that were necessary for the reorientation of African agriculture. Some of the less profitable investments that had been envisaged were put aside. The effects of the economic crisis on state budgets forced countries to reduce their agricultural ambitions in order to meet more urgent needs. To lessen the shock for the most deprived sections of their population, a number of these countries had once more to buy the products most urgently needed on international markets – falling prey to the old demons of dependency. These emergency expenditures were made at the cost of long-term investment, which alone will allow Africa permanently to escape the spectre of food shortage.

The breadbasket of humanity?

Will the earth manage to feed a population of 9 billion in forty years' time, an overall increase of more than 2 billion, including

1 billion in sub-Saharan Africa? The challenge is on an enormous scale. Yet analysis of the increase in the needs and production capacities of the different regions of the world shows that a narrow path does exist for the food security of humanity – a path that passes through Africa.

According to FAO research, Asia, having brought all possible land into cultivation and pressed productivity gains to a maximum, will show a substantial food deficit by 2050. Even by cultivating all the available space on its territory, and making the ambitious assumption of a 50 per cent increase in yields, a shortfall of 1 billion tonnes of cereals will still have to be filled in order to feed the Asian population, i.e. twice the present Chinese harvest of wheat and rice.[5] What parts of the world can supply such an increase in global production? Not Europe or the United States, which already use almost the whole of their available agricultural land, and whose intensive agriculture does not allow us to envisage great leaps in productivity. Latin America and Africa are the only continents where there are still substantial reserves of agricultural land – 80 per cent of the world's total – and major gains in productivity to be made.[6] It is on these portions of the planet, therefore, that the capacity to feed the extra 2 billion human beings expected over the next four decades will depend.

How can we ever imagine that Africa, where 400 million people today suffer chronic malnutrition, can in due course become one of the planet's breadbaskets? This prospect, however, lies on the critical path of world food security. If it can be risked, it is because Africa is on the eve of a great upswing in its agriculture.

Several Asian and Gulf countries are not mistaken. Since the turn of the century, major agribusiness companies, speculative and sovereign funds have taken an interest in African land and its productive potential. Land that a few years ago still had no marketable value is now leased or purchased by foreign investors in lots of several hundred thousand – even million – hectares.[7] Whether to ensure the long-term food security of states in the Arabian peninsula, to invest in the production of raw materials whose prices are predicted to rise, or to push forward the frontiers of international speculation in landed property, there are plenty of buyers – but they risk importing into Africa the food insecurity of more affluent societies. Between 2004 and 2008, more than 2.5 million hectares were leased to these new-style farmers by the governments of Ethiopia, Ghana, Mali, Mozambique, Sudan,

Tanzania and Madagascar. The Malagasy president decided to
meet the country's debts by conceding 1.3 million hectares to the
Korean company Daewoo, more than the whole surface area of
Lebanon, for the production of palm oil and maize – destined for
export to Korea. This one-sided contract, which was cancelled by
his successor, contributed to the wave of popular discontent that
overthrew him in April 2009. The government of Sudan – where a
large section of the population, settled in refugee camps, survives
thanks to food aid from the international community – has done
deals with Saudi companies, a public fund in Abu Dhabi and the
Syrian government.

Shocking as it might appear, this wave of purchases reveals the
growing value of African arable land now that the pioneering wave
in Asia has come to an end. It is true that a number of these agreements are based on the myth of an African Eldorado of unoccupied
land. In actual fact, the system of land ownership in sub-Saharan
Africa is very varied and often unregistered. The fact that farmers
are not formally the owners of their soil does not mean that they
have not acquired rights to it through using it. Some of the land
being leased out is actually cultivated by peasants or nomadic
stockraisers with no written property title. The arrival of foreign
buyers in territories that are partly occupied thus risks increasing
tensions over land, or depriving whole villages of the resources
on which their food security depends.[8] But if not all of Africa is a
space of unoccupied virgin land over which no one has rights, the
continent's reserves of cultivable land are still considerable.

For a European used to the mixed farming of much of our
countryside, an aerial survey of Central African territory from the
capital Bangui to the northeast of the country is a striking experience: scattered forests stretch over the horizon, punctuated here
and there by deserted clearings. Dwellings are strung along the
few earth roads that cross these spaces, lost in an immensity of
green in which there is no shortage of fertile land. The land actually cultivated in sub-Saharan Africa represents only a quarter of
that potentially usable for agriculture.[9] According to certain estimates, the combined agricultural potential of Angola and Zambia
is equivalent to that of Argentina, while the territory of the DR
Congo could feed as many inhabitants as India. Such compari-
sons are naturally only theoretical. It would be risky to cultivate
all the land potentially exploitable, as this would mean clearing

forests that are indispensable for regulating the environment. The exploitation of available land will also mean the relocation of large numbers of people in sub-Saharan territories, which will not be without its difficulties. It remains, nonetheless, that the critical path to planetary food security will involve the steady improvement of additional areas for agriculture in Africa – compatible with the preservation of the continent's major forest regions.

But extension of cultivated land will be far from enough in itself to feed the continent's growing population. It will have to be accompanied by a simultaneous take-off in yields. The productivity of a sub-Saharan farmer is about 200 times less than that of his European counterpart. If ecological conditions for agriculture south of the Sahara place the European level of yields out of reach, an increase in productivity represents nonetheless a considerable resource for world production. Despite major geographical disparities, and contrary to a widespread idea, the continent does have tremendous water resources that are insufficiently exploited. It also benefits from major reserves of labour-power. Why then has this productivity take-off not already happened? Can we believe this will be possible tomorrow, even though several competent agronomists have devoted their careers to it in vain over the past decades? The simple answer is that the conditions for take-off have not yet been met.

One of the limiting conditions on African agriculture, in fact, is that, over most of the continent, water is only available in a very haphazard fashion. The improvement of land thus requires the construction of dams and irrigated enclosures, costly both to create and to operate. Such expenditure, however, is only profitable above a certain level of demand and price for the goods produced. This threshold effect has long placed a substantial barrier on the intensification of an African agriculture that lacked solvent and structured markets. The weakness of infrastructure linking the cities to the countryside did not enable markets to organize themselves in such a way that the continent's countryside could supply its cities, with the result that African foodstuffs found little outlet apart from subsistence production or small-scale trade. As we have seen, international prices for agricultural raw materials, kept artificially low by subsidies from the countries of the North, penalized African products and thus limited the incentive to invest. These historical constraints that weighed on the African market explain why only between 4 and 7 per cent of arable land in sub-Saharan Africa is irrigated, and why only a very small proportion of farmers use fertilizers.

The new world environmental situation, and the increasing density of population in Africa, have today turned these determining factors of African agricultural productivity around. Those commentators who were disturbed in winter 2008 by the rising prices of food crops forgot to make clear how much sub-Saharan farmers had suffered from the low levels of agricultural prices for several decades. The perspective of a long-term increase in prices for agricultural products is excellent news for the continent, which will in future have at its disposal the largest exploitable agricultural surfaces on the planet.[10] With imported foodstuffs increasingly dear, African products will again become attractive for export, turning investments that were recently still unprofitable into lucrative ones. The continent's cities will also turn more to local markets for their supplies. The accelerated growth of the urban population, which presently suffers from the increasing prices on international markets, will ensure almost unlimited outlets for regional products: in Africa, as elsewhere on the planet, urbanization represents the future of agriculture.

The substantial improvement in road networks in the course of the last decade, and the patient work of organizing small producers, remove two major obstacles to the structuring of a regional agricultural market. Advances in agronomy also enable us to foresee the possibility of a far better balance between increasing productivity and protecting the environment. The techniques of agro-ecology, which privilege organic procedures over chemical and mechanical ones, make it possible to increase yields without degrading ecosystems. Their beneficial effects on the soil have been proved in Latin America over several decades, and they are gradually being imported to Africa – with already promising effects. At long last, African agriculture is emerging from two decades of neglect. Lenders of international funds, realizing how agricultural investment lagged behind in the period of structural adjustment, debt repayments and social programmes, are falling over themselves today with projects for increasing African production. As we have seen, foreign actors are also prepared to invest major sums in sub-Saharan agribusiness. If some of the projects envisaged present obvious political and environmental risks, there is no doubt that foreign investors can play a transforming role in the modernization of some forms of agriculture, by providing capital, technologies and the access to markets that have been wanting for several decades.

Now that the conditions for a take-off of sub-Saharan agriculture are at last in place, the continent is set to play a far more important role than it does presently in the new world agricultural economy. Newly on the radar of the international community after several decades of being forgotten, Africa's reserves of land and productivity represent one of the solutions to the global environmental crisis.

20

The Human Struggle

Sub-Saharan Africa is also caught in a fourth stalemate with the unsustainable exploitation of its ecological resources. Embarked on a race against poverty, the continent is running down its natural heritage at a frantic pace – totally inappropriate at a time of global environmental crisis.

Collective ecological suicide

Central Africa's forest capital makes this region one of the great regulators of global climate. With a total of some 220 million hectares, the forests of the Congo basin make up the second-largest forest reserve on the planet, after Amazonia. At a time when global emissions are out of control, this gigantic machine for capturing carbon dioxide forms one of the essential links in the world climate equilibrium. The Gabon forest alone stores four times more greenhouse gas than France produces each year. Yet deforestation rates are higher in Africa than on any other continent.

There is nothing surprising in this: wood represents around 80 per cent of African energy consumption. Rural populations, only a tiny fraction of whom have access to electricity, are forced to cut trees close to their dwellings as fuel for cooking: three-quarters of African households use wood or charcoal. This toll on the tropical forest was sustainable fifty years ago, but is no longer so at a time when population density is rapidly increasing. Along with the extension of agricultural surfaces, it is the primary cause of deforestation in sub-Saharan Africa. The DR Congo, which holds over half the African tropical forest, will see its population rise from 65 million to 125 million in the next twenty years. Lacking satisfactory alternatives, the Congolese population will continue to take what they need to feed themselves – to the detriment of major environmental balances. Once again, local and global problems come together here: the continent has already seen its forests reduced by 10 per cent between 1990 and 2005, or an annual loss of over 4 million hectares, i.e. more than half the total decline in the world's forest cover.[1]

Africa's biodiversity is also being extinguished at a great speed, as virgin land is occupied and the rural environment grows more crowded. Eight of the thirty-four global diversity hot spots are located in Africa, attesting to both remarkable richness and great vulnerability. A quarter of the 4,700 species of mammal catalogued on the planet are found in Africa. If the ecosystems that house this biodiversity degrade in the same way as in the more developed parts of the planet, an irreplaceable genetic capital will disappear – a capital from which humanity will have to draw responses to the health and agricultural challenges of future centuries. The hunting of wild animals and the degradation of their ecosystems threaten the survival of several species. Bush meat forms an essential nutritional supplement for poor populations. In times of economic crisis, in particular, fish, monkeys, antelopes and snakes are the only source of protein for millions of Africans. In one village in southern Cameroon, our host explained that each year he went a bit further into the forest to hunt. In the last few years, several species have disappeared from the places he stalked.

In zones of political instability, these daily losses of small game are accompanied by regular raids on nature reserves. In Chad, we were told that the guards in a wildlife park deserted by tourists themselves escorted poachers – tired of risking their skins in fighting them. In the Central African Republic, elephants are hunted with automatic weapons by men who arrive in pick-ups from neighbouring Sudan. At this pace, Central Africa could see elephants disappear from its territory in only a few years. The International Union for Nature Conservation estimates that more than 700 listed animals in Africa are threatened in the short term with extinction. Africa is therefore today one of the main actors in the erosion of global biodiversity.

The planet's lung?

Yet there is nothing unavoidable about this historical mistake. Africa's natural capital forms one of the continent's greatest treasures, and its value will only increase as the planet suffers the effects of the global environmental crisis. At a time when humanity is becoming aware of the value of biodiversity and the importance of forests in climate regulation, Africa has much to gain from acting as guardian of a natural heritage essential to human survival. If the treasure this represents is increasingly evident to the eyes of both Africans and their overseas partners, a race against the clock has started to find concrete incentives that will allow its preservation.

Very soon, a motley crew of actors will descend on the African forests. Contrary to the practices of recent decades, the money they invest will not be used to cut trees down but to preserve them. This development is a step in the right direction: if humanity considers the carbon storage capacity and genetic capital that the African ecosystems contain as global public goods, then their preservation deserves reward. Some pioneering countries such as Norway already devote several hundred million dollars of their development aid to the protection of tropical forests, aware that the countries that shelter these will not be able by themselves to pay the price of preserving the global climate. But what is the value of placing a 'carbon sink' such as the African forests at the disposal of humanity? If it is financially more profitable today to cut down a hectare of forest than to preserve it in a natural state or manage it in a sustainable fashion, this is precisely because no value has yet been attributed to the service of climate protection rendered by the forest. We know that this will demand financial flows well above the capacities of Norway or the major environmental NGOs. The time has thus come to move to a higher level in payment for the ecological services rendered by the world's forests: this is the price of global climate equilibrium.

It was believed for a long time that the only way to preserve such natural spaces as the tropical forest was to put them 'under wraps' by creating untouchable nature reserves. Today the model has changed: it is certainly essential to make sanctuaries of particularly vulnerable biological zones, but this is not a credible response on the scale of tens of millions of hectares. Trade in tropical woods represents 6 per cent of the GDP of the Central African countries, and 10 per cent of their foreign trade. It would be foolish to think that these countries will decide on their own to give up the income from their inheritance. Even if states agree to protect these spaces, the degradation of forests due to population pressure alone in the last twenty years shows that even putting millions of hectares of virgin forest under strict control would not guarantee their protection.

An alternative approach is that of seeing forest protection and exploitation as complementary rather than opposed. In Gabon, Cameroon, the Central African Republic and Congo, practices of sustainable forest management enable the essential part of their carbon capture capacity to be preserved. These projects unite all parties concerned in a common effort: forest operators, local populations, public authorities, wood certifying agencies and development banks. They build compromises between the interests of these different actors, combining policies of creating protected areas with the sustainable management of exploited forests. But this procedure comes at a cost for the exploiters, who are responsible for listing all the trees in their allotted sector and only felling a limited number per hectare; this is also a cost for the public authority charged with supervision, which has to check that management plans are respected, particularly by the use of satellite images.

International mechanisms are in the course of development to compensate for some of the loss of profit on the part of countries that choose to struggle against the degradation of their ecosystems.[2] These are based on setting a value on the stocks of forest carbon, estimated in relation to an alternative use of forested regions. Compensation is then granted in proportion to the tonnes of carbon not released into the atmosphere thanks to the preservation of forest cover. These mechanisms are still in a pilot phase, but will have to be rapidly generalized and extended to carbon stored in the soil, or even in the immense African savannah. Their financing can then be ensured by world funds, either based on public resources or tied to the vast carbon market being formed – worth a total of $126 billion in 2008. In the first case, a part of the receipts from this ecological taxation will have to support African countries in their efforts to preserve the carbon storage capacity of their ecosystems. In the second case, investors will be able to finance agro-ecological projects, projects of preservation or sustainable management of the forest with the aim of producing carbon credits, with a tonne of carbon preserved giving a right to credits exchangeable on the international carbon market.

This 'market' in avoided deforestation and storage of carbon in the soil could represent several billion euros in revenue for Central Africa – enough, for example, to finance the energy transition of its members by way of hydroelectric dams on the region's rivers. The environmental rent that payment for ecological services may ultimately provide for certain African states will not only bring international resources over a very long term, but also allow the preservation of all the *local* benefits of the ecosystems thus pre-served – including in the struggle against desertification, regulation of water supplies and the preservation of a tourist potential that is still only little exploited. It could become one of the essential motors of economic growth for Africa in the post-oil era.

A new model

Traditional economics taught us to plan development by consid-ering nature as abundant and free. This is now over: the form of growth based on short-term choices has foundered. Our econo-mies will now function under strong physical constraints. The climate, energy and food crises that are shaking our world in the early twenty-first century call for growth models to be rethought from scratch. The societies of sub-Saharan Africa cannot escape this as they move into economic take-off. They will also – even especially – have to go beyond conflicts between economic growth and availability of natural resources. Africa needs growth. Africa needs energy. But Africa, whose population would suffer most from an absence of global climatic regulation, also needs a stable environment.

Ecology was long conceived as a political ideology of struggle on behalf of nature. The global environmental crisis, whose out-lines are gradually becoming more clear, shows that this current of thought is more fundamentally a practical struggle on behalf of people. In the face of its premises we are all ecologists. This new ecology calls for courageous choices and a break with past models, in order to make the wellbeing of men and women today compatible with that of the men and women of tomorrow. Africans have no other choice but to wage this ecological battle – and their international partners with them. Then humanity will emerge from this crisis strengthened, enriched by a 21st-century model of development.

Part Eight

The Newcomer at the Feast of Nations

A forgotten continent in the twentieth century, Africa is now heading for a key position. Africa's billion will not be able to escape this 'recentring' on the world stage, in the same way as it was previously forced to accept a spectator role in the affairs of the previous century. The centrifugal forces that inspire this movement originate both in the upheavals that are shaking the continent and in the great structural movements of our planet.

Part Eight

The Newcomer at the Court of Nations

21

Africa Courted

A second independence

Let us consider for a moment the period that has just ended. It is hard to imagine a more subordinate and asymmetrical relationship than the one that tied the African nations to the great powers of the twentieth century – from its beginning to its end.

The colonial years were a time of one-sided and clearly possessive relationships. The European nations, in the full throes of industrialization, armament and subsequent reconstruction, experienced a vital need for raw materials. Africa, cut up into slices at the Berlin Congress of 1885, was therefore a continent to exploit according to the logic of the colonial pact: an imperial monopoly. But not only that: in the race for hearts and minds, missionaries and schoolteachers saw eye to eye. The 'civilizing mission' of the French empire under Jules Ferry, a relic of Rudyard Kipling's 'white man's burden', was to enlighten this part of humanity that had remained in ignorance for too long. A continent to exploit or to civilize, Africa was the passive 'object' of colonial designs. Only the kingdom of Ethiopia, which Menelik II and Haile Selassie managed to save from Italian control, seemed to escape this fate.

Everything changed with independence, but simply so that everything could remain as before. For the happy years of African emancipation were also those of the Cold War. Scarcely freed from their colonial masters, the African nations were forced to accept either Western, Russian or Chinese protection, swinging in a way from one empire to another. Ethiopia, a founder member of the

League of Nations that had triumphantly resisted the colonial episode, did not escape this patronage once it was deprived of its enlightened monarchs. Fearing the consequences of direct confrontation, it was on a more convenient battlefield that the great powers decided to fight – with proxies. Angolans, Mozambicans and Congolese still bear today the scars of a global war that was cold only in Moscow and Washington. As strategic pieces on a planetary chessboard, the room for manoeuvre of African leaders was restricted to changing camps or playing a double game – something that certain of their number did with considerable skill. Up to the fall of the Soviet empire, the logic of blocs locked African nations into relationships no less one-sided and subordinate to their protectors than those of the colonial era. Punished for their 'betrayals' – on the lines of Sékou Touré's Guinea that committed the offence of rejecting the offer of alliance with France – African leaders also saw their loyalty rewarded.

For the years of independence and 'cold' war were also the decades of the post-war boom. While Americans and Soviets fought each other through their Angolan and Cuban substitutes, European and North American societies emerged into the era of high consumption. Just like the industrialization, arms and reconstruction races of the first half of the century, the consumer revolution of these decades proved greedy for African raw materials. From Mobutu to Bokassa, via the Nigerian generals and P. W. Botha, presents, backhanders and other little deals with the continent's ruling classes enabled the great powers to continue the colonial pact by other means. As pawns in the Cold War, backyards of the neocolonial patchwork, the African nations thus remained essentially just objects of international politics. Relationships with their overseas partners remained marked by the seal of imbalance.

Then came the fall of the Berlin wall. As we have seen, from one day to the next the African nations lost any strategic interest in the eyes of their former allies. In a burst of solidarity, Europe and the United States dispatched cohorts of aid workers to bandage their wounded and bury their dead. Too occupied with refloating the countries of Eastern Europe, they let development aid fall by half. Above all, however, after the model of their governments, Western companies disengaged from a bankrupt continent, making way for the UN blue helmets and the NGOs. From the Security Council to television news, Africa in the 1990s was marginalized and became an object of concern, a continent to be treated with emergency aid – and also to be closely watched, a role assumed by the twin sisters of Washington[1] and the Club de Paris.[2]

In the 2000s Africa has embarked on a new era, one that closes the overly long chapter of decolonization. Largely free from debt, its states are earning ever greater sums. Steadily casting off the oversight of the IMF and the World Bank, African nations are taking back control of their economic policies. Courted by the new actors on the international chessboard, they are free to form political alliances with whomever they choose. For too long objects of foreign policy, they are now becoming full subjects of international relations.

The death of Omar Bongo, the doyen of African leaders and shadowy godfather of Françafrique, is a symbol of this page that has turned. On both sides of the Mediterranean, a new generation is changing the face of Africa's relations with its former colonial powers. For the new leaders who have never known French, British or Portuguese Africa, there is no longer anything natural about these relationships. The Chinese breakthrough in Africa, more a consequence than a cause of this change of era, reminds those who would prefer to forget that the continent is no longer anyone's private reserve. Freed from the control of the colonial powers, the superpowers of the Cold War and the Bretton Woods institutions, the African nations are thus masters of their own destinies more than ever before. At the dawn of the twenty-first century, sub-Saharan Africa can finally savour the first fruits of its independence.

African desires

This new African independence – the real independence, we are tempted to say – is accompanied by a change in the continent's status, after it was 'forgotten' for a while. Long perceived as marginal, it is becoming once more a strategic piece on the great planetary chessboard. Sub-Saharan Africa, with its 1.8 billion inhabitants, will have considerable effects on the planet as a whole – in terms of migration, security, environment and trade. This share of challenges and opportunities will constitute so many decisive issues of public policy.

Africa's natural resources are coveted by all in the early twenty-first century. In the age of world environmental crisis, this phenomenon can only grow in scale. There is no need here to repeat the importance of African land in world food production, or the value of the carbon sinks of the Congo basin forests. But it may still be useful to recall that, until the emergence of a post-oil economy, Africa's 'black gold' will be increasingly crucial for supplying the world's major economies. The oilfields of the Gulf of Guinea already provide 15 per cent of US oil consumption, on a level with Saudi Arabia. If we believe American information services, this figure could pass 25 per cent by 2015.[3] China already meets a third of its needs with African oil. Manganese, copper, uranium, coltan, bauxite, zinc and gold: the mineral assets in which the African subsoil is so rich are also increasingly important, particularly in this time of take-off of the great emerging economies. One study has assessed their value at $50 trillion.[4] Beyond this staggering figure, one thing is certain – Africa will remain in this century a source of desirable natural riches.

If sub-Saharan Africa is strategic for its exports to more developed countries, it will also be so for the market it provides – a vast space of 1.8 billion consumers. The African population of tomorrow will have to feed themselves, house themselves, move around and communicate. Chinese exporters have already grasped the opportunities that this new market offers, stimulated by Africa's growing population. From textiles through toys to electronics, machinery and household goods, inexpensive products 'made in China' open the gates of consumption to millions of Africans too poor to have access to European imports.

Africa's population is also creating an exponential demand for services: by 2012 the continent will have 500 million mobile phone subscribers, or more than the entire population of the European Union.[5] It is now in Africa that European operators see their turnover growing most rapidly. Heedless of the financial crisis raging across the planet, banking services have also continued their explosive growth in the late 2000s, as Africans found themselves able to save. Given that only 20 per cent of sub-Saharan households as yet use banks, the potential of the African savings market is a colossal one. Combining these two opportunities, entrepreneurs of 'mobile banking' have discovered a profitable niche:[6] in 2006, 2 per cent of Zambia's GDP was paid for in this way. No operator can fail to adopt this innovation, now also reaching Europe. Education, health, leisure – the continent's emerging middle class is steadily expanding its demand for services, opening a range of opportunities for African and foreign businesses. But this continent in the throes of catching up is also a space for construction. From ports to dams, via roads and fibre-optic 'highways', equipping the continent represents a market of 10 billion euros or more a year.

Its attractiveness, therefore, is not simply in the long term – 'when Africans get rich'. This is the lesson of the formidable paradox of savings distribution on a world scale in the course of this decade of financial torment.[7] Though more fragile in appearance, African financial markets have turned out to be both more profitable and more secure, since the beginning of the century, than the markets of the North, thanks in particular to the inherent profitability of the projects they finance. Should we be surprised? Any industry that wants its investments to be productive and its loans repaid must orient its activity towards the zones where the great majority of its customers will be found, both today and tomorrow – zones experiencing high rates of growth. The developed economies no longer have a monopoly on growth, or the developing ones a monopoly of risk. Anyone who doubts this need only turn to the business section of their favourite newspaper: the greatest losses suffered by several European banks in recent years were not in Asia, Latin America or Africa, but rather in the United States – between the Enron scandal, the bankruptcy of Lehmann Brothers and the incredible swindle of Bernard Madoff. A study carried out by the organizers of the World Economic Forum in Davos, moreover, classed Namibian and South African banks as among the most secure in the world, ahead of French banks (in 19th position, i.e. two places behind Namibia and four places behind South Africa), and well above the United States (in 40th position, behind a good number of African countries due to the chain of bankruptcies in the course of the year).[8]

As well as an economic partner, Africa will also be sought-after as a diplomatic one. In an international system where the big issues facing humanity arise on a planetary scale, no unilateral response to collective problems is possible. From trade to climate negotiations, from the UN General Assembly to the Human Rights Council, the votes of the forty-seven states of sub-Saharan Africa

count. Indeed, as democracy makes headway across the world, so
the principle of 'one person one vote' advances, making the power
monopoly of a handful of Northern states ever less legitimate. The
'democratization' of the instances of world governance is under
way, making a greater place for the regions historically under-rep-
resented. Would it be at all conceivable to manage world affairs
without China (population 1.3 billion today, 1.4 billion in 2050)
or India (1.2 billion today, 1.6 billion in 2050)? What about sub-
Saharan Africa, then, where the population of 1.8 billion expected
in forty years' time will be nearly double that of the United States
and Europe combined? Behind the crisis of representation of world
decision-making bodies lies a crisis of legitimacy, which reduces
the effectiveness of their resolutions.

The organizers of the high-level summit charged with responding to the global economic crisis were not mistaken: the twenty
countries invited to London in spring 2009 included in particular
the Chinese, Indian and South African presidents. The sharehold-
ers of the World Bank, for their part, have decided to grant an
additional administrative seat to Africa, which will give the developing countries a majority of seats on this decision-making board
– accused in the 1990s of being in the pocket of the industrialized
countries, and the United States in particular. In the many forums
of world governance where they sit, African representatives will
thus be led to take far more responsibility in the management
of international affairs. Evidence of this epochal change is that,
since the turn of the century, the emerging countries have greatly
increased their diplomatic missions in African capitals. The continent has never hosted so many ambassadors on its territory.

Independent and courted, sub-Saharan Africa cannot long leave
the old world powers indifferent – unless these are struck by an
incurable blindness. Its silent transformation will inevitably imply
a sea-change in the relationships that it has with its partners. The
incestuous proximity of colonial control lies in the past, as well
as the military patronage and financial trusteeship that followed.
A one-sided dialogue, since it was asymmetrical and forced, has
finally turned into a genuine exchange of views – and a negotiation that can only be based on equality. As a journalist for *Jeune
Afrique* wrote about China's flirtations with the new arrival in the
concert of nations, 'the time of arrogance is over'.[9]

A United States of Africa

If it is up to Africa's partners to take note of the opportunities offered by the continent's strategic emergence, it is up to Africans to seize them. The architecture of world governance, as it is shaping up in the early part of this century, rests on a series of forums and negotiation processes designed to draw up collective standards (on climate, trade, etc.). This liberated and sought-after Africa, now subject and master of its own fate, thus has no other choice but to endow itself with the institutional capacities that will enable it to defend its interests there and exercise its collective responsibilities.

A united Africa could become one of the major forces in international relations, along with Europe, China and India. Yet its component nations, so long seeking to assert their independence, are very far from a like-minded group; they act separately from one another, and consequently are not very audible in global negotiations and governance forums. Africa in fact suffers a great handicap: whereas, in terms of population, it is more or less in the same league as India or China, it lacks institutional unity. This fragmentation prevents it from asserting its due weight in international negotiations.

Profound questions remain regarding the way in which Africa will organize in order to tackle its internal challenges and defend its interests internationally. Will Africans remain loyal to their colonial political structures – the former British colonies playing the card of Anglo-Saxon solidarity and the French colonies that of the francophone community? Will they be convinced by Chinese 'soft power' and decide to follow the twenty-first century's leading emerging nation? Or by an ambitious and visionary offer of a Euro-African space of peace and prosperity? Will regional logics prevail instead, forming as many diplomatic blocs as there are African economic communities? Or will the continent mark its rise in world affairs in the form of a political organization of its own? None of this is yet decided.

Some African countries have indeed managed to mobilize effectively in certain periods, testifying to the strength of unity. In the course of the cotton saga, Burkina Faso, Benin and Mali waged a

real diplomatic offensive against the subsidies that the countries of
the North granted their producers. But, apart from such occasional
episodes, the individual African nations find it hard to make their
voices heard in the concert of nations. South Africa and Nigeria
have indeed imposed themselves in the last few years as serious
claimants to a permanent seat on the UN Security Council, in the
company of Brazil and Japan. This testifies to the distance travelled in half a century, but raises a new question: will these fortunate two manage to speak for the continent as a whole? After half
a century of monopoly of international governance by the world's
great powers, the expansion of the G-8 carries a new risk: that of
a confiscation of the voices of the 'South' by the club of emerging
countries. It cannot be taken for granted that the leg-up offered to
Africa in the major UN bodies, in the form of a South African or
Nigerian seat, meets the legitimate demand for participation of a
people who will soon make up a fifth of humanity.

Within Africa itself, even if the comforting myth is still maintained, the successive failures of pan-Africanism in the twentieth century have produced a certain disenchantment. They have
left a tangle of monetary, customs and economic communities:
UEMOA, CEMAC, CEDEAO, CEEAC, COMESA, EAC, SACU,
COI, SADC, IGAD, UFM, CEN-SAD;[10] despite the merits of some
of these bodies, the sheer number of communities harms the very
objective of regional cooperation that each of them is supposed to
promote – a cooperation that is essential for tackling the impending challenges.

It may be, nonetheless, that the wind is in the process of changing. From the beginning of the century, in fact, a wave of hope has
been inspiring African elites. With the end of apartheid, everything again seems possible. The New Economic Partnership for
Development (NEPAD), despite all its hesitations and the meagre-
ness of its achievements to date, is evidence of a new faith in the
private sector. An African political structure is emerging – further
evidence of this also being the growing assertiveness of the African
Union. This new entity is registering its first successes in the field of
peacekeeping and mediation. In Darfur, a joint UN-African Union
mission is in place – something unthinkable only ten years ago.
The Union is also asserting its own choices, sometimes open to
question. It decided in 2009 to support the Sudanese president
Omar el-Bechir, despite his being the target of an international

arrest warrant. African countries also met together in Addis Ababa in 2007 to reach a common position on Chinese penetration on the continent. They appointed a single spokesperson to make their voices heard at the climate negotiations in Copenhagen in December 2009. This new regional organization is a step in the right direction: the economic growth under way, the various crises within the continent and the rising power of outside actors can only increase the need for coordination, as well as the cost of a lack of it.

Step by step, therefore, Africa seems to be taking the road of integration. It now has a conference of heads of state that meets at least once a year at the organization's headquarters; an Executive Council of ministers; a Commission; a pan-African parliament; an Economic, Social and Cultural Council; an African Court of Human Rights; and a Court of Justice. The ambition of the African Union matches the need for regional cooperation. European unity was not made in a day, but is still an ongoing process, and it will be a long road towards a United States of Africa.

22

Africa's New Exploiters?

Certain actors on the international stage have lost nothing from this change of direction. With the continent's place reassessed in their foreign and trade policies, they are hurrying to build ties with the African nations. Despite the clumsiness of first love, they are seducing Africa with talk of its future, of mutual interests and a road to take together. The relationships they are forming with Africa challenge the continent's traditional partners. Two years after the third Sino-African summit was held in Beijing, India organized its first summit with Africa, South Korea its second, and Japan its fourth cooperation forum. The proliferation of these 'strategic partnerships' attests to the new attraction Africa exerts. If there can be no doubt that Africa has entered the world stage, the diplomatic chronicle of the past decade also shows that the world has entered Africa.

Chinafrique

The 'Chinese eruption' on the continent has led to a great deal of ink being spilled on both sides of the Atlantic.[1] The third summit of Sino-African cooperation held in autumn 2006, a regular high mass of Chinafrique, managed to bring representatives of forty-eight African states to Beijing – including forty-one heads of state – thus revealing a major development in international relations.

The relationship between China and Africa is certainly nothing new. The Chinese like to remind their European counterparts that their first connections with the continent preceded the Portuguese explorations. A seaborne expedition under the Ming dynasty, led by the Chinese captain Zheng He, coasted African shores in the fifteenth century and reached the southernmost point of the continent some decades before Bartolomeu Dias 'discovered' the Cape of Good Hope.

But what is striking in relationships between Beijing and the African capitals is, above all, their remarkable continuity. China and the first few independent African countries were together at the Bandung conference in 1955, before the successive waves of African independence expanded the ranks of a Third World that was largely Afro-Asian. From this time on, thousands of Chinese agronomists and 'barefoot doctors' supported the young African nations freshly freed from the colonial yoke. To keep its place in relation to the Western powers and its Russian neighbour, China supplied aid at this time to countries that were better-off than it was in terms of GDP per capita. Zhou Enlai's 'African safari' in December 1963 and January 1964 sealed this new partnership. It was on this occasion that Mao's prime minister announced, in a speech delivered in Ghana, eight founding principles of Chinese cooperation with the African nations – including equality between partners, the pursuit of mutual benefit, and respect for national sovereignty – three principles that continue to mark the rhetoric of Sino-African relations today. Each of these symbolized a break with the one-sided relationships that the African countries had long had with their Western partners. In its exchanges with Africa, in fact, China did not have a 'white man's burden' to cast off, but could present itself as a developing country as well, their own alter ego. It came to Africa to do business, under a 'win–win' sign. This posture, both humble and eminently practical, led many Africans to see Chinese cooperation as less hypocritical than the supposedly disinterested Western economic aid. The absence of political strings on Chinese development aid, contrasting with the requirements for democracy and good governance from European and North American states, likewise remains one of the hallmarks of the Chinese offer.[2] It lies at the heart of what has been called the 'Beijing consensus',[3] as opposed to the 'Washington consensus' and its lists of conditions, often viewed as doctrinaire.

The same continuity is also seen in the effectiveness of Chinese aid, celebrated by several African leaders. After the World Bank refused in 1973 to finance the Tranzam, a railway line to link Lusaka with Dar es Salaam – a length of some 1,600 kilometres – China agreed to build this new track. Begun the same year, the project was finished a year ahead of schedule in 1976, thanks to the ferocious work of 15,000 workers and engineers imported from China. Recently, when the China Road and Bridge Corporation launched its army of workers on asphalting several thousand kilometres of road in Ethiopia, it broke the isolation of the great northern plateaus in just a few years – something that the major development bodies had not achieved in several decades. The 'Chinese road', as it is sometimes called, has also connected other formerly inaccessible zones, permitting the access of emergency food aid in the times of crisis that continue to ravage the country periodically, as well as of fertilizer and seed. A secondary effect of Chinese penetration is that Ethiopia has started cycling! Visiting the north of the country, we came across teams of racers astride gleaming new bikes. Given the awards won by Ethiopian athletes, no doubt these cyclists will be crossing France in a few years and winning the famous Tour.

If one thing has altered in China's relationship with Africa, it is its sudden change of scale. This massive and varied investment contrasts strikingly with the disengagement of the former colonial powers. The Chinese penetration in Africa from the start of the century is remarkable, whether we consider the take-off of aid, trade flows or Chinese immigration.

The 'Beijing action plan' envisaged a doubling of Chinese aid to African countries between 2006 and 2009. It is in this context that Beijing announced in 2007 an aid 'package' of $8 billion to the DR Congo for infrastructure work, the equivalent of a whole year's GDP for that country. The financial assistance granted by China, suspended in an artistic vagueness and enveloped in a bureaucratic veil, is notoriously hard to measure.[4] It remains, nonetheless, that Beijing could shortly become Africa's no. 1 lender, while the G-8 countries have not managed to honour their solemn promise to double development aid between 2005 and 2010.[5]

The growth of this economic aid has been accompanied since the turn of the century by a flurry of commercial agreements between China and Africa – a practical demonstration of the theory of mutual interests. Securing access to African oil is a strategic issue for China, whose dependence on oil imports will increase steadily over the next few decades. China already imports more crude from Angola than from Saudi Arabia. But the relationship between Beijing and black Africa is not just in terms of oil. China is at a stage in development where it can offer Africa trade in both directions. Beijing ensures its strategic supplies of raw materials, while the African economies gain a source of revenue indexed to China's impressive growth rate – also, thanks to the import of cheap commodities, an entry ticket to mass consumption.

The army of Chinese traders now in Africa know how to take greatest advantage from this window of historical opportunity. Contrary to a widespread idea, they have established themselves there by investing in niches that are often neglected by their European counterparts. Very active in the construction sector, in mining, oil, timber and more recently agriculture, the thousand Chinese companies established on the continent include some of the world's biggest corporations. By requiring far narrower margins than their European equivalents, and having at their disposal an immigrant labour-force working for Chinese pay and conditions, these construction companies have considerably reduced the cost of infrastructural projects – at the risk of provoking a legitimate complaint from the young African unemployed, since local labour draws little benefit from this building fever.

For China the continent is an Eldorado, a Far West abandoned at the height of the storm by European companies who had grown tired of Africa. For all the qualifications that the ambiguities of a still-new presence impose, these big Chinese firms, along with the tide of individual shops that flourish in African capitals (restaurants, petty traders), show very well how there is nothing unrealistic in Africa's being a 'land of opportunities', that it's not simply a dream of 'Afro-optimists'. Sino-African trade passed the $100 billion mark in 2008, or twice that of Franco-African trade. As the continent's leading supplier ahead of France and Germany, China already represents, at the end of this decade, the second outlet for African exports after the United States. The creation of 'special economic zones'[6] on the African coasts, similar to those that flourished in Southeast Asia during the take-off period of the Asian tigers, is designed to reinforce this tendency. The first of these zones, established in Tanzania, was launched with great ceremony by president Hu Jintao in 2007. These commercial relationships enable Africa to tie itself to the engine of world economic growth.

Rising exports, lower consumer prices, new capital flowing into emerging services and workshops: a new growth engine has been switched on. Inevitably there will be some mistakes. But it will not be switched off again – and others will also appear.

However dynamic and structural they are, these commercial exchanges are not the whole of China's relationship with Africa. Beijing's investment in the continent is part of a long-term strategy. Evidence of this are the new 'Confucius institutes' – Chinese cultural centres that have sprung up in Kenya, Zimbabwe, Rwanda and Mauritius over the last decade. African students can learn Chinese there for free. The best of them are eligible for scholarships to go and study at the universities of Beijing, Shanghai or Guanxi. In just a few years, China has become one of the main destinations for African students. In 2007 the country enrolled 21,000 new entrants under these scholarships.[7] In the previous five years, the number of Africans who went off to study in China rose by 20 per cent a year. More than a commercial strategy, China is thus conducting a real educational and cultural policy towards Africa. Beijing also encourages the movement of people between the two continents. While the number of Chinese settled in Africa began to take off at the turn of the century, reaching a total of 750,000 by 2009, the number of Africans in China has risen sixfold in ten years. The Chinese authorities counted 230,000 of them in 2006.[8]

Finally, China has close diplomatic ties with a number of sub-Saharan countries. It uses its permanent seat on the Security Council to act as the spokesperson and even protector of friendly regimes. Following the principle of non-intervention, Beijing cossets in this way several pariahs of the international community. Sudan under Omar el-Bechir and Zimbabwe under Robert Mugabe, both exposed to international sanctions, have enjoyed precious support from the Chinese authorities while they trampled roughshod over the human rights of their citizens. More surprising, perhaps, China has sometimes acted against its own commercial interests in order to maintain its legitimacy as spokesperson for the Third World. This was particularly the case in the Doha round of trade negotiations, where Beijing opposed a reduction of customs duties for the countries of the South in order not to disassociate itself from the bloc of developing countries led by India.[9] Another striking symbol of this is the 'special present' given graciously to the African Union: its gigantic conference centre in Addis Ababa, twenty-five storeys tall and with 500 offices, was conceived, constructed and financed by China.

'Yellow China', the China of peasants, wide continental space and tradition, has long been opposed to 'blue China', that of the mandarins, the sea and exchange with the world. The staggering rise of China in Africa seems to confirm the ascendancy of blue China over yellow in this new century. By encouraging its private sector on the continent, by training young Africans and establishing Chinese cultural centres, by its development aid and its diplomatic charm offensive, Beijing is experimenting in Africa with a new and profoundly internationalist foreign policy.[10] A sign of changing times is that the traveller from Beijing to Lagos no longer has to go via London, Brussels or Paris. New airline routes are flourishing between the two continents. Does this Chinese-style 'soft power' herald an age of Asian leadership? The trials and errors of Chinafrique that we discover at the dawn of the twenty-first century would then mark the beginning of a new epoch, in which Europeans and Americans lose the 'monopoly of history'.[11]

All Africans!

If the rise of Chinese influence is undoubtedly the most striking development in Africa's relationship with the world in this decade, there is more to the story than this, as Indian, Latin American and Arab interests are also increasingly present on the continent.

Ever since its own independence, India has maintained close relations with the East African countries, where its diaspora has settled, as well as with Nigeria and Ghana, which are fellow-members of the Commonwealth. In 1961, Nehru visited his counterpart Nkrumah, hero of African independence and herald of pan-Africanism. In the last few years, New Delhi has also perceived the wind of change that is blowing over Africa. Though its pockets are less deep than Beijing's, since the turn of the century Indian diplomacy has not spared its efforts to extend its influence across the continent as a whole – playing alternately on its intact prestige as leader of the non-aligned movement, and on the attraction of trade relations and Indian technical cooperation. The Tata group has branches in many parts of the continent,[12] particularly in vehicle assembly. Textile companies have established joint ventures with African businesses, while Arcelor-Mittal is currently making West Africa one of its sources of mineral supplies.

If the secret of Chinese cooperation is infrastructure projects delivered in record time key in hand, Indian cooperation draws on the exchange of technology in high value-added industries.[13] It highlights the comparative advantages of Indian know-how in computers, agriculture and health, not to mention defence. Almost the whole general staff of the Ghanaian army have benefited from training in India, and New Delhi played a major role in the birth of the Nigerian Defence Academy.[14] On the civilian side, and at the request of the former Ghanaian president John Kufuor, New Delhi also contributed to the financing and establishment of the Ghanaian–Indian 'Kofi Annan' centre for the development of new computer technologies in West Africa. This centre of computing excellence, equipped with the latest technologies, can accommodate up to 1,000 scientists and technicians, students and apprentices, and works in alliance with institutions on all six continents.

During the food crisis of 2007–8, India's offer to assist the countries of West Africa to double their yields, after the pattern of the green revolution, also brought New Delhi much praise in the regional press. Behind these cooperation initiatives, beside the concern to diversify its sources of oil, lies the ambition to form a support network in international milieus. New Delhi's diplomatic activism in world trade negotiations and within the 'Group of 77' is part of this enterprise, along the lines of the Afro-Asian solidarity movement in which India exercised a natural leadership. By tenaciously struggling for the WTO cycle of trade negotiations to be favourable to the poorest countries on the planet, the Indian trade minister thus acted publicly as spokesperson for African interests.

If competition between India and China is felt in Africa, it is confined today to charm offensives towards African governments who are not so accustomed to parades of Asian delegations in their capitals. Beyond their tactical differences, the initiatives of both Asian powers towards black Africa are based on a similar analysis of the global issues they will have to face in the coming decades.

Nor are China and India alone in perceiving the benefits of involvement in Africa. The Gulf States are not prepared to leave Asia the monopoly on the world's last trading frontier – which happens to lie at their doorstep. With the runaway flight of oil prices in the early part of the decade, these oil and gas states saw the take-off of sub-Saharan growth as an opportunity to invest petrodollars that they no longer knew what to do with. The financial crisis that marked the end of the decade made Africa south of the Sahara an attractive zone for sovereign funds, whose investment strategies have a double requirement of yield and security. The United Arab Emirates, Saudi Arabia and Kuwait figure among the main foreign investors in the Sahel countries and West Africa. They benefit there from the network of Islamic development banks, and can draw diplomatically on the influential Organization of the Islamic Conference – whose members include more than half the sub-Saharan states. In the space of a few years, the Gulf monarchies have achieved a striking breakthrough in Senegal in this way, thanks to Dakar's encouragement. The big Dubai Ports World group was entrusted with managing the container terminal in the autonomous port of Dakar – a market that was winkled away from Senegal's traditional partner Bolloré in conditions that this company is still challenging – while the emir's Jebel Ali Free Zone Authority obtained the grant of a free zone of 10,000 hectares only 40 kilometres from Dakar, and the company of Tarek Bin Laden, Osama's half-brother, cornered the market for construction of the new Diass airport adjacent to this zone.[15] In both West Africa and Sudan, in Ethiopia and Madagascar, entrepreneurs from the Gulf are behind controversial projects in the field of foodstuffs, in direct competition with certain Asian investors.

Nor is North Africa lagging behind here, as shown by the breakthrough of Moroccan banks at the end of the decade. Along with their expanding customer base in Morocco itself, the country's banks are now orienting their growth strategy southward. Commenting on the purchase of five branches of Crédit Agricole in West and Central Africa at the end of 2008, the president of the Attijariwafa Bank explained to readers of the financial weekly *Les Afriques*: 'It's the future that we are building today in Africa.'[16] Moroccan entrepreneurs, who do not miss an opportunity to stress their African identity in the face of overseas competitors, are also increasingly present in West African foodstuffs and industrial sectors. Like Morocco, Tunisia is also making a southward turn, aware of the risks involved in too great a dependence on Europe and the United States. In the course of a conference organized in May 2009 at the Tunis chamber of trade and industry, under the title 'Tunisia in its African space: civilizational tie and partnership for mutually beneficial development', the head of the Tunisian employers' association encouraged his country's entrepreneurs to 'go and take their share of the [African] cake'.[17] The delegations of Tunisian businesspeople who have followed one another through the West African capitals did not lose any time in responding to this very rational appeal.[18]

Brazil, too, has decidedly taken an African turn, as a necessary step in its strategy of emergence in a multipolar world. It even boasts of being an 'African nation' itself. President Lula said at the United Nations in 2006: 'We feel ourselves bound to the African continent by historical and cultural ties. As the second largest black population in the world, we are committed to sharing the challenges and destiny of Africa.'[19] Under his leadership, Brazil has opened a dozen new embassies in Africa.

Programmes of South–South cooperation under the Brazilian Agency for Cooperation are increasingly geared towards non-Portuguese-speaking countries of black Africa. Major exchanges take place in the field of agro-ecology; Brazil established a model farm for cotton production in Mali in order to strengthen research and combat the 'unfair competition' of the Northern countries' agricultural subsidies. Kenyan and Tanzanian farmers have also been trained in techniques of conservation agriculture.[20] Just as in their relationships with the development organizations of the developed countries, Brazilians insist on a two-way partnership. The country's most striking diplomatic offensive towards Africa is in the field of biofuels. Brasilia in fact has every interest in sharing technologies linked with biofuels, in order to win allies in climate and trade negotiations. It is with a view to Africa's being able to 'join the biofuel revolution',[21] as Lula encourages it to do, that the Brazilian centre of agro-alimentary research opened a laboratory in Ghana in 2007. And, in the same context, Brazilian researchers have set out to map the potential for sugar production in several sub-Saharan countries – a task expected to change the pattern of agricultural production in whole regions.

In order to strengthen its footing on the international stage, Brasilia is not sparing its efforts towards Africa. Like India, Brazil presents itself as one of Africa's partners, and seeks to act as spokesperson for its interests in international forums. It was the lynchpin of the creation of the alliance with South Africa and India at Cancún in 2003, which is now one of the axes of the G-20 and has increasing weight in various international negotiations. The value of Brazilian exports to Africa, if still small in relation to that of other emerging countries, tripled between 2003 and 2006, a sign of the activism of the Afro-Brazilian chamber of commerce.

Old appetites, new friends

These new partnerships are keenly discussed on both sides of the Atlantic. The Chinese breakthrough in Africa, in particular, arouses the fear of Africa's being trapped in a new 'colonial pact'. China's political and business leaders are certainly not free from mistakes and contradictory policies – such as the support given to corrupt leaders. How could it be otherwise in this period of apprenticeship?

Each party will draw lessons from its own clumsiness. It is not in China's interest to ally itself with what is worst in Africa, to appear as exploiting the continent, let alone as its corrupting evil genius. Beijing is acutely aware that one of the greatest challenges of this partnership will be to avoid disappointing the immense expectations of Africans. Equality between partners, pursuit of mutual advantage, respect for national sovereignty – the rhetoric is not insignificant. Africans are sensitive to the pillars on which their relationships with China are based, and will undoubtedly remind their interlocutors of these in case they fail to live up to their principles. Despite the fears that are apparent in certain European discourse, it is quite unlikely that the freedom to choose their own relationships that African states have regained will lead them to hurl themselves into the mouth of the dragon. Africans have already lost the fruits of their independence once. Now that this independence is finally restored, they will not let it slip away again.

Chinese stranglehold on Africa, the buying-up of the continent by the Gulf's petrodollars, new Asian colonialism, yellow peril... these fantasies around the emergence of new and unscrupulous partners hide a very real development: just like Brazil, India and a number of Arab states, China has taken the measure of the changes at work on the continent, and reconsidered the nature of its relationships with Africa. These new forms of collaboration are rich in lessons for Europe and the United States. Because they compete with Western discourse, vision and projects for the continent, they oblige Africa's traditional partners to reflect on the relationship they themselves propose. Their successes teach us that Africans want to speak of the future as partners – but also of long-term mutual interests.

23

Acknowledging Africa

Acknowledging Africa is an intellectual reversal that the United States broadly undertook by re-assessing the place that Africa was expected to occupy in 21st-century international relations. While a Pentagon study of 1995 had concluded that the United States had 'only very little strategic interests in Africa',[1] the continent became a substantial objective of foreign policy again under George W. Bush. Barack Obama's America, for its part, has offered Africa a 'partnership based on responsibility and mutual respect'. A minor revolution, therefore, in the space of a decade and a half. Will Europe do the same, half a century after the wave of independence?

From 'war on terror' to 'mutual responsibilities'

It is impossible to understand George W. Bush's presidency without taking the measure of the traumatic experience of the attacks of 11 September 2001. Threatened at its very heart, the United States had to defend itself by relentlessly hunting down the terrorists on their own ground. Three years earlier, however, East Africa had already marked itself out as a target. The car bomb attacks carried out against the US embassies in Kenya and Tanzania, which killed 229 people, including a dozen Americans, were claimed by the Islamic Army for the Liberation of the Holy Places, a group affiliated to Al-Qaeda. The transformation of the Salafist 'Group for Preaching and Combat' along with the strengthening of the 'Shebabs' Islamic militias, in a Somalia prey to anarchy, could only

strengthen Washington's idea that sub-Saharan Africa was one of
the rear bases of international Islamic terrorism – and thus a ready-
made target for the crusade against the 'forces of evil'. According to
the right wing of the Republican party, in power at this time, such
a crusade had to be waged simultaneously by force, economics and
faith. These three pillars of the neo-conservative credo characterized the re-emergence of sub-Saharan Africa in American foreign
policy during George W. Bush's two presidential terms.

Let us look, first of all, at the reappearance of Africa on the
radar screens of US foreign policy, which took place via the armed
forces – whose influence in Washington was greatly expanded
by the anti-terrorist crusade. It was in the context of the 'war on
terror' that the United States installed a base of over 1,000 men
in Djibouti, in 2002, in a camp previously occupied by the French
Foreign Legion. Not content with this foothold on the Horn of
Africa, the US army decided in 2007 to provide itself with a pur-
pose-built military command centre on the continent. But though
the US government continued to present the new structure as a
centre of support for humanitarian missions and Africa's own
peace-keeping operations, the ambiguities of the Africom mandate
rapidly surfaced in the analyses of Washington think tanks – one
of whose roles is precisely to say out loud what the administration
thinks privately.

Aware of the growing dependence of the United States on West
African oil, the administration's strategists saw the Chinese breakthrough on the continent as threatening American interests. The
instability of the Middle East and the declared hostility of certain
Latin American leaders towards their North American big brother
pressed the United States to diversify its source of supply. West
Africa then presented itself as a necessary bridgehead for applying this strategy. Analysts agreed that, beyond its humanitarian
component, Africom would have the mission of securing one of
the sources of American oil supply, deterring a Chinese advance in
Africa and serving as a base for the anti-terrorist struggle. Having
lived for nearly half a century with French army bases, Africans
were not fooled by American intentions. As shown by the difficulties of both the Bush and Obama administrations in their search
for a country in which to establish their advance base in Africa, the
African Union, led by the continent's emerging powers, looks with

distrust at this new military interference, as the sign of an impending re-militarization of the continent.

Then there is economics. The sudden resurgence of interest in sub-Saharan Africa was expressed in a splurge of American aid, which rose four times over in the eight years following the attacks of September 2001.[2] When Bush came to power, his administration immediately suspended American finance to the UN population programme, accused by the conservative right of offering family planning advice and thus encouraging abortion. It was in this context that the 'President's Emergency Plan for AIDS Relief' (PEPFAR) was outlined, in which the deeply moralistic dimension of Bush's foreign policy was abundantly clear. (Beneficiaries of the programme must promise not to resort to prostitution, and PEPFAR even finances activities promoting sexual abstinence.) In 2009, close to $18 billion was spent to bring free anti-viral drugs to some 2 million Africans – whose survival now depends on the continuation of this Republican programme. But the Bush administration also set under way a second major aid programme, the Millennium Challenge Corporation (MCC), a structure designed to reward developing countries who choose the path of democratization and liberalization – two mantras of neo-conservative foreign policy. In order to be eligible for MCC subsidies, candidate states have to obtain a sufficient score on a battery of indicators of 'good governance' and economic liberalization. The funds allocated, which come to several hundred million dollars over a few years, are invested in the promotion of economic growth by way of infrastructure development. Independent of the State Department, this body rapidly became a major competitor to USAID, the established American aid agency deemed too bureaucratic and too close to the Democrats.

Whatever the domestic policy reasons lying behind their respective creation, it is undeniable that PEPFAR and MCC together represent a substantial financial effort in African development, and express a real re-engagement of the United States on the continent. This investment in Africa by George W. Bush might be surprising, coming from a president criticized for his lack of international culture, at the head of a party that has traditionally been sceptical about development aid. But this would be to ignore the influence of American lobbies.

Finally, we should consider faith. American civil society is the third actor in the return of the United States to Africa. Embracing both the most militant liberals and the most fervent conservatives and religious figures, a varied group of associations of all kinds has made itself the self-proclaimed representative for Africa in Congress and at the White House. If liberals had already succeeded in placing Africa rather higher on the agenda in the Clinton years, conservatives no doubt contributed to the spectacular investment of American foreign policy in Africa under George W. Bush. It is in fact hard to separate the breakthrough of Christian NGOs in sub-Saharan Africa from the striking rise of the North American evangelical movement in this zone over the past twenty years. Deliberately maintaining confusion between their missionary and their humanitarian efforts, hundreds of religious organizations have waged their race for African souls with the blessing of the White House – and the financial support of Congress, by way of tax relief on donations and legacies. In return, these NGOs and foundations present on the ground have exerted a powerful lobbying activity in Washington, particularly in relation to the conflicts in southern and western Sudan – both followed very closely by the Bush administration.

For Washington, these three pillars of US African policy go hand in hand. In fact, neo-conservative think tanks such as the Heritage Foundation, the Department of Defense (and particularly the demonic deputy secretary for defense, Paul Wolfowitz[3]), the White House (and Bush's neo-conservative vice-president Dick Cheney) and the American religious NGOs were united in their strategic vision of sub-Saharan Africa as one of the fault lines in the clash of civilizations. The Sudan–Sahel zone and the Horn of Africa, frontier zones between 'Western' (read 'Christian') and Islamic influence, should not be abandoned to poverty, with the risk of providing soil for the 'enemies of freedom'. In addition to the vigilance of American GIs who were increasingly present, and the battle for democracy and against poverty waged by American aid, the conversion of African animists to Christianity was intended as a further rampart against the Islamic peril.

Then, by one of those fabled upheavals of history that American democracy displays from time to time, came the most African of US presidents. Prague, Cairo, Accra: in a series of path-breaking speeches, Barack Husein Obama started in 2009 to reforge US foreign policy. By holding a hand out to the 'Islamic world', a mirage dreamed up by his predecessor's neo-conservativism, the new president pulled the rug from under the feet of the champions of the 'clash of civilizations' at a speech delivered at the Egyptian university of Al Azar. Though this had been expected in Kenya, his father's country that had recently been shaken by election violence, it was in the Ghanaian capital that Barack Obama chose to look into the face of tomorrow's Africa. Before the parliament of this young African democracy, freshly converted to a multiparty system, the US president exhorted African peoples to take the destinies of their countries in hand, so as to put an end to the years in which Africa was always associated with charity. 'Africa doesn't need strongmen, it needs strong institutions', he proclaimed in Accra, spelling out that 'in the twenty-first century, capable, reliable and transparent institutions are the key to success' – thus breaking with an ideological conception of 'good governance' focused on form rather than institutional practice.

It is clear that neither the struggle against terrorism, nor the securing of energy supply, will disappear from the equation of American policy in Africa. But a rebalancing of priorities towards human security and economic relations harks back to the tradition of American 'soft power'. Obama's Accra speech, and Hillary Clinton's African tour in summer 2009, show Washington's eagerness to pose as the partner of African nations – a desire based on an analysis of Africa's new place in the world: 'the twenty-first century will be shaped by what happens not just in Rome or Moscow or Washington, but by what happens in Accra as well... Your prosperity can expand America's. Your health and security can contribute to the world's.' As the first decade of the century is coming to an end, Washington is in turn persuaded that Africa will contribute to writing the century's history.

Continental drift

If the United States has embarked on remoulding its African policy, Europe is still waiting.

The 1990s was the decade of a great disconnection between Europe and Africa. The stakes of the Cold War had disappeared.

The feeling of colonial responsibility had gradually faded. A new generation of leaders came to power on both sides of the Mediterranean, reducing the historical closeness between African leaders on the one hand, and British, French and Portuguese on the other. Relations between the former imperial powers and their erstwhile colonies no longer went without saying; Paris, London and Lisbon all believed they had more to lose than to gain from a costly tête-à-tête with an Africa shaken by crisis – and branded now by the Rwandan trauma. While the former colonial powers had never spared their efforts in the wake of independence to preserve a monopoly in their respective 'backyards', at the end of the century they were in a hurry to shake off these burdensome bilateral connections. Once they became multilateral, political relationships that had previously been stifling were transformed into weak compassionate ones, tinged here and there by echoes of post-colonial guilt. Whether in the political, economic or strategic domain, this disengagement was striking.

The difference of intrinsic interests between the former imperial powers and their erstwhile colonies was healthy enough, for Europe as well as for Africa – a necessary break. But the change of generations could have provided an opportunity for re-inventing these relationships on the basis of a dialogue free from complexes, as the seedbed of a new partnership. It has to be noted that this second point has not yet been reached. While the leading players in the multipolar world have perceived the wind of change blowing over the continent, Europe, despite being closer to Africa in many respects, finds this hard to believe – as if blind to the upheavals taking place outside its gates. Burdened by their historic baggage, European countries seem caught in a posture of strategic indecision, torn between compassion towards societies perceived as wretched, greed at the thought of a treasure once possessed, and indifference towards a neighbour who is unknown because it is believed to be known too well. The absence of strategic vision on the part of decision-makers, financial and industrial in particular, is matched by the disinterest of public opinion, grown tired of Africa.

This European disinvestment from Africa – psychological, commercial and financial – shapes the terrible contradiction of a missed opportunity: after several decades of proximity to a suffering continent, Europe has abandoned its South at the very time this is preparing to take off. While Africa is weaving strong relationships with its new partners, European society is turning its back on it.

This distancing represents a historical error, whether Africa succumbs to the perils of its metamorphosis or grasps the opportunities it offers.

If, in the first case, entire parts of Africa were to collapse for lack of support for its transformation, the consequences for its neighbours would be catastrophic. The 1990s, with their tens of millions of dead, offer only a glimpse of the long-term risks that Africa and its neighbours would run in case of failure. One study has estimated the financial cost of the wars in sub-Saharan Africa between 1990 and 2005 at around $300 billion – i.e. $20 billion per year, or nearly twice the average sum of development aid received by its states throughout this period.[4] We should realize that no emergency bandage, no humanitarian transfusion, would be able to stem the ills arising from a sick Africa. Europe cannot allow itself to have at its doorstep an Africa of fire and blood.

It is beginning to discover the risks represented by a fragile Africa in terms of the drug trade and the traffic in human beings. To get round the controls at European ports and airports, which are particularly attentive to goods arriving from Latin America, the South American cartels are now bringing their supplies in through West Africa by boat or plane (sometimes in the bellies of Nigerians who are specially stuffed for this sinister trade), before distributing them in Europe. A UN study estimates that more than a quarter of the cocaine consumed in Europe in 2006 arrived via West Africa.[5] Guinea-Bissau, Africa's leading narcostate, has become in a few years a regular turntable for cocaine traffic destined for the European market. It makes an ideal prey: the country's judicial system is in tatters, it has no more prisons since the war of 1998, and its army is underpaid. Its territory, bordering on Senegal, is no longer controlled. When it finally decided to clean up its act in response to pressure from the international community, the head of state was assassinated. The drug barons now lay down the law in Bissau, with the complicity of the leading officials of this dissolving state. In Guinea, as elsewhere in Africa, citizens often suffer not from their state being strong but rather from its being weak.

The poorest and most fragile regions of Africa will also be the incubators of global health risks, in a century in which mobility is expected to grow steadily. At the time of the AIDS, Ebola and SARS epidemics, of 'bird flu' and H1N1, access for all to basic health and medical systems is not only a moral imperative, but also one of public health: the battle for European health is also waged in Africa.

As we have seen, no fortress can protect Europe from waves of immigrants trying to escape their ruined countries, even if these represent only the most recent wave of the African demographic and migratory storm. The hundreds of small craft that sink each year off the Mediterranean island of Lampedusa or the Canaries would be only the advance guard of a generation deprived of any future. Without economic growth strong enough to respond to the challenges of Africa's growing population, it will not be some thousands of economic, political and environmental refugees that Europe and the Maghreb have to face, but millions. Europe therefore has everything to lose from abandoning Africa in its moment of transformation.

In the opposite case, if the majority of African nations succeed in following the paths traced by its development pioneers, then Europe, by its disinterest in Africa, would simply leave others to profit from the emergence on its doorstep of a young and dynamic continent. This divorce would be all the more puzzling in that European nations invested a great deal in Africa when it was doing badly. Between EU aid and that of its member states, Europe continues to provide close to 60 per cent of the world's total aid budget. More than a third of this sum is devoted to Africa. Yet the share of Africa's trade with Europe has steadily shrunk since the beginning of the century. Those disturbed by the assertion of 'new actors' in Africa fail to realize that these have positioned themselves above all in sectors that European companies abandoned in the 1980s and 1990s. Busy fighting for new trading opportunities in Asia, the majority of these no longer perceive the potential of African markets – where they continue to lose ground year after year. This is no small paradox when we know that it is precisely Chinese, Indian and Brazilian investment in Africa that has proved tremendously profitable. Europeans, however, have at their disposal a whole range of tools and expertise that can respond to the new needs of Africa's population explosion. Besides, after an initial wave of enthusiasm, ever more Africans are adopting a more critical stand towards certain practices of their new partners and seeking European institutional, environmental and social know-how. This request for European re-engagement has so far remained unmet, for lack of any genuine common strategy towards our African neighbour.

On paper, to be sure, Europe is on the right track. The term 'aid' had been exchanged for that of 'partnership'; arrangements between capitals have given way to an inclusive approach that links civil society on both sides of the Mediterranean. In 2005 Europe adopted a 'European Union Strategy for Africa' based on an action plan and five partnerships in fields of common interest. But this language of partnership is often belied by practice. Several signs indicate that Europe has still not taken the real measure of the issues at stake in Africa.

The most telling of these signs is the fiasco of the 'Economic Partnership Agreements' (EPAs) between the European Union and seventy-nine 'ACP' countries (Africa, Caribbean, Pacific). The negotiation process was designed to draw up reciprocal free-trade agreements to replace the so-called 'preferential' agreements of Lomé and Cotonou, deemed incompatible with WTO rules. The EU's stated objectives were to help the countries concerned profit fully from the spin-offs of market opening, and to create a movement that would be fruitful for development by promoting regional integration. The negotiations would supposedly be marked by a relationship of trust between Africans and Europeans.

Nothing of the kind. Conducted briskly by the 'trade' division of the European Commission, these negotiations gave the lie to both the spirit and the letter of the new Euro-African partnership on which the ink had barely dried. This test of the Commission's 'development' orientation failed to take into account the hesitancy of the African countries, concerned as they were about the effects of trade liberalization on their export sectors. Worse still, while the deadline of 1 January 2008 was approaching, Europe chose to play on divisions between its prospective partners, at the risk of undermining the economic cooperation that was in the process of construction. Intended to embody a renewal of Afro-European relations, the EPA negotiations were the unhappy beginning of a partnership that is still to be found.

Europe's declining role among Africa's trading partners in the last two decades expresses this distance between the two sides – and casts doubt on talk about European re-engagement.[6] Scarred

by the debt crisis, by corruption, by the legal and physical insecurity of the 1990s in West and Central Africa, many European
businesses grew tired of Africa. The retreat of French companies,
historically very active on the continent, illustrates a decline in
trade ties that were previously dynamic: investment in sub-
Saharan Africa, which now represents no more than 1.5 per cent
of France's direct foreign investment, has stagnated or fallen
from one year to the next, even while that of other world economic actors has steadily advanced since the turn of the century.
The fall in the number of French expatriates confirms this economic retreat: under 100,000 French nationals are now living in
francophone Africa, as against nearly 140,000 in 1985. The major
French banks' ownership share in the West African banking system
has likewise fallen from 80 per cent to 33 per cent in the course of
the decade. While West African economic indicators have turned
green, these banks are still continuing their withdrawal strategy
– to the profit of their Nigerian, Moroccan or Chinese counterparts. When European banks undertook a massive withdrawal of
their capital at the time of the financial crisis, the Industrial and
Commercial Bank of China, the largest bank in the world, took
advantage of the fall in prices to increase its investment on the
continent: it acquired 20 per cent of the capital of the Standard
Bank of South Africa, one of the continent's largest banks, for
some $4.85 billion.[7]

More fundamentally, perhaps, the rhetoric of Euro-African
partnership is itself flawed, inasmuch as it continues to convey
a compassionate and rescuing stance towards Africa. Behind the
talk of 'mutual interests', Europe finds it hard to escape the 'charitable' position it adopted throughout the 1990s. As if nothing had
changed, the Europe–Africa strategic partnership was thus given
the objective of 'putting Africa back on the path of sustainable
development and reaching the Millennium Development Goals
by 2015' – ignoring Africa's forceful request for business and its
no less passionate rejection of compassion. Europe's diplomatic
stance is unique: where Washington speaks of geopolitical interests, and Beijing of 'win–win' trade, Europe sticks to development
goals. Whilst the prominence of strategic interests on the part of
the two great powers is seen as a token of credibility, the 'disinterested' stance of Euro-African partnership is deemed by many
Africans as unbelievable or even contemptuous. Whereas 85 per

cent and 75 per cent of Nigerians and Kenyans, respectively, said in 2009 that they have a favourable opinion of China, only 61 per cent and 62 per cent of them had a favourable opinion of Europe.[8]

The contrast is all the more striking in that Europe was able to offer Central Europe and the countries of the Mediterranean basin the construction of a common space of peace and prosperity, by its policies of expansion and the Union pour la Méditerranée. Blinded by the past, Europe has relegated sub-Saharan Africa to the margin of this great space of exchange of goods, people and ideas. The president of Senegal, Abdoulaye Wade, shocked Paris by denouncing the Union pour la Méditerranée as a new relegation of sub-Saharan Africa. If this was certainly excessive, does it not reflect African perceptions – and a reality that others exploit?

From its African history, Europe acquired a certain intimacy with the continent. But if in the late twentieth century, Europe was able to recognize the opportunity to invest to its east, it finds it hard to realize that the space of nearly 2 billion people that will come into being to its south as the year 2050 approaches amounts to a fundamental stake, in terms of competitiveness and influence, in a twenty-first century that is set to be multipolar. Economics, climate, international health, conflict management, energy, migration – the ingredients are combined for a partnership oriented towards the future and matters of common interest. But an ageing Europe finds it hard to question the patterns of the past, without realizing that the African nations are moving ahead at high speed and will not wait for it.

Conclusion: Can Africa Reject Development?

With the twenty-first century, Africa is opening a new chapter in its history. As with every new era, the page is blank; this part of the story is still to be written.

We recalled at the start of this book how, for the author of *War and Peace*, neither Napoleon's genius nor that of General Kutuzov took into account, with the triumphant arrival of the French in Moscow and their humiliating retreat, the force of European history on the march at that time, which transcended the genius of great men and the changing fates of nations. There is something deeply Tolstoyan about the demographic, economic and social forces at work in Africa in the early twenty-first century; the continent's transformations offer it the tools for internally generated growth that its painful history had long removed. Ecological, economic, migratory, social and identitarian upheavals are in this sense unavoidable in Africa: like the hero of a Greek tragedy moving towards his fate, this people on the march can no more reject development than they could formerly free themselves from the tragedy of economic cycles. As we have seen, this journey will not enable Africa to avoid crises or sufferings, or the setbacks that punctuate all great leaps forward.

But here lies the paradox: these are the same forces that, in company with the main evolutionary trends of the world as a whole, are irresistibly propelling Africa from the status of a mere object to that of an independent subject of public policy and international relations. Whether in demography, ecology or economics,

Conclusion 263

this Africa in movement, independent and sought-after, is retaking its place in history – and thus becoming the agent of its own destiny.

Everything suggests that this process will continue to be bumpy. If, as Barack Obama said in Accra, no strongman is needed for the continent to succeed, nor is any wrong-doer needed for it to fail. There are many possible causes of skidding out of control: while Africa's population explosion creates the markets and conditions for take-off, it also threatens the viability of this dearly acquired growth; it makes social balances fragile and it compromises access to resources; it provokes transformations of identity that are both structuring and explosive. Africa will undoubtedly remain, for a long time to come, a political terrain that is risky in relation to the opportunities it offers. Its invaluable diversity will form at the same time one of its great handicaps. Its political unity, however desirable, is not close. Its youth, a healthy asset in an ageing world, will simultaneously present a major challenge, for both Africa and the world.

The historic moment of a swing from disaster to progress faces each actor involved with new choices, which will guide the story of the new era. What then should be done? It is up to Africans to decide for themselves. The most well-intentioned of their friends cannot stand in for them in their choices about savings, migration and investment, or in their struggles for democracy, regional integration and growth.

Their partners equally have choices to make. Europeans may continue to show the same kind of disdain, whether compassionate or complacent, that has prevented the realization of so many good ideas over the last twenty years. Not knowing how to turn the page of a burdensome history, they may turn their backs on an emerging continent. Far better would be an economic reinvestment that seeks mutual advantage; a more global partnership than the sham offered in the Cotonou agreements, necessary but not sufficient; an upward adjustment on migration; a healing of the sensitive relationship between former colonizers and former colonized that would free this for good from the decaying odour of 'Françafrique' and its like; an overall social project, in other words, along the lines of what Europe succeeded in building with the countries of the East, and plans to build with those of the

Mediterranean. The stage of stifling closeness is past, and the time is come to construct a Euro-African space of growth built around common interests – not just between a handful of leaders whose interests are mixed, but between countries, peoples and economies. Let us be clear: it is only in this way that the old continent will survive without too much difficulty its coexistence with this young, impetuous and coveted neighbour. In the face of the challenges and opportunities of the African transformation, indifference cannot take the place of politics.

Some people maintain that the winners from the historic game being played in Africa will be the major emerging countries, given how greatly their determination contrasts with European indecision. Yet nothing is less certain: they may well continue to exploit African resources, its markets as well as its nature, in an extraction mode, take no interest in institutional and human construction under the dishonest pretext of political neutrality, and go on exporting their emigrants to the African tropics without worrying about the tensions this will unavoidably generate. But what will they really gain from supporting repellent regimes that will in due course fall? From risking the over-indebtedness of a continent that will not repay them? From becoming suppliers of markets that exploitation will bankrupt? Some actors from Asia and the Gulf cherish the illusion that a strategy of seizing African land will ensure their food security. They can certainly expect to fail along these lines. Genuine food security consists in producing enough for all, which their financial resources can assist, but not in a stranglehold on spaces that poverty and hunger would make uncontrollable.

America, finally, may continue to see Africa as a pawn in its 'hyperpower' strategy – whether its aim is planetary democratization, oil supplies or security operations. It would also lose this game, in the face of a continent that is rapidly rising and set to join the major emerging powers in the 'great game' of the twenty-first century. Who is in a better position than the United States to measure the risks and prospects of a young continent in transformation, or to bet on its future?

Each actor involved will have to revise their position. This is a difficult act, as it requires them to remove their blinkers and see the African continent for what it is – beyond talk that is falsely reassuring or needlessly alarmist. The time has come to change our rear-view mirrors for telescopes. The pace of Africa's transformation forces us to reconsider what we see in its full complexity, in the risks it generates as well as the opportunities it offers.

This re-assessment, to be successful, should not borrow from the register either of compassion or of charity – even if it does authorize friendship and fraternity. The point of this change of perspective is to receive this newcomer at the feast of common prosperity. Its destiny may upset our own: a wrong path on its part would trigger a chain of conflict, while its headlong feverish rush to development can make its swarming youth one of the engines of world growth. The pillage of its resources would ruin our own search for sustainable development, while their preservation would bear the seed of our own reconquest of ecological stability.

On reflection, perhaps Tolstoy was wrong: the genius of Kutuzov – that of having grasped History on the march – may well have prevailed over that of Napoleon, who proved unable to perceive his collapse. Like the Russian winter, the tumultuous flow of African history leaves a place for the wisdom of human choice.

Maps

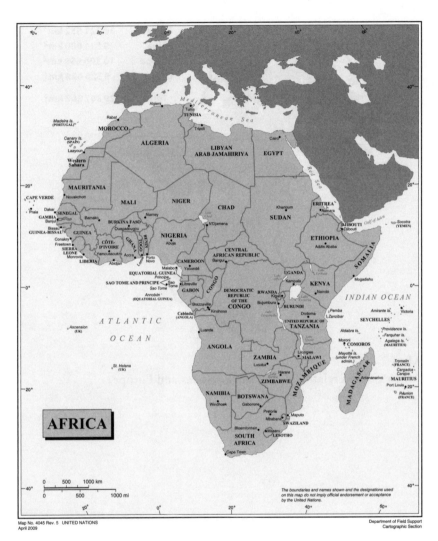

Map No. 4045 Rev. 5   UNITED NATIONS
April 2009

Department of Field Support
Cartographic Section

Map 1
Political map of Africa.
Source: Africa, Map No. 4045 Rev. 5, April 2009.

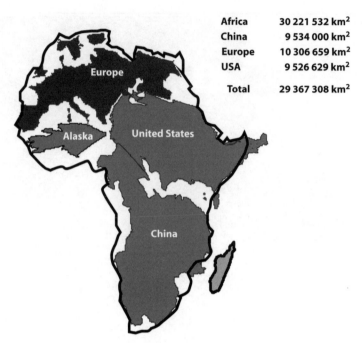

Africa	30 221 532 km²
China	9 534 000 km²
Europe	10 306 659 km²
USA	9 526 629 km²
Total	29 367 308 km²

Map 2
Africa's size in relation to the United States and Europe.

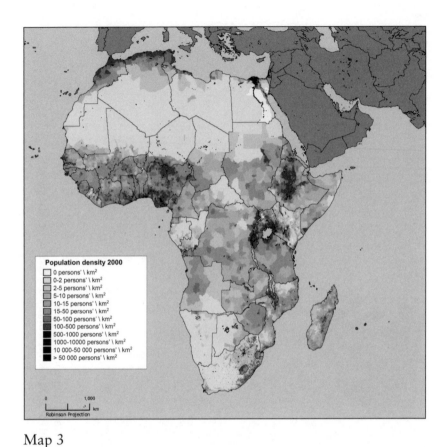

Map 3
Africa: population density.
Source: © Center for International Earth Science Information Network,
PLACE II.

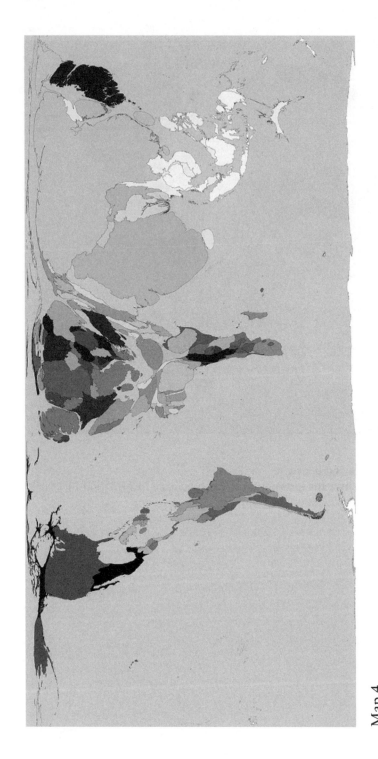

Map 4
World population distribution at the time of African independence (1960).
Source: 2006 SASI Group (University of Sheffield) and Mark Newman (University of Michigan).

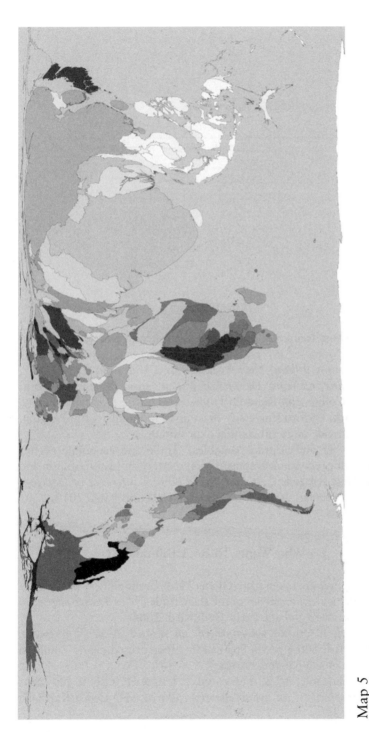

Map 5
World population distribution projected for 2050.
Source: 2006 SASI Group (University of Sheffield) and Mark Newman (University of Michigan).

Notes

Foreword

1 In this short foreword, I have not the space to provide underpinnings for some of my arguments and assertions. My three books (*The Bottom Billion*, New York: Oxford University Press, 2007; *Wars, Guns and Votes: Democracy in Dangerous Places*, New York: Harper Collins and Random House, 2009; *The Plundered Planet*, New York: Oxford University Press and Harmondsworth: Penguin, 2010) provide more substantial expositions.

2 Paul Collier and Antony Venables, 'Trade and economic performance: does economic fragmentation matter?' in Justin Yifu Lin and Boris Plescovik (eds.), *Annual World Bank Conference of Development Economics, 2008*, Washington, DC: World Bank, 2010.

3 Ibid.

1 Who Wants To Be A Billionaire?

1 These figures are taken from Olivier Pétré-Grenouilleau, who gives a detailed historical analysis of the slave trade in *Les Traites négrières: essai d'histoire globale*, Paris: Gallimard, 2004.

2 S. Brunel, *L'Afrique, un continent en réserve de développement*, Paris: Bréal, 2003, p. 58. Spanish flu alone caused nearly 2 million fatalities in sub-Saharan Africa.

3 J.-P. Guengant, in B. Ferry (ed.), *L'Afrique face à des défis démographiques, un avenir incertain*, Paris: AFD-Ceped-Karthala, 2007, p. 27.

4 This average conceals tremendous regional differences. While Gabon and the Central African Republic have very low densities (5 and 6 inhabitants per square kilometre, respectively), Rwanda and Nigeria have, respectively, 390 and 171.

5 The combined populations of India, Bangladesh and Pakistan came to 1.5 billion in 2010.

6 J.-N. Biraben, 'L'évolution du nombre des hommes', *Population et Sociétés* (INED), 2003, 394.

7 This first phase sees mortality fall without a decline in the birth rate, producing a sharp natural increase. The second phase sees the birth rate fall to the same degree as mortality, leading to a reduction in natural growth.

8 A study conducted in forty-four African countries shows that AIDS tends to increase fertility rates and reduce rates of school attendance. S. Kalemli-Ozcan, 'AIDS, "reversal" of the demographic transition and economic development: evidence from Africa', National Bureau of Economic Research, working paper, May 2006.

9 Including the countries of East-Central Europe, but excluding Russia.

10 J.-C. Chasteland, 'La population du monde: géants démographiques et défis internationaux', *Les Cahiers de l'INED*, 2002, 149.

11 A term coined by the demographer Alfred Sauvy.

12 By definition this lies outside the 'official' economy that provides the greater part of production of goods and services in the industrialized economies. This 'informal sector' is marked by a combination of subsistence production and small-scale trade, with occasional or family employment.

2 Malthus on CNN

1 J.-F. Bayart, *The Illusion of Cultural Identity*, Chicago: University of Chicago Press, 2010.

2 J.-F. Bayart, 'Culture et développement: les luttes sociales font-elles la différence?' contribution to AFD-EUDN conference of 5 December 2007.

3 J.-F. Bayart, *The State in Africa: The Politics of the Belly*, New York: Longman, 1993 (first published 1989).

4 The Organization for Economic Cooperation and Development has some thirty member countries, including the world's richest economies.

5 With the notable exception of Chinese aid, especially since the middle of the 2000s.

6 T. R. Malthus, *An Essay on the Principle of Population*, 1798.

7   Ibid.
8   J.-M. Jancovici, presentation to the Agence Française de Développement (AFD), 2008.
9   J. M. Diamond, *Collapse: How Societies Choose to Fail or Succeed*, New York: Viking, 2005.
10 J.-P. Olivier de Sardan, *Analyse rétrospective de la crise alimentaire en Niger*, Document de travail no. 45, AFD, August 2007.
11 This inter-governmental body is charged with establishing the scientific facts on climatic changes, and their impacts on the different regions of the globe.
12 Fourth report of the IPCC, *Climate Change 2007: Impacts, Adaptation and Vulnerability*, Cambridge: Cambridge University Press, 2007.
13 P. Schwartz and D. Randall, *Abrupt Climate Change, Scenario and its Implications for United States National Security*, report to the Pentagon, October 2003.
14 See 'Pax Africana? Le nouvel interventionnisme libéral', *Politique Africaine*, June 2005, 98.
15 Laurence Gbagbo wrote: 'We are making progress, but it is hard and inevitably causes damage: we are asked to replay 1789 in the presence of Amnesty International.' Cited by Jean-Pierre Foirry, *L'Afrique, continent d'avenir?* Paris: Ellipses, 2006.
16 The treaty of Westphalia, negotiated by the European states in 1648, is viewed as the starting-point for the organization of the world into independent sovereign states.
17 Chapter VII of the UN Charter particularly permits member states of the Security Council to authorize a military intervention in a sovereign state when they establish the existence of a threat to international peace.

3   A Black Peril?

1   UN estimates give a figure of 16 million, which is probably conservative; other sources suggest twice as many. Cf. P. Hugon, *L'Économie de l'Afrique*, Paris: La Découverte, 2009.
2   CEPII, *Les Dossiers de la mondialisation*, November–December 2006, 5. France only receives 2 per cent of these immigrants, or 5 million individuals.
3   The balance of migration measures the number of arrivals in a given territory minus the number of departures.
4   F. Héran, *Le Temps des immigrés: essai sur le destin de la population française*, Paris: Le Seuil, 2007, p. 56.
5   Ibid.

6 *La Cohérence des politiques au service du développement: migration et pays en développement*, OECD report, 2007, pp. 22–3.
7 Immigration cannot be equated with its irregular component (only 6 to 15 per cent of immigrants settled in Europe are irregular), and irregular immigration cannot be equated with the 'boat people' who loom so large in the media. A major part of irregular immigrants in Europe have arrived in a regular situation but overstayed their authorized time.
8 'The reality is that borders are beyond control and little can be done to really cut down on immigration', the Nobel prize-winner Jagdish Bhagwati explained in a 2003 article for *Foreign Affairs*, 'Borders beyond control'.
9 Ferry (ed.), *L'Afrique face à des défis démographiques*, p. 58.
10 The expression used in Mali for emigration means 'going off on an adventure'.
11 Cf. *Populations et Sociétés*, January 2004, no. 397, INED; Hein De Haas, 'Turning the tide? Why development will not stop migration', *Development and Change*, 2007, 38 (5), p. 13; and *Overcoming Barriers: Human Mobility and Development*, UNDP Development Report, 2009.
12 H. De Haas, 'Irregular migration from West Africa to the Maghreb and the European Union', *International Organization for Migration*, 2008, p. 26. See also H. De Haas, *The Myth of Invasion: Irregular Migration from West Africa to the Maghreb and the European Union*, IMI Research Report, International Migration Institute, Oxford University, 2008.
13 De Haas, 'Irregular migration', p. 18.
14 *Rapport de la Commission pour la libération de la croissance française, présidée par Jacques Attali*, 25 January 2008, La Documentation Française.
15 UNDP, *Overcoming Barriers*.
16 I.e. the difference between the number of births and the number of deaths in a given territory.
17 Héran, *Le Temps des immigrés*.
18 Ibid.
19 Ibid., p. 82.
20 Report from the McKinsey Institute, *Germany 2020*, May 2008.
21 UNDP, *Overcoming Barriers*.
22 The substantial rise in the share of skilled workers in migration flows has been particularly shown by M. Beine, F. Docquier and H. Rapoport, 'Brain drain and human capital formation in developing countries: winners and losers', *Economic Journal*, April 2008, 118 (528), pp. 631–52.

23 'De nouvelles données sur l'émigration des médecins africains', *CAP Afrique*, 15 August 2006; INSEE (French National Institute of Statistics and Economic Studies) 2009.

24 Figures from the report of the Center for Global Development, 'A new database of health professionals', Working Paper 95, August 2006.

25 The bulk of 'temporary immigrants' in the post-war period eventually remained in Europe. See A. Sayad, *La Double Absence: des illusions de l'immigré aux souffrances de l'immigré*, Paris: Le Seuil, 1999.

26 See 'Le codéveloppement à l'essai', rapport d'information no. 417 (2006–7), produced for the Commission des Affaires Étrangères of the Assemblée Nationale, 20 July 2007.

27 N. Ruiz, *Managing Migration: Lessons from the Philippines*, World Bank report, August 2008.

28 And considerably more if reliable figures could be obtained for informal flows. The global economic crisis certainly reduced these return flows in 2009, but they are expected to rise again from 2010 on. See 'Migration and development brief', World Bank, July 2009.

29 W. Shaw, 'Migration in Africa: a review of the economic literature on international migration in 10 countries', Washington, DC: World Bank, 2007; and the interview with Catherine Wihtol de Wenden in *Le Monde*, 6 October 2009.

30 See, on this subject, the pioneering study by T. Mélonio, *Balances migratoires: concept, hypothèses et discussions*, Document de travail no. 74, AFD, October 2008.

31 The sending of money back to the home country is certainly a long-established practice for emigrants. The phenomenon can, however, be characterized as 'new' in terms of the scale it has acquired since the late twentieth century.

32 As classified by the Human Development Index of the UN Development Programme, 2007.

33 De Haas, 'Turning the tide?'

34 Report for the French ministry of the interior by C. Milhaud, 'L'intégration économique des migrants et la valorisation de leur épargne', September 2006.

35 Ibid. This report, moreover, refrained from taking a position on the economic usefulness of the transfers.

4 Crowded Roads

1 Figures provided by the French ministry of the interior (2005), and migration profiles established by European Commission delegations in the Africa–Caribbean–Pacific countries (2007).

2 *Migration*, OECD Sahel and West Africa Club, August 2006.

3 Figures from the WALTPS study, cited in ibid.

4 Guengant, in Ferry (ed.), *L'Afrique face à des défis démographiques*, p. 52; United Nations, *Trends in International Migrant Stocks: The 2008 Revision*, UN, 2009.

5 M.-A. Pérouse de Montclos, 'L'Afrique rejette ses propres immigrés', *Le Monde diplomatique*, December 1999.

6 R. Banégas and F. de Akindès, *Patientez-vous, la guerre va finir*, a study by the Agence Française de Développement (AFD), Paris, July 2008.

7 'Autochthonous' in the sense of people originating from the place in which they live, and 'allochthonous' referring to those not originating there.

8 J.-P. Chauveau, 'Question foncière et construction nationale en Côte-d'Ivoire: les enjeux silencieux d'un coup d'État', *Politique Africaine*, June 2000, 78, pp. 94–125.

9 The Bretton Woods institutions are the World Bank and the International Monetary Fund (IMF), which have their headquarters in Washington, DC. They were created by an international conference that met at Bretton Woods in New Hampshire in June 1944.

10 Structural adjustment plans were programmes to apply conditions imposed by the IMF for the rescheduling of developing countries' debts, from the 1980s on. Aiming to restore the external balance of trade and currency, they insisted on reduction in public expenditure, and such structural measures as privatizations and free movement of capital.

11 Extract from Curdiphe, 1996, cited by Banégas and Akindès, *Patientez-vous*.

12 According to the demographer N. Robin.

13 Estimates of the number of immigrants in South Africa are contested. For a critical analysis of the figures, see the annex by S. Ellis, L. Landau, D. Vigneswaran and A. Wa Kabwe-Segatti, *Migration in Post-Apartheid South Africa: Challenges and Questions to Policy-Makers*, Notes and Documents no. 38, AFD, 2008.

14 Guengant, in Ferry (ed.), *L'Afrique face à des défis démographiques*, p. 56.

15 The great bulk of these refugees were living in South Africa irregularly.

16 For more details of these migrations and the issues involved for South Africa, see Ellis, Landau, Vigneswaran and Wa Kabwe-Segatti, *Migration in Post-Apartheid South Africa*.

17 A. Bensaâd, 'Agadez, carrefour migratoire sahélo-maghrébin', *Revue Européenne des Migrations Internationales*, 2007, 19 (1).

18   See Fabrizio Gatti, *Bilal, sur la route des clandestins*, Paris: Liana Levi, 2008.
19   De Haas, 'Turning the tide?' p. 47.
20   Ibid., p. 21.
21   See De Haas's analysis, ibid., p. 13.
22   *Migrations*.
23   Bensaâd, 'Agadez'.
24   O. Jacob, 'Les juifs du Mali', *La Voix des Séfardes*, September 1997, 28.
25   For an analysis of Indian emigration in this period, see Thomas Metcalf, *Imperial Connections: India in the Indian Ocean Arena, 1860–1920*, Berkeley: University of California Press, 2007.
26   Gandhi lived in South Africa for more than two decades.
27   According to Jean-Raphaël Chaponnière, the Chinese presence in Africa does not appear in the *Atlas des diasporas* compiled by G. Chaliand (Paris: Odile Jacob, 1991).
28   See the study by Serge Michel and Michel Beuret, *La ChinAfrique: Pékin à la conquête du continent noir*, Paris: Grasset-Fasquelle, 2008. See also M. Dupré and W. Shi, *La Présence chinoise en Afrique de l'Ouest: le cas du Mali et du Bénin*, Documents de travail no. 69, AFD, August 2008.
29   Michel and Beuret, *La ChinAfrique*, p. 70.
30   *La Lettre du Continent*, 22 February 2007. Cited in ibid.
31   Ibid.
32   The number of living languages in Africa, recently counted by linguists.
33   De Haas, 'Turning the tide?' p. 20.

5   The Undiscoverable Curse

1   This is the position taken by Steven Smith, for example, in his essay *Négrologie: pourquoi l'Afrique meurt*, Paris: Calmann-Lévy, 2003.
2   W. Easterly and R. Levine, 'Africa's growth tragedy, policies and ethnic divisions', *Quarterly Journal of Economics*, November 1997, 112.
3   R. Dumont, *False Start in Africa*, London: André Deutsch, 1966.
4   G. Myrdal, *Asian Drama: An Inquiry into the Poverty of Nations*, New York: Pantheon, 1968, and A. Kamarck, *The Economics of African Development*, New York: Praeger, 1967.
5   According to the 2008 list of the NGO Transparency International, nineteen of the fifty most corrupt countries are African.
6   *Human Security Report: War and Peace in the XXIst Century*, Oxford: Oxford University Press, 2005, p. 4.

7   W. Easterly, *The White Man's Burden: Why the West's Efforts to Aid the Rest Have Done So Much Ill and So Little Good*, Harmonds-worth: Penguin, 2006, p. 45.

8   R. J. Barro, 'Economic growth in a cross-section of countries', *Quarterly Journal of Economics*, 1991, 106, pp. 407–33.

9   P. Collier and J. W. Gunning, 'Why has Africa grown slowly?' *Journal of Economic Perspectives*, 1999, 13, pp. 3–22.

10 Cf. in particular J. Sachs and A. Warner, 'Sources of slow growth in African economies', *Journal of African Economics*, 1999, and J. Sachs, 'Tropical underdevelopment', Boston, CID working paper, December 2008, no. 62.

11 Easterly and Levine, 'Africa's growth tragedy', pp. 1203–50.

12 P. Guillaumont, 'On the economic vulnerability of low-income countries', mimeo, CERDI-CNRS, University of Auvergne, 1999.

13 See the very title of a paper by Xavier Sala-I-Martin of Columbia University, 'I just ran two million regressions', *American Economic Review*, May 1997, 87 (2).

14 Cf. for example the debate between the geographical school and the institutionalist school on the causes of African underdevelopment.

15 In a more or less 'robust' manner, we are told. Cf. R. Levine and D. Renelt, 'A sensitivity analysis of cross-country growth regressions', *American Economic Review*, September 1992, 82 (4), pp. 942–63.

16 D. Moyo, *Dead Aid: Why Aid Is Not Working and How There Is Another Way for Africa*, New York: Farrar, Straus and Giroux, 2009. (*L'Aide fatale* is the French title.)

17 D. Bloom and J. Sachs, 'Geography, demography, and economic growth in Africa', *Brookings Papers on Economic Activities*, 1998-2, 29, pp. 207–96; October 1998 (revised), p. 4.

18 A term used by L. E. Harrison in 1979, in a *New Scientist* article 'The curse of the tropics': 22, p. 602.

19 Aristotle, *Politics*, Book VII, 7.

20 Montesquieu, *The Spirit of the Laws*, Book XIV, ch. 2, 'How much men differ in the various climates'.

21 Term used by Daniel Etounga Manguelle in *L'Afrique a-t-elle besoin d'un programme d'ajustement culturel?*, Libramont-Chevigny: Édi-tions Nouvelles du Sud, 1991.

22 Bloom and Sachs, 'Geography, demography, and economic growth in Africa', p. 4.

23 An expression used by Bono in his preface to Jeffrey Sachs's book *The End of Poverty*, Harmondsworth: Penguin, 2005.

24 Cf. S. Amin, *Imperialism and Unequal Development*, New York: Monthly Review Press, 1979.

25 Brunel, *L'Afrique*, p. 38.

26 Demand made at the 'summit of the poor' held parallel to the G-8 summit of July 2008.

27 Moyo, *Dead Aid*.

28 Etounga Manguelle, *L'Afrique a-t-elle besoin d'un programme d'ajustement culturel?*

29 The exceptions are therefore all the more praiseworthy. Particular reference is made here to the writings of the political scientist Jean-François Bayart on the 'politics of the belly'.

30 M. Delafosse, *L'Âme nègre*, Paris: Payot, 1921.

31 Readers interested in the genealogy of this idea may refer to Hegel's *Philosophy of History* (New York: Dover, 1956, pp. 93ff.: 'Introduction. Geographical Basis of History'), which contains a long commentary on black Africa and its place in history.

32 L. E. Harrison and S. P. Huntingdon, *Culture Matters: How Values Shape Human Progress*, New York: Basic Books, 2000.

33 A. Kabou, *Et si l'Afrique refusait le développement*, Paris: L'Harmattan, 1991.

34 On this subject, see J.-F. Bayart, 'Culture et développement: les luttes sociales font-elles la différence?', as well as the works of Alain Henry and Philippe d'Iribane: 'Revolution by procedures in Cameroon', *Successful Companies in the Developing World. Managing in Synergy with Cultures*. Notes and Documents, no. 36, Paris: Agence Française de Développement, 2007.

35 Gunnar Myrdal, the great Swedish economist and Nobel economics laureate in 1974, published his trilogy *Asian Drama* (Harmondsworth: Penguin) in 1968.

6   The Great Wheel of Growth

1 Pearson Report, World Bank, 1969.

2 Brunel, *L'Afrique*.

3 See the analysis by Gilles Duruflé, *L'Ajustement structurel en Afrique: Sénégal, Côte-d'Ivoire, Madagascar*, Paris: Karthala, 2008.

4 A law passed at the beginning of the century to reassure the anti-colonial lobby required the French colonies to be self-financing.

5 Cf. C. Rodrik, 'The real exchange rate and economic growth', Working Paper, Harvard University, 2007, revised October 2008. The author shows how an undervalued exchange rate is favourable to growth in general, particularly via the development of industry. On the other hand, overvaluation may have very damaging consequences for an economy.

6 Cf. the analysis by B. Losch, 'À la recherche du chaînon manquant: pour une lecture renouvelée de l'économie de plantation ivoirienne',

in B. Contamin and H. Memel-Foté (eds.), *Le Modèle ivoirien en question*, Paris: Karthala, 1997, p. 213. Cited in Banégas and Akindès, *Patientez-vous*.

7 Brunel, *L'Afrique*, p. 73.

8 'Central African Republic: anatomy of a phantom state', *Africa Report 136*, International Crisis Group, 2007, p. 7.

9 Tied aid being economic aid granted on condition that the beneficiary uses the funds to buy goods and services from suppliers in the donor country.

10 This is economic assistance from international organizations.

11 Hugon, *L'Économie de l'Afrique*.

12 This refers to a historic period marked by a simultaneous fall in the prices of raw materials (oil and minerals, but also coffee and cocoa) and a worldwide rise in interest rates.

13 J. Sachs, *Understanding Shock Therapy*, Social Market Foundation occasional paper, London: Social Market Foundation, 1994.

14 A term used by Jean-Pierre Foirry, *L'Afrique: continent d'avenir?* Paris: Ellipses, 2006, p. 62.

15 This analysis is based partly on the work of Patrick and Sylviane Guillaumont, which shows the significance of governmental development aid as a counter-cyclical instrument.

16 In his speech at La Baule on 20 June 1990, French president François Mitterrand presented economic aid as conditional on the commitment of African heads of state to a process of democratization.

17 World Bank, '50 Things You Didn't Know about Africa', 2007: http://web.worldbank.org/WBSITE/EXTERNAL/COUNTRIES/ AFRICAEXT/0,,contentMDK:20563739~menuPK:1613741~page PK:146736~piPK:146830~theSitePK:258644,00.html.

7 The Great Shake-Out

1 See, in particular, Duruflé, *L'Ajustement structurel en Afrique*, and J. Stiglitz, *Globalization and Its Discontents*, New York: W. W. Norton, 2002.

2 The median sovereign debt of the sub-Saharan countries. Cf. IMF, *Global Economic Outlook, 2008*, Washington, DC: IMF, p. 14.

3 IMF, *Regional Economic Outlook: Subsaharan Africa*, Washington, DC: IMF, May 2009.

4 Despite the steep rise in the agricultural prices and oil, the average rate of inflation on the continent stayed at around 8 per cent in 2007, as against 15 per cent in 2000.

5 Terms of trade are defined by the ratio of an economy's import and export prices. An improvement in the terms of trade means either

that a country's exports fetch a higher price, or that its imports cost less.

6 Africa has 30 per cent of world mineral reserves. Cf. Brunel, *L'Afrique*, p. 27.

7 This was from 2004 to 2005.

8 Figure from the FAO, cited in Devèze et al., *Défis agricoles africains*, Paris: Karthala, 2008, p. 57.

9 Developed in *The Wealth of Nations* from the example of pin manufacture.

10 See H.-M. Cour, 'Afrique de l'Ouest: le grand bond en avant', *Vivre Autrement*, May 1996.

11 A. Maddison, *The Contours of the World Economy, 1–2030 AD*, Oxford: Oxford University Press, 2007.

12 This rose from 10 to 30 per cent of the West European population between 1800 and 1890, i.e. a development similar to that of sub-Saharan Africa in just forty years.

13 *Min* for *nongmin*, 'peasant', *gong* for *gongren*, 'worker'.

14 This is only one reason behind the difference in effectiveness of investments between Africa and Asia.

15 These 'clearings' are forcible expulsions carried out by the authorities to dislodge people who have settled without title to the land they occupy.

16 Ester Boserup, development economist, cited in Devèze et al., *Défis agricoles africains*.

17 Tractebel Development Engineering, *Étude sur la qualité de l'air à Ougadougou*, December 2002.

18 The rate of dependence of a population expresses the number of young (under 15) and old (over 65) people who depend on the income generated by the active population (between 15 and 65).

19 This demographic 'dividend' or 'bonus' refers to the economic advantages of the demographic transition stage characterized by a low rate of dependence.

20 J. Arabache and J. Page, *More Growth Fewer Collapses? A New Look at Long Run Growth Strategies in Subsaharan Africa*, Washington, DC: World Bank, November 2007.

8 Emerging Africans

1 See the photographic and sociological study coordinated by Joan Bardeletti, 'Les classes moyennes en Afrique', online at www.classes-moyennes-afrique.org.

2 Cf. 'SA middle class booming', *South Africa Good News*, 21 May 2007, and 'South Africa's middle class – young, black and driving a BMW', *Guardian*, 13 April 2004.

3   J. Gettleman, 'Kenya's middle class feeling sting of violence', *New York Times*, 11 February 2008.

4   Depending on whether one uses the World Bank statistics or the broader definition of the 'Africa 2's' given by Vijay Mahajan in his book *Africa Rising* (Upper Saddle River, NJ: Pearson, 2008), the African 'middle class' today counts between 15 and 30 million individuals. Beyond the absolute figures (which depend on arbitrary definitions), what matters is its rate of growth.

5   J. Santiso, 'Pourquoi l'Afrique intéresse les marchés financiers', *Telos*, 8 September 2007.

6   Safaricom is the country's largest telecommunications company. Cf. 'Africa: new sources of finance energize economy', *Financial Times*, 27 May 2008.

7   Between 2004 and 2006, direct foreign investment in sub-Saharan Africa doubled to reach US$36 billion: UNCTAD, *World Investment Report, 2007*, Geneva: UNCTAD, 2007.

8   Report on the *Capital* television programme.

9   These 'ratings' being a qualitative evaluation of bonds issued by a company or state with regard to its solvency.

10 World Bank, *Beyond Aid: New Sources and Innovative Mechanisms for Financing Development in Subsaharan Africa*, Washington, DC: World Bank, 2008; Standard and Poor's, January 2010.

11 IMF, *IMF World Economic Outlook*, Washington, DC: IMF, April 2008.

12 Arabache and Page, *More Growth Fewer Collapses?*

13 P. Guillaumont and S. Guillaumont, 'Big push versus absorptive capacity: how to reconcile the two approaches', Working Paper 200614, CERDI 2006; P. Collier, *The Bottom Billion: Why the Poorest Countries are Failing and What Can be Done about It*, Oxford: Oxford University Press, 2007.

14 Pew Research Center, *Global Attitudes Report 2007*, Washington, DC: Pew Research Center.

Part Five   Between God and Mammon

1   Over 40 per cent of the population of black Africa in 2008 were under fifteen, and over 60 per cent under twenty-five. Cf. UN, *World Population Prospects: The 2008 Revision*.

2   For an analysis of the 'transition crisis' at work in the Islamic world, see Y. Courbage and E. Todd, *Le Rendez-vous des civilisations*, Paris: Le Seuil, 2007.

3   Durkheim used this word to describe a social situation characterized by a weakening of the values (civic, moral or religious) that governed a society, and the associated feeling of alienation and loss of

bearings. He saw the anomie of European societies in the nineteenth century as one of the causes of suicide.

4 It may be useful here to dwell for a moment on the questionable notion of 'modernity'. James Ferguson, *Expectations of Modernity: Myths and Meanings of Urban Life on the Zambian Copperbelt*, Berkeley: University of California Press, 1999, shows very well the limitations of the 'mythology of modernization' based on a teleological approach to history and development. We are thus very cautious here in using the term 'modernity' in contrast with 'tradition' – a concept that is equally imperfect, referring to recurring social practices. Where many writers conceive modernity as the culminating point of a linear trajectory, and judge the modernity of a society by its proximity to standards or styles of living of the industrialized societies, we conceive it rather as something eminently plural and evolving. Chapter 11 below, which takes us from the *Big Brother* television programme to the Nollywood cinema industry and Nigerian tele-evangelism, illustrates some constitutive elements of an 'African modernity'.

5 For more detail on this subject, cf. Ferguson, *Expectations of Modernity*; also 'Africa has never been "traditional". So can we make a general case? A response to the articles', *African Studies Review*, September 2007, 50 (2), pp. 183–202, cited from J.-F. Bayart, 'La démocratie à l'épreuve de la tradition en Afrique subsaharienne', *Pouvoirs*, 2009/2, 129, pp. 27–44.

9   Urban Compositions

1 See Claude-Hélène Perrot, 'Chefs traditionnels et crise nationale: le cas du sud-est de la Côte d'Ivoire', *Afrique Contemporaine*, 2006, 217.
2 According to ibid.
3 J.-F. Bayart, *La Politique par le bas en Afrique noire*, Paris: Karthala, new edition 2008.
4 Alain Touraine, *La Société invisible*, Paris: Le Seuil, 1977.
5 In particular, Louis Wirth's work on Jewish immigrants in Chicago, *The Ghetto*, 1925, cited in Thomas Bossuroy, 'Déterminants de l'identification ethnique en Afrique de l'Ouest', *Afrique Contemporaine*, 2006, 220.
6 C. André and J.-P. Plateau, 'Land relations under unbearable stress: Rwanda caught in the Malthusian trap', *Journal of Economic Behaviour and Organization*, 1998, 34 (1).
7 See M. Morelle, 'Les enfants des rues, l'État des ONG: qui produit l'espace urbain? Les exemples de Yaoundé et d'Antananarivo', *Afrique Contemporaine*, 2006, 217.

8   There are few reliable statistics on street children. These estimates
    come from B. Pirot and Y. Marguerat, *Enfants des rues d'Afrique
    centrale*, Paris: Karthala, 2004, and from Médecins du Monde in
    N'Djamena.
9   See M. Debos, 'Les limites de l'accumulation par les armes: itiné-
    raires d'ex-combattants au Tchad', *Politique Africaine*, March
    2008, 209.
10 See, in particular, Ahmadou Kourouma, *Allah n'est pas obligé*,
    Paris: Le Seuil, 2000.
11 This illustration is drawn from Véronique Moufflet, 'Le paradigme
    du viol comme arme de guerre à l'est de la République démocratique
    du Congo', *Afrique Contemporaine*, 2008, 227.
12 Cited in ibid.

10   Crescent and Cross

1   See, on this subject, J.-F. Bayart (ed.), *Religion et modernité poli-
    tique en Afrique noire: Dieu pour tous et chacun pour soi*, Paris:
    Karthala, 1993.
2   *Zakat*, the third pillar of Islam, is the obligation of charity towards
    the most deprived.
3   M. Mohamed-Abdi, 'Retour vers les *dugsi*, écoles coraniques
    en Somalie', *Cahiers d'Etudes Africaines*, 2003, 169–70,
    pp. 351–69.
4   A visionary quote, but perhaps apocryphal.
5   Richard Banégas coined this concept in relation to the 'domestica-
    tion of democratic modernity'.
6   A phenomenon that Pierre Bourdieu called the *hysteresis* of habitus.
    This concept denotes the way in which a person who has been
    socialized in a particular social world maintains some of its habits
    even if these have become inappropriate, for example in the wake of
    a sudden historical development.
7   This list is taken from G. Nicolas, 'Géopolitique et religions au
    Nigéria', *Hérodote*, 2002, 106.
8   See Ruth Marshall-Fratani's study, 'Prospérité miraculeuse: les pas-
    teurs pentecôtistes et l'argent de Dieu au Nigéria', *Politique Afric-
    aine*, 2001, 82.
9   The term 'Salafi' is inexact, but used here for lack of a satisfac-
    tory alternative. If the growing influence of strict interpretations
    of Islam is readily apparent, both in West Africa and across the
    whole Sudan–Sahel belt to the Horn of Africa, the phenomenon
    of Islamic renewal is wider than just the Salafi current, including
    Shiism and various local forms of a modern and transnational
    Islam.

10 See R. Otayek, *Le Radicalisme islamique au sud du Sahara: Da'wa arabisation et critique de l'Occident*, Paris: Karthala, 1993; M. Miran, 'Vers un nouveau prosélytisme islamique en Côte-d'Ivoire: une revolution discrète', *Autrepart*, October 2000, 16.
11 A term used by R. Guolo in 'Le fondamentalisme islamique: radicalisation et néotraditionalisme', in A. Piga (ed.), *Islam et ville en Afrique au sud du Sahara*, Paris: Karthala, 2003.
12 The Islamic *sheikh* denotes an individual respected for his religious function and his knowledge of the Koran. Traditional African Islam is organized in religious brotherhoods.
13 M. Lasseur, 'Cameroun: les nouveaux territoires de Dieu', *Afrique Contemporaine*, 2005, 215.
14 This is a theoretical opposition, which largely vanishes as certain Protestant churches gain wealth and build links with the state.
15 Cf. B. Meyer, 'Les Églises pentecôtistes africaines, Satan et la dissociation de la "tradition"', *Anthropologie et Société*, 1998, 21 (1), pp. 63–83; S. Fancello, 'Sorcellerie et délivrance dans les pentecôtismes africaines', *Cahiers d'Etudes Africaines*, 2008, 189–90; C. Hamès, 'Problématiques de la magie-sorcellerie en islam et perspectives africaines', *Cahiers d'Etudes Africaines*, 2008, 189–90.
16 R. Marshall-Fratani, 'Prosperité miraculeuse: les pasteurs pentecôtistes et l'argent de Dieu au Nigéria', *Politique Africaine*, 2001, 82.
17 Murray Last made the point in his intervention at the FASOPO conference on 1 February 2008 that rigorist Islam in Nigeria became populist by freeing itself from the intellectual class of the *oulemas*.
18 *Da'wa* denotes the missionary activity that various Islamic currents practise in order to extend their area of influence.
19 The 'SARPed generation', as young Nigerians say, referring to the Structural Adjustment Programmes of the 1980s and 1990s.
20 Lasseur, 'Cameroun'.
21 See Nicolas, 'Géopolitique et religions au Nigéria'; M. A. Pérouse de Montclos, 'Le Nigéria à l'épreuve de la "sharia"', *Études*, 2001/2, 394; Murray Last, 'La charia dans le Nord-Nigéria', *Politique Africaine*, 2000, 79.
22 It is unnecessary here to dwell on the uselessness of this concept, proposed by Samuel Huntingdon in 'The clash of civilizations', *Foreign Affairs*, summer 1993. See, for example, E. Said, 'The clash of ignorance', *The Nation*, October 2001, or E. Said, 'The myth of the clash of civilizations', lecture at the University of Massachusetts, 1998.
23 The sources that report this agree that the scope of this 'presence' is very hard to establish with any precision.

24 For a more detailed analysis of this phenomenon, see 'Économie morale et mutations de l'islam', *Afrique Contemporaine*, supplement, 2009, 231.
25 R. Marshall-Fratani, 'Mediating the global and local in Nigerian pentecostalism', *Journal of Religion in Africa*, August 1998, 28.

11 Switched-on Africa

1 We have used here information from the study by Sean Jacobs of the University of Michigan, 'Big Brother, Africa is watching', *Media, Culture and Society*, 2007, 29, 6.
2 Quotes here from ibid. (retranslated from the French publication in *Politique Africaine*, December 2005 – January 2006, 100).
3 E. Akpabio, 'Attitude of audience members to Nollywood films', *Nordic Journal of African Studies*, 2007, 16.
4 Cf. Thomas J. Bassett's analysis in '"Nord musulman et Sud Chrétien": les moules médiatiques de la crise ivorienne', *Afrique Contemporaine*, 2003, 206.
5 *Janjawid* is a generic term for the Darfur militias.
6 Cf. R. Marchal, 'Tchad/Darfour: vers un système de conflits', *Politique Africaine*, June 2006, 102, pp. 135–54, and J. Tubiana, 'Le Darfour, un conflit identitaire?' *Afrique Contemporaine*, 2005, 214.
7 On the Nigerian case, see Murray Last's presentation at the FASOPO meeting of 1 February 2008.
8 www.keneya.org.ml.
9 Source: Internet World Statistics, February 2010: www.internetworldstats.com.

12 The End of Ethnicity

1 In particular, J.-F. Bayart, *The Illusion of Cultural Identity*, Chicago: University of Chicago Press, 2010; J.-L. Amselle, *Mestizo Logics: Anthropology of Identity in Africa and Elsewhere*, Stanford: Stanford University Press, 1998.
2 J.-P. Dozon, *Ethnicité et histoire: productions et metamorphoses sociales chez les Bété de Côte-d'Ivoire*, Paris: Karthala, 1981; and J.-L. Amselle and E. M'Bokolo, *Au coeur de l'ethnie: ethnie, tribalisme et État en Afrique*, Paris: La Découverte, 2005.
3 G. Prunier and J.-P. Chrétien, *Les Ethnies ont une histoire*, Paris: Karthala, 2003.
4 Mwai Kibaki, the incumbent president, of Kikuyu ethnicity, was opposed by a Luo candidate, Rail Odinga, himself supported by

many Kikuyus. But these Kenyan ethnic groups are also somewhat arbitrary: the Kalenjin, for example, made up of a number of different peoples, forged an ethnic identity from scratch in the second half of the twentieth century, in the course of their struggle for territories which they claimed to have been deprived of.

5 This 'nationalist moment' was particularly bloody, from its beginnings in the French Revolution and the ensuing Napoleonic wars to its collapse after the shock of the Second World War.

6 S. Fancello, 'Akanité et pentecôtisme: identité ethno-nationale et religion globale', *Autrepart*, 2006, 38 (2).

7 These large districts closed to non-residents are well developed in the major South African cities, just as in the United States and Brazil.

8 J.-B. Onana, 'Cameroun, le sport contre les ethnies', *Outre-Terre*, 2005, 11.

9 T. Boussuroy, 'Déterminants de l'identification ethnique en Afrique de l'Ouest', *Afrique Contemporaine*, 2006, 220.

10 Ibid.

11 Nicolas, 'Géopolitique et religions au Nigéria'.

13   African Democracy

1 F. Fukuyama, *The End of History and The Last Man*, New York: Simon & Schuster, 1992.

2 François Mitterrand's foreign minister, Roland Dumas, summed up the La Baule speech as follows: 'The wind of freedom that has blown in the East will inevitably blow one day in the direction of the South.' See 'L'inflexion du discours de La Baule', March 1998, www.voltaire.net.

3 Launched in the early 1990s in several sub-Saharan countries (Benin, Burkina Faso, Mali, Congo...), these 'sovereign national conferences' took the form of broad discussion forums on a national scale, involving representatives from all levels of society. This was particularly the occasion for the emergence of demands for the establishment of multiparty systems and rotation of political power by way of free and transparent elections. In several cases, they made it possible to define new democratic institutions and propel major constitutional revisions.

4 J.-P. Olivier de Sardan, 'L'espoir toujours repoussé d'une démocratie authentique: dramatique déliquescence des États en Afrique', *Le Monde Diplomatique*, February 2000.

5 See, in particular, the analysis by Achille Membe, 'Esquisses d'une démocratie à l'africaine', *Le Monde Diplomatique*, March 2000.

6   See the analysis by Achille Membe, 'Situations de la démocratie en Afrique', *Courrier International*, 28 June 2008.

7   P. Nzinzi, 'La démocratie en Afrique: l'ascendant platonicien', *Politique Africaine*, March 2000.

8   B. Guèye, 'La démocratie en Afrique: succès et résistances', *Pouvoirs*, 2009, 129, pp. 5–26.

9   See 'François Traoré, héraut de la révolte des cotonniers africains', a portrait by Philippe Bernard published in *Le Monde*, 10 July 2005.

10   J. S. Mill, *On Liberty*, London, 1859.

14   The Dangers of Rent

1   The mineral coltan which occurs abundantly in sub-Saharan Africa (particularly in the Congolese province of Sud-Kivu) is used in the manufacture of electronic chips.

2   Including Africa north of the Sahara, Africa represented around 16 per cent of world exports of crude oil in 2007: OECD, 'Oil and gas', in *Atlas on Regional Integration in West Africa*, April 2007, p. 3.

3   PFC Energy, 2003 report. This figure is based on the conservative hypothesis of an average price of $60 per barrel over the period in question, and does not take into account recent discoveries of new sub-Saharan oilfields.

4   This 'curse' is studied in particular in J. Sachs and M. Warner, 'Natural resource abundance and economic growth', NBER working paper series, Cambridge, Mass.: National Bureau of Economic Research, December 1995, and more recently in Collier, *The Bottom Billion*.

5   R. Pourtier, *Afriques noires*, Paris: Hachette, 2001, p. 233.

6   A. Gelb and S. Grasmann, *Confronting the Oil Curse*, Agence Française de Développement – European Development Research Network lecture, November 2008.

7   Pourtier, *Afriques noires*, p. 233.

8   Victor T. Le Vine, 'African patrimonial regimes in comparative perspective', *Journal of Modern African Studies*, 1980, 18, pp. 657–73. For a more recent study of the concept of the neo-patrimonial state, see G. Erdmann and U. Engel, 'Neopatrimonialism revisited – beyond a catch-all concept', *GIGA Working Papers*, February 2006, 16.

9   Paul Collier et al., *Breaking the Conflict Trap: Civil War in Development Policy*, Oxford: Oxford University Press / World Bank, 2003.

10   Although the death count from the conflict in RD Congo is par-
       ticularly hard to establish, several estimates give figures of over 4
       million since 1998, the majority of them civilians.
11   Collier, *The Bottom Billion*, p. 21.
12   This is supported by the results of the econometric studies made by
       Paul Collier and Anke Hoeffler, 'Démocraties pétrolières', *Afrique
       Contemporaine*, 2005, 216.
13   Collier and Hoeffler, 'Démocraties pétrolières'.
14   See, in particular, D. Acemoglu, S. Johnson and J. A. Robinson, 'An
       African success story: Botswana', MIT Department of Economics
       Working Paper no. 01–37, 2001.
15   The annual growth rate was an average of 7.7 per cent between
       1965 and 1998.
16   French senate report of 1998.
17   This original method lies at the heart of the work of Kirk Ham-
       ilton and his team, *Where is the Wealth of Nations?* Washington,
       DC: World Bank, 2006. See also P.-N. Giraud and D. Loyer, *Capital
       naturel et développement durable en Afrique*, Document de travail
       no. 33, AFD, 2006.
18   This is the so-called 'Solow–Hardwick rule'.
19   We are using here the typology developed by Pierre-Noël Giraud in
       'Rente et croissance en Afrique subsaharienne', a study conducted
       for the AFD, December 2007.

15   The Vanguard of Development

1   Figures for the real growth of GDP (annual average) from 2000
      to 2006: World Bank, *Africa Development Indicators*, Washington,
      DC: World Bank, 2008–9.
2   For an analysis of the Ghanaian developmental state, see Christian
      Chavagneux, *Ghana, une révolution de bon sens: économie poli-
      tique d'un ajustement structurel*, Paris: Karthala, 1997.
3   'Ghana: managing oil revenue for brighter tomorrow', March 2008,
      on www.allAfrica.com.
4   The meaning of *burkina faso* in the Mooré and Dioula languages.
5   Classification according to average growth figures from 1995 to
      2007: IMF, *Regional Economic Outlook: Subsaharan Africa*, Wash-
      ington, DC: IMF, October 2008, p. 31.
6   The 'Washington consensus' is named after an article by the econo-
      mist John Williamson ('What Washington means by policy reform',
      in Williamson (ed.), *Latin American Readjustment: How Much Has
      Happened*, Washington, DC: Institute for International Economics,
      1989), which put forward ten recommendations taken up by the

Bretton Woods institutions for countries suffering from payments crises (fiscal discipline, redirection of public spending from subsidies towards broad-based provision of services, tax reform, market-determined interest rates, competitive exchange rates, trade liberalization, liberalization of inward foreign investment, privatization of state enterprises, deregulation, legal security for property rights). The granting of adjustment finance has long been dependent on public policy respecting these principles.

7   Nicolas Meisel and Jacques Ould Aoudia, *Une nouvelle base de données institutionnelles: 'profils institutionnels 2006'*, Document de travail no. 46, AFD, September 2007, p. 18.

8   Commission on Growth and Development, *The Growth Report*, Washington, DC: Commission on Growth and Development, 2008: www.growthcommission.org.

9   W. Easterly, 'Trust the development experts, all 7 billion of them', *Financial Times*, 29 May 2008.

10 This is the argument of Meisel and Ould Aoudia in 'La gouvernance dans tous ses états, économie politique d'un processus endogène', in S. Bellina, H. Magro and V. de Villmeur (eds.), *La Gouvernance démocratique: un nouveau paradigme pour le développement?* Paris: Karthala – Ministère des affaires étrangères et européennes, 2008.

11 This thesis, particularly as put forward by the economist Jeffrey Sachs in his book *The End of Poverty* (London: Allen Lane, 2005), was the inspiration for the Millennium Development Goals.

12 The analysis offered in this paragraph is inspired by the publication of Meisel and Ould Aoudia, *La 'bonne gouvernance' est-elle une bonne stratégie de développement?* Document de travail no. 58, AFD, January 2008.

13 See D. Rodrik, 'Getting governance right', paper distributed by Project Syndicate, May 2008: www.project-syndicate.org.

14 The World Bank, in allocating its envelope of subsidies to the least-developed countries, makes use of the Country Policy and Institutional Assessment (CPIA), a grid for evaluating beneficiaries that classifies them according to the quality of their policies. The more a country is 'well governed', according to these criteria, the more entitled it is to a substantial aid package – according to the principle that aid will be more effective in a 'well-governed' country. The United States went further in setting up the Millennium Challenge Corporation (MCC) in 2004, a body that only grants subsidies to countries whose indexes of governance are deemed satisfactory.

15 Meisel and Ould Aoudia, *La 'bonne gouvernance'*, p. 35.

16 J.-P. Olivier de Sardan, 'L'économie morale de la corruption en Afrique', *Politique Africaine*, 1996, 63, pp. 97–116.

17 For an analysis of the various modes of corruption, see also J.-F. Médard, 'Les paradoxes de la corruption institutionnalisée', *Revue Internationale de Politique Comparée*, 2006, 13.

18 We are basing ourselves here on the levels of perceived corruption measured each year by the NGO Transparency International.

19 Meisel and Ould Aoudia, *La 'bonne gouvernance'*.

16 Fragile Africa: One Crisis after Another

1 Paul Collier et al., *Breaking the Conflict Trap*.

2 We thank Kersten Jauer for this information, obtained from the Central African Republic's ministry of public functions.

3 'Like the political institutions historically preceding it, the state is a relation of men dominating men, a relation supported by means of legitimate (i.e. considered to be legitimate) violence': Max Weber, *Politics as a Vocation*, in Weber, *The Vocation Lectures*, Indianapolis: Hackett, [1919] 2004.

4 A. Field, 'Crise somalienne: fondements et enjeux pour la communauté internationale', study carried out for the HCCI, DGCID and AFD, June 2007 (unpublished).

5 Statements cited by the International Crisis Group, *République centrafricaine*.

6 See M. Debos, 'Fluid loyalties in a regional crisis: Chadian "ex-liberators" in the Central African Republic', *African Affairs*, 2008, 107 (427), pp. 225–41.

7 It is estimated that only 7 per cent of violent deaths in the African conflicts of the 1990s were directly due to fighting. See M. Marshall, *Conflict Trends in Africa, 1946–2004: A Macro-Comparative Perspective*, British government report for the Africa Conflict Prevention Pool, October 2005.

8 Bayart, *The State in Africa*.

9 See the analysis by C. Arditi, 'Les violences ordinaires ont une histoire: le cas du Tchad', *Politique Africaine*, October 2003, 91, pp. 51–67.

10 See the study by Debos, 'Fluid loyalties in a regional crisis'.

11 The number of hectares of arable land per inhabitant in Côte d'Ivoire is expected to fall from its 1960 level of 0.69 to 0.10 in 2025; FAO figure from 1996, see P. Hugon, 'Prospectives de l'Afrique subsaharienne', *Futuribles*, October 2000, 257, p. 35.

12 André and Plateau, 'Land relations under unbearable stress'.

13 Catherine André and Jean-Philippe Plateau, cited by Jared Diamond (2006), pp. 325–6.

14 World Bank, *Kenya Country Social Analysis*, Washington, DC: World Bank, 2007.
15 Desertification means the degradation of land in arid zones due to either climatic variation and/or human activities. It is expressed in the deterioration of plant cover, soil and water resources, leading to a decline in the biological potential of the land and its capacity to feed the populations living there.
16 For an analysis of the developmental trends in African conflicts, see *The Human Security Report*.
17 The most representative thinker of this vision of aid is the economist Jeffrey Sachs, whose argument for aid is presented in the book cited above: Sachs, *The End of Poverty*.
18 Though this is not the only example, these positions have recently been the object of a wide polemic around the – bad – book by Dambisa Moyo, *Dead Aid*.
19 Along the lines of the Cold War, when economic transfers were more concerned to keep zones of influence in the 'right' camp than to promote their economic and social development.

17 The Limits to Growth

1 The Physiocrats and classical economists viewed land as a factor of production. But in neoclassical economic models, the only factors of production are labour and capital. Natural capital did not reappear in economic models until a few years ago.
2 Giraud and Loyer, *Capital naturel*.
3 The value of natural capital is assessed as the sum of actualized revenues arising from the use of resources. See K. Hamilton et al., *D'où vient la richesse des nations?* Washington, DC: World Bank, 2007.
4 N. Kimani, *Environmental Pollution and Impact on Public Health: Implications of the Dandora Municipal Dumping Site in Nairobi, Kenya*, Nairobi: United Nations Environment Programme, 2007.
5 Article on www.rfi.fr, 'Côte-d'Ivoire. Pollution: inquiétudes, rumeurs et arrestations', September 2006.
6 'Le climat et les changements climatiques', *Atlas de l'Intégration Régionale en Afrique de l'Ouest*, Club du Sahel, OECD, January 2008.
7 Oli Brown and Alec Crawford, *Assessing the Security Implications of Climate Change for West Africa*, Winnipeg: International Institute for Sustainable Development, 2008.

8   United Nations Environment Programme report on Sudan: http://
    postconflict.unep.ch/publications/UNEP_Sudan.pdf.
9   Also referred to as the 'digital revolution'.

18   Light against Darkness

1   Agence Française de Développement – Institute for Sustainable
    Development and International Cooperation, *Regards sur la Terre
    2007: Biodiversité, nature et développement*, Paris: AFD-IDDRI,
    2007, p. 74.
2   IMF, *Regional Economic Outlook: Sub-Saharan Africa*, Washing-
    ton, DC: IMF, October 2008.
3   Note by AFD/EDF/ADEME, 2008 (unpublished).
4   Average consumption per capita, excluding South Africa. See
    'State and trends of the carbon market 2009', World Bank, 2009,
    pp. 37–8.
5   AFD-IDDRI, *Regards sur la Terre 2007*, p. 75.
6   The Commonwealth of Independent States includes eleven of the
    fifteen former Soviet republics.
7   *World Energy Technology Outlook to 2050* ('WETO-H2'), Brus-
    sels: European Commission, 2007.
8   Values expressed in US dollars 2006.
9   The expense of leasing generating capacity to deal with power cuts
    can be as high as 4 per cent of GDP in certain countries. See *Diag-
    nostics des infrastructures en Afrique*, AICD, June 2008.
10 Note by AFD/EDF/ADEME, 2008.
11 Geothermal power consists in extracting the heat contained in the
    subsoil with a view to heating homes or producing electricity.
12 World Bank, *L'Explosion historique des prix des produits de base
    prend fin avec le ralentissement de la croissance mondiale*, Washing-
    ton, DC: World Bank, December 2008.
13 A. Labey, 'L'Afrique se met au Vert', *Jeune Afrique*, 22 March 2009.
    Figures updated in 2010.
14 Ibid.
15 Strategic intervention framework of the AFD on 'urban develop-
    ment', 2009. This figure includes North Africa.
16 P.-N. Giraud and B. Lefèbvre, 'Les défis énergétiques de la crois-
    sance urbaine au sud: le couple "transport–urbanisme" au coeur des
    dynamiques urbaines', in AFD-IDDRI, *Regards sur la Terre 2006*.
17 See J. Kenworthy, cited by B. Lefèbvre, 'Soutenabilité environnemen-
    tale des villes émergentes: le couple "transport – usages des sols"
    au coeur des dynamiques urbaines', Institut Français des Relations
    Internationales seminar, 2006.

19   The Hunger for Land

1 B. Davison and N. Bricas, 'Note préliminaire sur l'évolution des fondamentaux des marchés alimentaires mondiaux', Centre de Coopération Internationale en Recherche Agronomique pour le Développement, 12 May 2008.
2 Animal farming consumes large quantities of grain for feedstuffs. Beef needs six times more land area than cereals to produce the same number of calories.
3 M. Griffon, *Nourrir la planète*, Paris: Odile Jacob, 2006.
4 P. Collomb, *Une voie étroite pour la sécurité alimentaire d'ici à 2050*, Rome: Économica-FAO, 1999.
5 Ibid.
6 Gunther Fischer et al., *Global Agro-ecological Assessment for Agriculture in the XXIst Century*, Laxenburg, Austria: International Institute for Applied Systems Analysis (IIASA), 2001.
7 *Land Grab or Development Opportunity? Agricultural Investment and International Land Deals in Africa*, Rome: IIED-FAO-FIDA, 2009.
8 We draw here on the article by José Tissier and Emmanuel Baudran, 'La faim de terres: une conséquence attendue de la crise alimentaire mondiale', AFD, 2009.
9 Griffon, *Nourrir la planète*, p. 177.
10 Fischer et al., *Climate Change and Agricultural Variability*, Laxenburg, Austria: IIASA, 2002.

20   The Human Struggle

1 *State of the World's Forests*, FAO, 2007.
2 Cf. in particular the REDD system for reduction of emissions from deforestation and degradation.

21   Africa Courted

1 The IMF and World Bank.
2 The Club de Paris is an informal group of public creditors who meet occasionally to agree on solutions to be found for countries having payment difficulty (rescheduling of payments and possible debt relief). The nineteen industrialized countries who form the Club de Paris hold close to 30 per cent of the debt of developing countries, and have rescheduled the debts of nearly eighty of these.
3 *Global Trends 2015*, Washington, DC: National Intelligence Council, 2000.

4   *Les Afriques*, 4 June 2009, 78.
5   *Africa Progress Panel*, 2009.
6   This technology enables customers to settle bills and transfer funds via their mobile phone. See Stéphane Ballong, 'Afrique: le téléphone portable devient une banque', *AfrikEco.com*, 22 May 2009.
7   This analysis draws on that made by Luc Rigouzzo in 'Crise financière: et si on avait tort de ne prêter qu'aux riches', *La Tribune*, 28 October 2008.
8   'Les banques canadiennes seraient les plus sûres au monde', Reuters, 9 October 2008.
9   'Chine: le grand bond vers l'Afrique', *Jeune Afrique*, 14 July 2008.
10 These are, respectively, the West African Economic and Monetary Union; the Economic and Monetary Union of Central Africa; the Economic Community of West African States; the Economic Community of Central African States; the Common Market for Eastern and Southern Africa; the East African Community; the Southern African Customs Union; the Commission de l'Océan Indien, Maurice; the Southern African Development Community; the Intergovernmental Agency for Development; the Union for the Mediterranean; and the Community of Sahel–Saharan States.

22   Africa's New Exploiters?

1   This section owes a great deal to the work of Jean-Raphaël Chaponnière, economist with the AFD, who has a fine knowledge of economic relations between Asia and Africa. See, in particular, 'Les trajectoires de la Chine-Afrique', special issue of *Afrique Contemporaine*, 2008, 228.
2   This rhetorical element of the Sino-African partnership naturally needs qualification: the first condition of Chinese aid was, for a long time, recognition of the unity of China, in the sense of non-recognition of Taiwan. But this does not make it any less fundamental in the speech of both Chinese and African leaders.
3   J.-C. Ramo, *The Beijing Consensus*, London: Foreign Policy Centre, 2004.
4   On this subject, see E. Guérin, 'Bailleurs émergents: où en est la Chine en Afrique?' in 'Les trajectoires de la Chine-Afrique'.
5   *Independent* (London), 11 July 2009.
6   These are industrial zones benefiting from tax concessions. Their origin goes back to Deng Xiaoping, who took the initiative in this direction in the 1980s.
7   'Les étudiants africains s'intéressent de plus en plus à la Chine', *Chine Informations*, January 2008.

8 J.-R. Chaponnière, 'La dérive des continents: l'Asie et le futur de l'Afrique', *Futuribles*, March 2009, 350.
9 J.-R. Chaponnière, 'Un demi-siècle de relations Chine-Afrique: évolution des Analyses', in 'Les trajectoires de la Chine-Afrique'.
10 E. Guérin, 'Chinese assistance to Africa: characterization and position regarding the global governance of development aid', in IDDRI, *Idées pour le débat*, 2008, 3.
11 This is Chaponnière's hypothesis in 'La dérive des continents'. The concept of 'monopoly of history' is taken from Hubert Védrine, *Continuer l'Histoire*, Paris: Fayard, 2007.
12 F. Lafargue, 'L'Inde en Afrique: logiques et limites d'une politique', *Afrique Contemporaine*, 2006, 219.
13 Ibid., p. 147.
14 S. Singh, 'India and West Africa: a burgeoning relationship', Chatham House Briefing Paper, April 2007.
15 'Nouveaux amis', *Jeune Afrique*, 2 March 2008.
16 Interview with Mohamed El Kettani in *Les Afriques*, December 2008, 55.
17 Conference 'La Tunisie dans son espace africain: lien civilisationnel et partenariat pour un développement solidaire', organized in May 2009 by the Chambre de commerce et d'industrie de Tunis.
18 'La Tunisie à la conquête de l'Afrique', *Les Afriques*, June 2009, 80.
19 F. Lafargue, 'Le Brésil, une puissance africaine?' *Afrique Contemporaine*, 2008, 228, pp. 137–50.
20 Ibid.
21 Agence France Presse dispatch of 15 October 2007, cited in ibid.

23 Acknowledging Africa

1 'US oil politics in the Kuwait of Africa', *The Nation*, 4 April 2002.
2 Information report of the French foreign affairs commission on 'France's policy in Africa', chaired by Jean-Louis Christ, Paris, December 2008.
3 Paul Wolfowitz left the Department of Defense in spring 2005 to take up the presidency of the World Bank. Here, too, he immediately defined Africa as a priority zone.
4 Aid received by sub-Saharan states over this period rose to an average of $12 billion per year. See 'Africa's missing billions', International Action Network on Small Arms, Oxfam and Saferworld, October 2007.
5 'L'ONU s'inquiète de l'explosion des trafics en Afrique de l'Ouest', *La Tribune*, 9 July 2009.

6   The European Union strategy for Africa speaks of 'a leap forward in EU–Africa relations'.
7   *Les Afriques*, 4 October 2009.
8   PEW Global Attitudes Project, 2009.

Index